INDUSTRIAL RELATIONS IN JAPAN
CONTEMPORARY TRENDS AND CHALLENGES

INDUSTRIAL RELATIONS IN JAPAN

CONTEMPORARY TRENDS AND CHALLENGES

Dr. JOHN ZECHARIAH
Former Dean
Graduate School of Business Administration
Spicer Memorial College
Pune (India)

Foreword by

Prof. KOZO KAGAWA
Dept. of Industrial Relations
Doshisha University
Kyoto (Japan)

DEEP & DEEP PUBLICATIONS PVT. LTD.
F-159, Rajouri Garden, New Delhi - 110 027

INDUSTRIAL RELATIONS IN JAPAN
Contemporary Trends and Challenges

ISBN 978-81-8450-167-4

Printed in India at MAYUR ENTERPRISES
WZ Plot No. 3, Gujjar Market, Tihar Village, New Delhi - 110 018

Published by DEEP & DEEP PUBLICATIONS PVT. LTD.,
F-159, Rajouri Garden, New Delhi - 110 027 • Phone : 25435369, 25440916
E-mail : ddpubs@gmail.com • ddpbooks@yahoo.co.in
Showroom :
2/13, Ansari Road, Daryaganj, New Delhi - 110 002 • Telefax : 23245122

Contents

Foreword xi

Preface xiii

I. JAPAN AND THE JAPANESE WORKER : AN OVERVIEW **1**

1. Japan's Background 1
2. Japanese Worker 5
   - (a) Women Worker 19
   - (b) Part Time Workers 23
   - (c) Senior Workers 25
   - (d) Child Labor 27
   - (e) Foreign Workers 28
   - (f) Japanese Job Seekers 30
3. Changing Trends in Japanese Worker and Management 32
   - (a) Characteristics of Japanese Work 32
   - (b) Labor-Management Relations 35
   - (c) Rights and Duties of Employee and Employer 37
     - (i) Employee's Duties 37
     - (ii) Employer's Duties 38

(iii) Employee's Rights 42

(iv) Employer's Rights 43

4. Working Conditions 43

(a) Working Hours 46

(b) Over Time 48

(c) Rest Period 50

(d) Holidays 51

(e) Annual Vacation with Pay 52

(f) Education and Training 55

(g) Promotion 60

(h) Retirement 63

(i) Dismissal/Lay-Off 65

(j) Accident 67

(k) Labor Mobility 68

(l) Working Conditions in Public Sector 69

5. Key Aspects of Human Resources Management System—The Toyota as an Example 70

2. BASIC CHARACTERISTICS OF JAPANESE INDUSTRIES RELATIONS : AN EMPIRICAL SURVEY 79

1. Life Time Employment : An Introduction 79
2. Life Time Employment: Nature and Practice 81
3. Workers' Commitment 90
4. Employment System in Japanese Companies : An Example 94
5. Life Time Employment: Survey Interpretation 101

Life Time Employment 103

3. ENTERPRISE-BASED UNION 112

1. Nature and Classification 112
2. Organization of Japanese Company Union : An Example 121

3. Characteristics of Enterprise Union 123
4. Functions of Enterprise Union 124
5. Spring Offensive or Shunto 126
6. Trade Unions and Government 131
7. Unification of Trade Unions 132
8. Trade Unions and Employer's Associations 135
9. Future of Enterprise Trade Union 137
10. Enterprise Union : Survey Interpretation 140

4. SENIORITY (NENKO) WAGE SYSTEM 148

1. Meaning and Payment of Wages 148
2. Wage and Labour Productivity 156
3. Characteristics of Wage System 162
4. Seniority Wage System—Nenko 168
5. Wage Determination—Shunto 173
6. Basis of Seniority Wage: Survey Interpretation 174

5. LABOR DISPUTES 180

1. Labor Disputes : General View 180
2. Types of Industrial Disputes 197
3. Acts of Disputes 189
   (a) Strikes 192
   (b) Go-slow and Work to Rule 196
   (c) Picketing and Sit down 197
   (d) Taking Holidays 198
   (e) Pasting Posters and Wearing Ribbons 199
   (f) Control of Means of Production 199
4. Lock-Outs 200
5. Disputes in Small Enterprises 201
6. Disputes in Public Sector 202

7.	Labor Disputes—Country Comparison	205
8.	Prevention of Labor Disputes	209
6.	**DISPUTE SETTLEMENT MACHINERY IN JAPANESE INDUSTRIAL RELATIONS**	**212**
1.	Mutual Settlement	215
2.	Labor Relations Commissions	222
	(a) Unfair Labor Practice Cases—Adjudication	223
	(b) Conciliation	234
	(c) Mediation	235
	(d) Arbitration	237
3.	Emergency Dispute Settlement Machinery	248
4.	Dispute Settlement in Public Sector	249
5.	Dispute Resolution through Courts	251
	(a) Provisional Disposition Orders	252
	(b) Interpretational Application of Collective Agreements	254
	(c) Employment Contract Conflicts	257
6.	Controversy over the Jurisdiction of Labor Relations Commissions Courts	260
7.	**COMPARATIVE INDUSTRIAL RELATIONS IN JAPAN AND INDIA : A GENERAL VIEW**	**263**
1.	Industrial Relations in India	263
2.	Concept of Employment, Trade Union and Wage System in Japan and India	266
	(a) Different Meaning of Employment	266
	(b) Different Meaning of Wage System	268
	(c) Different Meaning of Labor Union	269
3.	Similarities and Differences between Japan and India	272
	(a) Labor Laws	272
	(b) Labor Administration Machinery	273

(c) Collective Agreement and Bargaining 274
(d) Acts of Disputes 277
(e) Unfair Labor Practices 278
(f) Dispute Settlement Machinery 280
4. Can We Learn from Japanese Experience? 286
5. Review of Japanese Industrial Relations 292

Index 295

Foreword

Dr. John Zechariah was a visiting scholar of industrial relations at the Department of Industrial Relations, Doshisha University, Kyoto, Japan from April 1990 to March 1991. During this time he was awarded a research fellowship by the Japan Society for the Promotion of Science. His research project was to do a "Comparative Study of Industrial Relations System in India and Japan". In order for him to best utilize his time he has researched on Japanese industrial relations through questionnaire and discussion with workers, job-seekers, trade union leaders and personnel staff of companies. Dr. Zechariah, in his own lucid style has been able to bring out this book, for those who share concern for industrial relations. As a result of his hard work and initiation, I am happy that he could bring out this book with just one year of study and experience, in spite of Japanese language barrier. I think this book has following features:

1. Recently, we find books and materials on Japanese industrial relations written in English, by non-Japanese writers or collaborations between Japanese and non-Japanese. Dr. Zechariah's contribution is most timely and welcome at a time when Japan is witnessing dramatic changes in its economy and society. The book is useful to non-Japanese and particularly Indian readers, as it explores the possible lessons.

2. Of late many are trying to probe the "mysteries" of the present-day industrial society of Japan and sought to explain the Japan's "miraculous" economic growth, in the "unique" nature of Japanese industrial relations. The so-called unique "pillars" (Life-time employment, Enterprise-based union and Seniority wage system) of Japanese industrial relations, have been explained quite successfully in this book based on survey.
3. This volume attempts to clarify and interpret all aspects of Japanese industrial relations. So this is like an "encyclopedia on Japanese industrial relations". The vital information and relevant statistics on various topics, which are normally not available, are in this book. Therefore, I am confident that this book will help particularly Indian people to understand Japan.

This is the first attempt of Dr. Zechariah, to introduce Japanese industrial relations; I hope he will make improvements in the next edition. It is a timely endeavor and would create interest and awareness of Japan, among people who are interested in industrial relations.

KOZO KAGAWA
Dept. of Industrial Relations
Doshisha University
Kyoto, Japan

Preface

Generally speaking, people in many countries know little about Japanese industrial relations and at the same time, more and more people seem to be eager to study Japan's present day economy and industrial relations. Many attempts have been made to describe the Japanese industrial relations but unfortunately, vast literature is not easily accessible. This is the main reason why I wrote this book, to give a practical and easy to understand the Japanese industrial relations, without getting bogged down in complex issues.

Industrial relations have made considerable progress in recent years. In the last five decades Japanese economy has attained a remarkable growth and has been the center of world attention. The unique characteristics/pillars of the Japanese industrial relations, that have been responsible for such an international attention and economic miracle, can be summarized as: Life Time Employment, Enterprise-based Union and Seniority Wage System. The attitude/preferences of workers and job seekers-towards the so called 'pillars' of the Japanese industrial relations, have been investigated with the help of a questionnaire, to elucidate how long and how far these pillars can influence the Japanese worker and Japanese industrial relations.

I admit that it is a complex task to describe industrial relations of Japan by an individual, but I have tried to provide a map for readers. It gives an overall view of Japanese industrial relations. I do not claim that this book is a complete, perfect and specialized study. My intention is to offer a useful starting point and guide for further deeper studies. However, many of my Japanese friends and academicians consider this volume as a complete guide to everyone who is interested in industrial relations of Japan. My friend Prof. Kozo Kagawa, in his foreword calls this work as an "encyclopedia of Japanese industrial relations". The book is expository, analytical and illustrative and seeks to explain the intricacies and complexities of various aspects of Japanese industrial relations. There is a growing interest and need in knowing more about the Japanese industrial relations among academic and non-academic circles. Therefore, a detailed bibliography, footnote, charts, table and figures have been provided.

The progress in industrial relations research has been very slow in developing countries including India, although a great stress is given on it. Since India is passing through rapid social and economic change, it is necessary for Indian industrial relations to make adjustment with these changes. Labour specialists like Vogel, Dore and OECD suggest that valuable lessons can be learned from Japanese experience. I feel the study in industrial relations is of vital concern for the country's growth. India can look for some tips and learn from Japanese experience.

The purpose of this book is: 1. To assist those who are interested in acquainting themselves with the Japanese industrial relations in general and by bringing research material within their reach. I have given detail statistics pertaining to various aspects which are not easily accessible, 2. To expose the Japanese labour management by describing the unique characteristics of the Japanese industrial relations, 3. First chapter will provide an overall view of the general working conditions in Japanese companies. I am sure Toyota and Matsushita Electric Company's examples though short will be of interest and benefit all those who are interested in labour study, 4. To highlight the unity of purpose among the Japanese population, discipline and devotion of work on the part of worker and a degree of paternalism on the part of employer and moderate role of government, 5. To highlight the disputes settlement machinery, i.e. Labour Relations Commission and Courts of Japan, and 6. To compare the Japanese industrial relations with India and see how we can benefit.

The preceding discussion gives some indication of the structure of this book. An introductory chapter provides a descriptive background of the Japanese labour relations. This chapter deals with the nature and characteristics of the Japanese worker, labour-management relations and general working conditions. In order to get better overall picture of the labour relations of Japanese company, the Toyota's human resources management system has been dealt in short.

My original intention was just to highlight the characteristics of Japanese industrial relations however, in the process of writing; I consider the necessity of including other aspects of Japanese industrial relations. This book is intended to benefit the students of personal management, trade union workers, labour officers and all those involved with labour welfare.

Chapters 1, 2, 3 and 4 are devoted to highlight the basic characteristics of Japanese industrial relations, based on empirical survey and statistics. Chapter 2 deals with the nature and practice of life time employment, worker's commitment and survey interpretation on the concept of life time employment. In order to understand fairly well the Japanese employment system, personnel management practice of Matsushita Electric Company has been explained in short.

It is hoped that Chapter 3 will be of great value particularly for trade union workers. This chapter deals with nature, classification, functions and characteristics of 'Enterprise-based Union'. Enterprise-based union is a type of union where employees of the same firm, irrespective of whether they are blue or white collar workers are organized together in a single union. In Japan, wages are negotiated between labour and management in spring. This unique kind of wage negotiation called as 'shunto' or 'Spring Offensive' is explained. This chapter also deals with the relations between trade union and government, unification of trade union, trade union and employer's association, future of enterprise-based trade union and Matsushita Electric Worker's Union.

Japanese wage system differs and exhibits unique characteristics. Chapter 4 deals with the meaning and payment of wage, wage determination or 'shunto' and survey interpretation which describes worker's attitude towards seniority wage system.

At the end of Chapters the attitude of workers and job-seekers of life time employment, enterprise-based union and seniority wage system, on the basis of survey has been highlighted.

Industrial relations in Japan although is peaceful in major industries, labour disputes have now become evident. Chapter 5 describes the nature, types of labour disputes, different acts of dispute, lock-outs, disputes in small enterprises and public sector, labour disputes country comparison and measure to prevent labour disputes.

Peace, harmony and efficiency are essential for the development of industrial relations. Chapter 6 deals with dispute settlement machinery of Japan but not intended to examine the legal framework. In other words, it explains what is being done? And how it is being done? Rather than what is the best way of doing? This chapter therefore, highlights the scope and use of mutual settlement system, the existing system of Labour Relations Commission (Conciliation, Mediation, Arbitration and Adjudication in cases of unfair labour practices), emergency disputes settlement machinery, settlement machinery in public sector, dispute resolution through courts and controversy over the jurisdiction of Labour Relations Commissions and Courts.

The last Chapter 7—A comparative study of industrial relations of Japan and India, has been devoted to stimulate thinking and to help the readers to draw their own conclusion. The basis of comparison is mainly on the concept of employment, trade union and wage systems. An attempt has been made to explain how the Japanese concept of employment, trade union and wage system differs from other countries particularly from India. The similarities between Japan and India, can India learn from Japanese experience and review of Japanese industrial relations has also been dealt in length.

In this book I have attempted to draw an image of the Japanese industrial relations on the basis of questionnaire survey, interviews and observations. If you were to visit Japan for yourselves, you might draw a completely different conclusion.

Beyond mere formality or courtesy, I would like to thank many people whose cooperation has made this book possible. This book is the outcome of my study in Japan as a visiting scholar during 1990-91, which I consider as a rare opportunity. I am deeply grateful to the Japan Society for Promotion of Science, which gave me a fellowship and generous research and travel grant which has made this work possible.

My stay at the Doshisha University, Kyoto was extremely pleasant. It is impossible for me to express adequately how deeply I appreciate the hospitality and kindness I received from my host Prof. Kozo Kagawa. He was kind enough to take time off to see my manuscript, gave me elaborate comments and wrote foreword of this book. I should not fail to mention Prof. Akio Nishiguchi, who rendered me intellectual guidance and help whenever I was in need. Mr. Motoyuki Yoshida, Prof. Yoshi Nakata, Prof. Sin-Ichi Ohta, Prof. Fujimura Hiroyuki, Rev. Hirata and Yoshiaki Nakano, all extended me significant assistance during my study. My intimate working association with these was very refreshing, pleasant and highly rewarding. I am very much indebted to these people for their very kind personal interest in me and my work and for their constant help and encouragement.

My obligations are far too many to acknowledge. The officials of the Japan Institute of Labour, Tokyo; the Kansai Labour Relations Commission, Kyoto; the Kyoto Labour Economic Institute, Kyoto; the Japan Foundation Office, Kyoto; the Matsushita Electrical Industries Co., Ltd, Ikeda City, Osaka; Unitika Ltd., Kaizuka, Osaka; Kyoto Mazda Group, Uji, Kyoto; Hirata Industrial Machineries Co., Kansai Factory, Yasu-gu, Shiga; Kaikin Osaka; Kubo Pearl Co., Ltd. Kusatus, Shiga and students of Doshisha University from whom I have benefited immensely through discussion and questionnaire.

If this book of mine would serve as a token of my gratitude for what I received from Japan, I shall have done my duty, to some extent.

Special thanks are due to Prof. Dr. P. Jegadish Gandhi, Former Professor of Economics, Voorhees College, Vellore, University of Madras, India for his guidance in publication. Thanks are also due to Mr. G.S. Bhatia, Managing Director, Deep and Deep Publications (P) Ltd., New Delhi for his willing cooperation in bringing out this elegant book within a short period.

JOHN ZECHARIAH

1

Japan and the Japanese Worker : An Overview

1. JAPAN'S BACKGROUND

Japan as an Asian country is often cited as a capitalist alternative to the socialist model, because of her exceptional economic performance. Japan is endowed with youthful energy and vital spirit and is constantly seeking to improve the older and discover the new. It has shown throughout history an aptitude for the assimilation of foreign ideas and the adoption of foreign technique to its own tradition. Today Japan is a meeting point between the new and old, as well as the East and West, which are fused into a unique harmony. The strength of Japanese culture of productivity is based on its powerful socio-cultural support system of people's deep love and concern, spiritual orientation of people and strong climate of cooperation amongst production actors, i.e. industry, trade, labor and government. Thus Japan has achieved a high level of prosperity and deserves to be considered an "Economic Super Power".

Japan is a small country with adequate supplies of labor but generally limited supplies of natural resources and land.[1] The modernization of Japan started in 1886, the year of the Meiji Restoration. Though some argue that the roots of modern development can really be found in the Tokugawa period, (prior to the Meiji Restoration) interest in Japanese economic performance centers around 1886—Meiji Restoration. Japan laid a deliberate ground work for modern economic growth between 1860 and 1900's. This groundwork was based on special features of the Japanese system and in addition some important policy measures:[2]

1. There was (and still) is a unity of purpose—discipline and devotion to work on the part of laborer and a degree of paternalism on the part of the employer.
2. The state has performed important functions in the Japanese experience, functions that are truly multi-dimensional.
3. Japanese historical experience.
4. Military activity has been an important factor in Japanese economic history.

The rapid pace of development after the 1860's through World War I was fostered by military activity. Thereafter, at least until 1946, war was a dominant theme in the Japanese economy. The World War II also had tremendous impact on the Japanese economy and later American occupation and policies. Japan lost all of its overseas territories, one-third of national wealth, and suffered heavy damage of production facilities. The Japanese economy, which had been completely ravaged and was totally confused at the close of the war, almost recovered its pre-war peacetime level in respect of national product and consumption level by 1953. The rapid industrialization and economic rehabilitation along with American assistance and people's efforts, Japan achieved remarkable economic growth. In 1960's Japan achieved high economic growth rate, unique in the world due to technological innovations and policy, giving priority to heavy and chemical industries. In the early 1970's Japan maintained higher growth rate than the developed countries and found itself achieving the second largest GNP in the free world in 1981. The year 1975 is considered a period of soft landing on the stable growth. Due to high appreciation of Yen in 1985, the economic environment has dramatically changed. The growth has resulted not only in a change in the industrial structure, but also in the concentration of industries and population in urban and metropolitan areas. The living standard of people was improved remarkably.

Japan is experiencing negative factors such as: aging labor force, changing values of younger generations, increasing uncertainty in politics, increasing tax burden, social welfare costs, skyrocketing land price and trade frictions with trading partners, yet her overall economic performance is very high.

The Japanese economic experience is of great interest mainly because of rapid and high economic growth. Apart from economic factors, non-economic factors such as: role of state, human element, end of military expenditure and limiting of low-growth sector are equally responsible for rapid economic growth. Many other factors are also responsible for high Japanese economic performance. Masaya Miyoshi classified these factors as overall factors, macro and micro-factors. Overall contributing factors are:

1. Dynamic competition,
2. Close government-industry communication,
3. A cultural and social status of business, etc.,
4. Political stability, and
5. Favorable international economic environment leading to Japan's export expansion.

The macro and micro-factors further classified as capital, labor and technology. Japan has reached present level, after variety of 'ups and down' in the last decades. The economy and industrial structure is homogeneous which is typical from the other economics.

Human element has been very important factor in Japanese economy. The favorable labor factors responsible for an impressive economic performance are:

1. High level education,
2. Flexible supply (labor) for growing industries,
3. Moderate labor movement,
4. Wage increase kept within productivity gains (macro),
5. Permanent employment, promotion by seniority, on-the-job training,
6. Consensus decision-making system,
7. Enterprising-based labor unions, and
8. Smooth labor transfer within a company and between affiliated companies (micro).

In Japan there is a peculiar and growth conductive attitude of labor toward industry—the 'permanent employment' system and the submissive attitude of labor towards the industrial establishment. The Japanese virtue of working hard and being content with simple life can be regarded as the Japanese version of the 'protestant work ethic' of Max Weber.[3] Managements and unions in Japan dreamed to 'catch up' with America and European countries after World War II. The labor unions adopted "wage as high as European countries", while management were active in investing in mass production and automation under widely accepted slogan, "let us catch up to the West European level". For both reaching the level of the US would have been like touching a twinkling star in the sky. They believed in "Do it or Perish".[4]

Interpersonal relations in a Japanese corporate organization are very harmonious. This harmony is a product of favorable human relations, labor management relations and relations in business operation. Japan government facilitates and encourages autonomous industrial relations and refrains from active intervention. The following factors are responsible for such harmonious relations in Japan:

1. Constitution in which all men are equal, encourage friendliness and harmony,
2. Labor Standard Law,
3. Trade Union Law,
4. Labor Relations Adjustment Law, and
5. Work rules where superior-subordinate relations are fair.

2. JAPANESE WORKER

Labor market is stratified by various factors in Japan, just as in any other industrialized courtiers. Stratification by sex, age, permanent and temporary is noteworthy. In this chapter we shall have birds-eye-view of Japanese labor, labor-management relations and working conditions. I feel it is essential to know these issues well, before we go into industrial relations in Japan.

It is true that Japanese worker works hard and his productivity is very high. Kasutoshi Koshiro, has analyzed five industrial relations factors contributing to high productivity in manufacturing industries. He considers these are "holy secretes":

1. Trade union policies towards technological change,
2. Low propriety to strike,
3. Flexible employment adjustment under the system of 'life time commitment',
4. Low separation rate of worker, and
5. Low absenteeism and high moral in Japanese factories.

The Japanese labor market is flexible from following perspective:[5]

1. Entry to and exist from the internal market,
2. The external labor market, and
3. Internal labor market.

It is interesting to see how Japanese companies adjust their labor during recession without dismissals. While core (permanent) employees retain their jobs because of Life Time Employment practice, the peripheral labor force—mainly female workers in their 30's serves as a shock absorber. The role of the external market to reallocate resources is comparatively small, labor resources are mainly supplemented by the inflow of new graduates. Regarding the internal market, it is common that flexibility is maintained to some extent even in large scale enterprise, by reallocating over time to adjust the size of the work force to fluctuations in production, suspension of new hiring, transfer or leasing of workers to subsidiaries. Thus

Japanese labor market depends more on the adjustment of quantity (employment) than on the adjustment of price (wage).

Japanese labor force employed in 1989 was 61.28 million out of a population of 99.74 million (15 years old and over) and 1.42 million (2.3%) unemployed. It is interesting to note the increase in population, 15 years old and over, from 1975 (84.43 million) to 1989 (99.74 million) and labor force employed from 53.23 million to 61.28 million. This resulted in an increased rate of unemployment from 1.9% to 2.3%, during the same period. Among employed, male constitute 36.54 million and female 24.74 million. As result 8.3 million male and 5.9 million female unemployed are found in 1989. Labor participation rate was 62.9 million in the same year (Table 1.1). The share of employment in secondary industry achieved a significant increase during the high-economic growth period when basic industries made strong growth and its share reached its peak of 36.6% in 1973. The share of employment in secondary industry was 33.8% in 1989. On the contrary, the percentage of persons employed in tertiary industry showed a rising tendency. The expansion of service industries led the share of employment in tertiary industry up from 47.3% in 1970 to 58.2% in 1989. Especially important is that the number of persons employed in service industries rose by 520,000 people or 4.0% from previous year to 13.36 million, scoring the biggest increase since 1983 (Chart 1.1, 1.2 and 1.3).

With change in industrial distribution, the structure of the employment status of working force has changed drastically. The percentage of wage earners among gainfully employed has increased. Participating rate is high (82%) at 40-49 age group, male 97% while female about 68%. There is a marked decline in worker's participation rate among young, especially between 15 and 19 years mainly because of higher education and recent decline in birth rate. The change in the supply structure of labor is evident particularly due to aging of the labor force, a rise in the worker's educational level, and increasing female participation in the labor force. These have led to gradual alternations in the 'life-long employment' system and 'seniority-based wage' system which are traditional in this country. The decline in worker's participation is also due to reduction in aggregate female participation ratio. However, in recent years

TABLE 1.1
The Labour Force and Rate of Unemployment

The population Classified by working Status *(Units : 10,000 Persons, %)*

		1986	*1987*	*1988*	*1989*
Population over 15 years old		9 587	9 720	9 849	9 974
	Male	4 662	4 726	4 790	4 854
	Female	4 925	4 994	5 059	5 120
Labour Force		6 020	6 084	6 166	6 270
	Male	3 626	3 655	3 693	3 737
	Female	2 394	2 429	2 473	2 533
Employed		5 853	5 911	6 011	6 128
	Male	3 526	3 551	3 602	3 654
	Female	2 327	2 360	2 409	2, 474
Unemployed		167	173	155	142
	Male	99	104	91	83
	Female	68	69	64	59
Rate of Unemployment		2.8	2.8	2.5	2.3
Labour force Participation rate		62.8	62.6	62.6	62.9
Population not in Labor force		3 513	3 584	3 635	3 655
	Male	1 007	1 043	1 071	1 091
	Female	2 506	2 541	2 564	2 564

Source : Monthly Statistic of Japan, Statistics Bureau, Management and Coordination Agency.

there is a growth in the number of female employees due to the shortage of labor. Chart 1.3 shows labor force participation rate by sex, where small participation is higher than female on all age groups except 15-19 year age group.

Table 1.2 highlights employed persons by industries and occupation. The largest percentage of employed are in manufacturing, wholesale and retail trade, and service industries. Except service industry the percentage of male employed is more in every industry. The average rate of

CHART 1.1
Structure of Employment

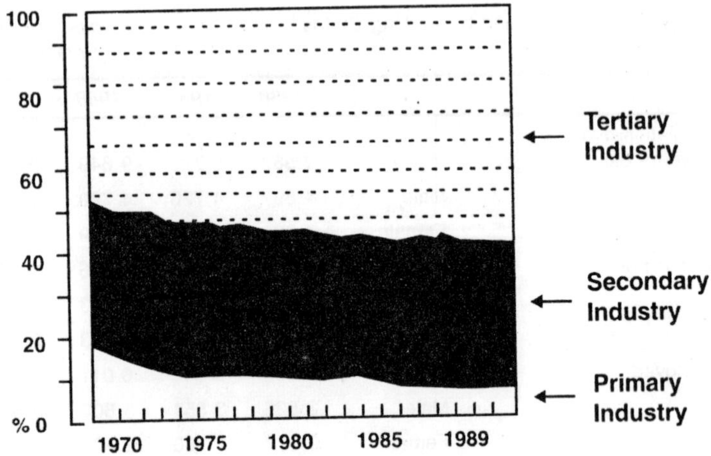

CHART 1.2
Unemployment Rate and Job Opening Rate

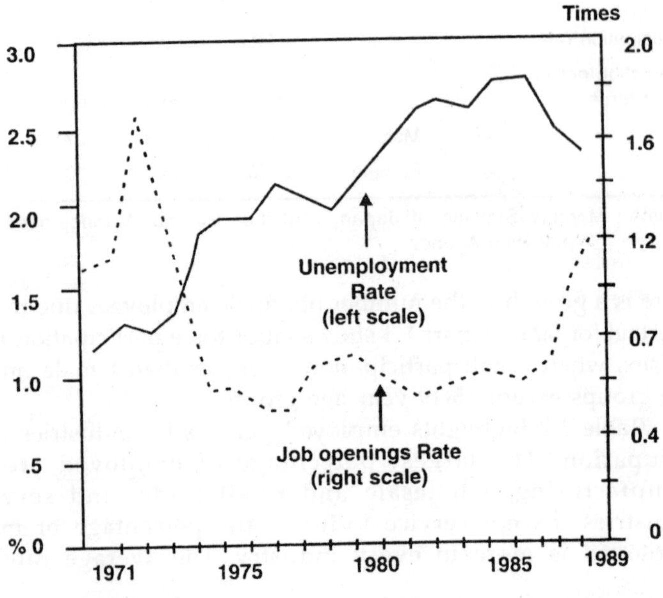

CHART 1.3
Labour Force Participation Rate by Sex (1989)

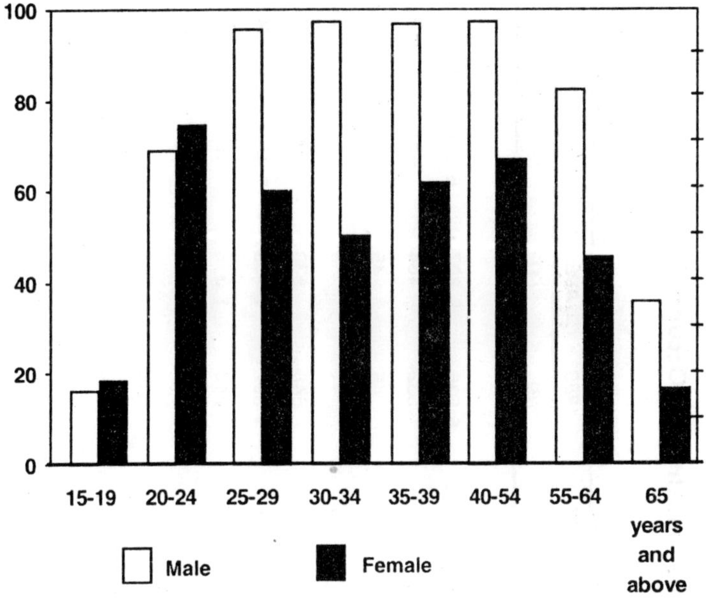

unemployment in Japan was 1% during high-economic growth period. However, due to the recession after the first oil crisis in 1973, the employment situation deteriorated and thus the unemployment rate rose from 1.4% in 1974 to 1.9% in 1975. Unemployment after reaching a peak of 3.1% in 1987 declined substantially and average 2.5% in 1988. The average number of unemployed 1989 was 1.42 million, a drop of 130,000 or 8.4% from year earlier. The average unemployment rate for 1989 was 2.3% the lowest annual average since 1981 when it stood at 2.2% (Chart 1.2).

The distribution of the labor force has changed completely with a change in the industrial structure in the post-war period. The percentage of labor force employed in primary industry declined, while portion of the labor force employed in secondary and tertiary industry increased. Within secondary industry, the increase in those employed in manufacturing industries has been remarkable, and within this category the

TABLE 1.2
Employed Persons by Industry and Occupation

(10 thousand)

(1)	1975 (2)	1980 (3)	1985 (4)	1988 (5)	1989 (6)	Male % (7)
Industry						
Total	5 223	5 536	5 807	6 011	6 128	59.6
Agriculture and Forestry	618	532	464	431	419	50.4
Fisheries	43	45	45	40	44	72.7
Mining	16	11	9	7	7	85.7
Construction	479	548	530	560	578	84.3
Manufacturing	1 346	1 367	1 453	1 454	1 484	60.2
Wholsale and retail trade eating and drinking places	1 127	1 248	1 318	1 389	1 400	51.6
Finance, insurance and real estate	170	191	217	236	243	51.4
Transport and communication	332	350	343	353	368	86.1
Electricity, gas and water	32	30	33	31	30	83.3
Services	855	1 1	1 173	1 284	1 336	49.3
Government	196	199	199	194	189	82.5

Occupation						
Total	5 223	5 536	5 807	6 11	6 128	59.6
Professional and technical workers	364	438	538	633	665	57.9
Administrative and managerial workers	206	220	211	228	235	91.9
Clerical and related workers	320	924	1 21	1 65	1 101	40.8
Sales workers	738	797	861	930	937	62
Farmers, woodsmen and fishermen	654	570	502	649	459	52.5
Mining workers	9	5	4	4	3	100
Transport and communication workers	237	248	227	222	230	95.7
Craftsmen and production process workers	1 580	1 653	1 689	1 668	1 687	68.5
Labourers	148	168	230	252	263	56.3
Protective service and other service workers	457	501	501	512	519	45.5

Sources : Statistics Bureau, Management and Coordination Agency.

CHART 1.4

Items Evaluated to be Important at the Interview

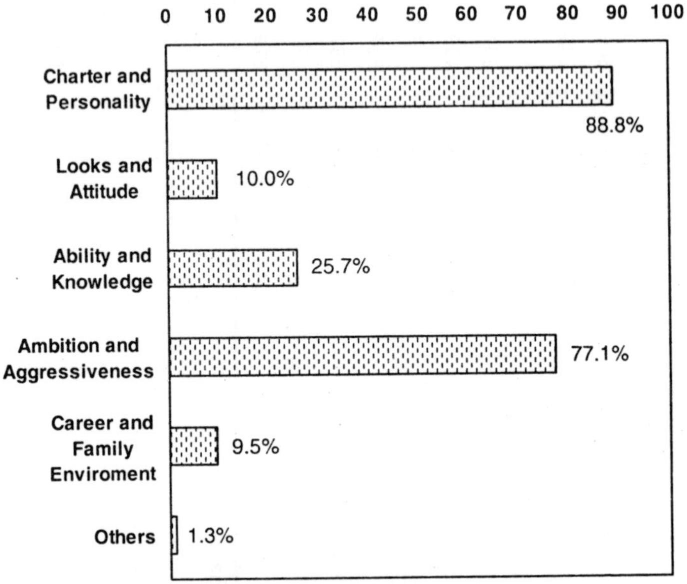

Source : Recruit 1974, Japan Recruit Center, 1974.

portion of those employed in heavy and chemical industries has increased, while the portion employed in light industries has declined. The percentage labor force employed in metal, machinery and related industries as against all manufacturing increased. However, the proportion of secondary industry as a whole stopped increasing after 1970 while that of tertiary industry increased steadily.

The largest number, around 35.8 million were employed by private industry and 5.2 million were employed in public sector. The public sector employees can be divided into four categories: National government employees, local government employees, public corporation employees and national government enterprises and employees in local government enterprise.

One of the most important characteristics of Japanese labor market is the differences in working conditions, including wages, according to the size of enterprise. Though it is believed that income distribution in Japan is generally more equal, employees in smaller enterprise get less than larger enterprises.

At least legally speaking in Japan, the distinction between blue collar and white collar workers is almost irrelevant. The more important distinction in Japanese daily employment relationships is the one between permanent employee and temporary employee. Permanent employees are those who are employed with an indefinite term contract and who are expected to stay in the enterprise until they reach retirement age. Temporary employees are either employed for a definite or and indefinite period. Permanent employees refer to graduates hired from junior and senior high school as well as colleges and universities, during April every year (Fig. 1.1). Such hiring during last school year has been criticized because it interferes with the last months of students' education. These employees are fresh without any work experience nor have they been self-employed. The permanent employees constitute the central labor force for the company. Employees not hired at this time of the year are considered temporary employees. In addition to these two groups, there are seasonal workers who may be employed up to six months. Due to recent shortage of labor, difference between permanent and temporary employees has been reduced, while permanent employee number is increasing. Table 1.3 highlights the ratio of enterprise and measures for obtaining work force, i.e. hiring new graduates, hiring career employees, accepting transfers, temporary workers and hiring part timers.

FIG. 1.1
Time Schedule for Recruitment

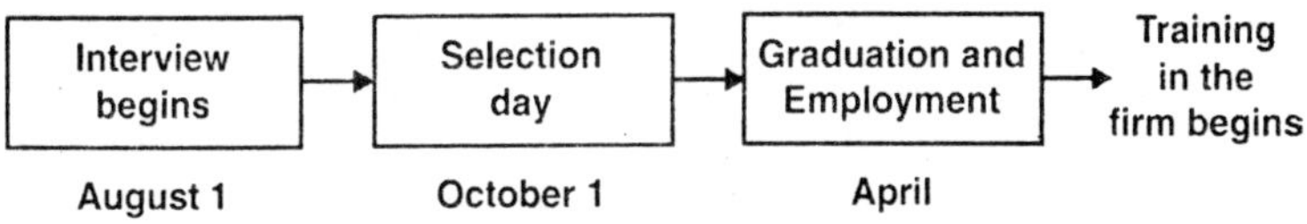

Generally, permanent employees largely out number temporary employees in most enterprises, except perhaps in small enterprises. For the last several years, temporary workers have amounted less than 20% of the total Labor mobility ratio,

TABLE 1.3

Ratio of Enterprise—Measures for Obtaining Workers (All Industries)

(*M.A.* %)

Establishment of new section, reorganization of existing section:	77.3
Hired new graduates	51.0
Hired-career employees	52.9
Accepted temporary transferees from subsidiaries or related companies	15.1
Used dispatched (temporary) workers	6.1
Hired part-timers	30.9
Establishment of new section:	
Transferred from other sections	80.2
Hired new graduates	42.3
Hired mid-career employees	49.0
Reorganization of existing section	
Transferred from other sections	74.0
Hired new graduates	51.9
Hired mid-career employees	48.6

Sources : Year Book of Labour Statistics, 1988.

percentage of new employees and percentage of separations of regular, full time and part time workers (male and female) has been highlighted in Tables 1.4 and 1.5. The employees' separation rate in Japan is very negligible. The important reasons for separation are: termination of contract, employers convenience (temporary transfer, re-employment to previous company), fixed retirement age, ones own responsibility, ones own convenience (marriage, delivery and child care) and sickness and injury. Against the background of favorable economic conditions, corporations are making plans for increased hiring across the spectrum of educational backgrounds, from high school to college. The Japanese companies are looking for mid-career workers, because to prepare for introduction of new technology, it is difficult for obtain new graduates as replacement, of expansion of current business, to revitalize organization through hiring persons with

TABLE 1.4

Newly-hired Employees by Gender and Age

(*in thousands*)

Industry	*Total*	*19*	*20-24*	*25-29*	*30-34*	*35-44*	*45-54*	*55-59*	*60-64*	*65 above*
(1)	*(2)*	*(3)*	*(4)*	*(5)*	*(6)*	*(7)*	*(8)*	*(9)*	*(10)*	*(11)*
Industries covered (All) Total	4 549 6	817 5	1 250	7 541 9	416 5	782 0	471 8	158 5	84 2	26 3
Male	2 169 5	384 7	619 6	279 9	195 7	296 9	212 2	102 4	60 2	17 6
Female	2 380 1	432 8	631	0 262 1	220 8	485	259 6	56 1	24 1	8 5

Source : Year Book of Labour Statistics, 1988.

TABLE 1.5
Trends in Hired Labour, Classified by Gender

(Units: 10,000 Persons, %)

Industry	Total		Female		Male		Proportion of female to total employees
	Number of empoyees	Change from the previous year	Number of empoyees	Change from the previous year	Number of empoyees	Change from the previous year	
(1)	(2)	(3)	(4)	(5)	(6)	\	
1980	3 971	2.5	1 354	3.4	2 617	2.0	34.1
1985	4 312	1.1	1 548	2.0	2 764	0.6	35.9
1986	4 379	1.6	1 584	2.3	2 795	1.1	36.2
1987	4 428	1.1	1 615	2..0	2 813	0.6	36.5
1988	4 538	2.5	1 670	3..4	2 868	2.0	36.8

Source : Women's Labour conditions, Ministry of Labour, Japan.

varied experiences, of shorter training period compared to new graduates so they can be used more quickly, it needs staff with highly specialized knowledge and experience, to replace retiring staff and to rectify imbalances in age composition of employees. These days' mid-career workers are increasing. Table 1.6 shows the ratio of enterprise and hiring channels. They are public employment service office, national personnel banks, part timers banks, private sector employment referral office, head hunters, introduced by customers or affiliated company, introduced by economic or industrial organizations with which enterprise has relations, introduced by university or research institute professor, personal relationship, friend or acquaintance of employees, want advertisement, flyers, etc. Table 1.7 highlights reasons for hiring mid-career workers. They have to prepare for new technology or entry into new, difficulty in obtaining new graduates as replacements, expansion of current business, to revitalize organization through hiring persons with varied experience, short training period as compared to new

TABLE 1.6
Ratio of Enterprise—Hiring Channel for Mid-career and Part-time Workers (All enterprise)

	(M.A. %)
Enterprises hiring	100.0
Public employment services office national personnel tanks, part-timers banks	53.2
Private sector employment referral office	6.1
Headhunters	2.8
Introduced by customer or affiliated company	16.5
Introduced by economic or industrial organisation with which the enterprise has relations	1.4
Introduced by university or research institute professor	2.4
Personal relationship (friend or acquaintance of employees)	51.3
Want ad, want ad in specialized publication	43.5
Flyer, posted notice	17.1
Others	7.4
Enterprise not replying	1.2

TABLE 1.7

Ratio of Enterprise—Reason for Hiring Mid-career Workers (All enterprise)

(*M.A.* %)

Enterprise hiring	100.0
To prepare for introduction of new technology or entry into new	9.4
Difficulty in obtaining new graduates as replacements	30.7
Expansion of current business	37.4
To revitalize organization through hiring persons with varied experience	14.5
Short training period compared to new graduates so they can be used more quickly	21.3
Needed staff with highly specialized knowledge and experience	14.3
To replace retiring staff	71.0
To rectify imbalances in age composition of employees	6.2
Others	6.6
Enterprises not replying	0.7

Sources : Year Book of Labour Statistics, 1988.

graduates so they can be used more quickly needed staff with highly specialized knowledge and experience, to replace retiring staff, to ratify imbalances in age composition of employees, etc. The job opening ratio has increased and in particular, the rate of high school graduates in 1990 will approach the all-time high of 3.88 which was reached in 1975. I will discuss more about permanent and temporary employee in Chapter 2.

Article 14 of the Labor Standard Law of 1947 states, "Labor contracts with the exception of those without any set period, shall not be concluded for a period longer than one year, except in the case of those requiring a definite period for the competition". This means employee has no legal obligation to stay in a particular enterprise longer than one year. The employer too does not have legal obligation to keep his employee, he may dismiss his employee with or without notice, depending on the reason for the dismissal. But in reality however, conditions in Japan to-day make dismissals extremely difficult. There are several judicial decisions in which the court found that the employer had abused its rights of dismissal.[6]

According to the Article 20 of the Labor Standards Law, the employer must give at least a thirty days advance notice before dismissal or pay a compensation amounting to thirty days average wage, "except when the continuance of the enterprise is made impossible by reason of some natural calamity or other inevitable cause or when the dismissal is caused by the employee's own behavior". For employees, the period of notice is decided depending on the term of wage calculation, in accordance with civil law principles, so far those whose wage is calculated on the daily basis it is 14 days. For those whose wage is calculate for a certain period, notice should be given in the first half of the period and the contract terminated from the next periods. For instance, monthly wage earners may terminate the contract from the next month if they give notice in the first half of the month. For those whose wage or salary is calculated for a period longer than six months the term of notice is three months (civil law Article 627). Employees are protected, as per the Labor Standard Act, by extending the period of notice for up to 30 days in the case of dismissal by the employer, regardless of the length of wage calculation. In the case of termination by the employee the civil law principles still apply. As far as both parties are concerned, notice is not necessary when there is cause of terminating the contract at once. However, with regard to just cause, the Labor Standard Law provides some protection for employees and certain principles have been developed through legal precedents in this connection.

The Labor Standard Law excludes from its coverage domestic employees in the home and family workers who work in plants. Apprentice worker is one who is on probation for a specified period by the contract, during which the employee's performance and ability is monitored and evaluated; and during which either of the parties can terminate the contract as soon as they wish to do so.

(a) Women Worker

Article 14 of the constitution prohibits the discrimination in working conditions because of sex and guarantees equality of the sexes. The Labor Standard Act, in Article 4 also prohibits discrimination against women in the field of wages and protects women worker with regard to hours of work, night work and guarantees maternity leave for six weeks, (in case of multiple birth, 10 weeks leave before the expected date of birth, 8 weeks after child birth. But if a woman request to work after 8 weeks, she can work) and equal opportunity in employment. Article 5 of the Labor Standard Act, prohibits employer not to force workers to work against their will, by means of violence, intimidation, imprisonment or any other unfair restraint on the mental or physical freedom of the workers.

Women are appearing in the work place in increasing numbers (About 16.7 million women were employed in 1988; an increase of 550,000 relative to the previous year. The proportion of women in the work force also increased to a historical high of 36.8% compared to 36.5% in 1987). More than 90% of unmarried women in their 20's, excluding students are employed, compared to about 60% of married women[7]. Table 1.7(a) highlights ratio of female employment classified by martial status. Chart 1.4 shows trends in distribution ratio of women labors, classified by martial status (excluding agricultural and forestry industry) and Table 1.6 deals with trends in hired labor and classified by gender. According to 1988 white paper on working women, newly hired female employees by educational background, 13.5% had college or university diplomas and 23.19% had junior college diplomas. University and junior college female graduates represented 22.0% of total employees. The number of women workers is increasing due to shortage of workforce in recent years. Housewives, who had not been working, started to work and younger female workers who had been leaving work after marriage began to stay in employment. Thus the percentage of female employees over 30 years and percentage of married women has been increasing steadily. The proportion of married women among total number of women employees exceeded 50%. Part time women workers account for a significant portion of this increase. Women workers have become a last resort for much needed additional labor.[8]

In spite of laws, discrimination still prevails. The difference between men and women according to Nakamura, reflect not only worker's characteristics including age, length of service, educational background and position in the household, but also employment factors such as industrial sector, size of enterprise, job and position classification where women are employed. Many companies will employ women only in temporary, part-time or low paying jobs. According to the Labor Ministry Survey on Personnel Management of women workers in 1981, only 27% of companies that recruited university graduates offered employment to female graduates. As per the Ministry of Labor Report of 1987, about recruitment and employment of female, over 80% of the respondents claimed that they "did not discriminate against women even before the law enforced or that the system has improved since". Ninety-six to ninety-eight percent said that they improved in recruitment, those conditions which had been discriminating toward women, such as setting an upper age limit and recruiting only those who commute to work from the home of their parents. As for job assignment and transfer, about 56.1% said they had not discriminated against women. Regarding this 53.8% said they had not discriminated against women before the law went to enforcement. A 1990 poll by the Sendai Bar Association reports, that many women complain that working conditions have worsened rather than improved since the Equal Employment Opportunity Law, enacted four years ago. According to poll survey only 16% of the respondents, mainly women workers at large companies feel working condition have improved since the law has been enforced, while 84% say they have seen no change. The most notable changes cited by respondents were that overtime work had been increased, discrimination in promotions had diminished, wages were in greater parity with men and menstrual leave had been abolished. Only 25% of the respondents say contract terms for recruits are equal for both sexes. The survey also shows that female workers at larger companies work fewer hours in principle and have more paid holidays than those in smaller companies. But in reality they are reportedly forced to work more overtime and face difficulties when taking holidays. About 20% of respondents say they do not have the 14 weeks of maternity leave that is guaranteed by law. Respondents also complain of low wages, strained relationship with co-workers, difficulties in taking holidays and hard work.

Discrimination also prevails in retirement policies, promotion and training. The Labor Ministry has issued guidelines for the abolition of a lower retirement age for women with some success. Early retirement of women worker has been declared as illegal by courts in Japan. According to Supreme Court's decision, a disparity in the retirement age between men and women is unconstitutional, even if employer is phasing in a common retirement age. An early retirement system is sometimes put into effect for special categories of employees particularly for women. Such a system applied regardless of sex is legal, only in so far as it is reasonable to have early retirement because of the nature of the work. This is however very exceptional.

Women workers are over protected and given higher treatment. Women workers are allowed to do overtime amounting to 2 hours a day, 6 hours a week or 150 hours a year. However, women workers engaged in accountancy may work more than 6 hours' overtime a week provided they do not work more than 12 hours in 2 weeks. Women are not allowed to work at night, underground or on the weekly holiday. Dangerous jobs and jobs which involve the carrying of heavy weights, as specified by an ordinance of the labor ministry are prohibited for women.

The labor ministry's survey showed that fewer than 40% of companies employ women in positions above the level of supervisor and 20% of these companies provide no training whatsoever for women workers. Forty percent provide different kinds of training for women and men. In spite of the legal principle of equal pay for equal work in 1982, the average wage for women workers was 52.8% of that of men. On many occasions sex discrimination remains difficult to prove in Japan.

Koike Kazuo acknowledges that to some extent, women workers in Japan are not an advance as women workers in other industrialized countries. For example, as there are fewer Japanese women in administrative positions and in their prime age, the male-female wage difference is considerably greater than those in some other advance countries. He also maintains, however, that the major explanation of the phenomenon is the highly developed internalization of Japanese labor markets, particularly for large firms. He claims therefore, Japanese women workers lag far behind men in terms of their labor force participation and working conditions because of the backwardness of social and institutional arrangements for working women.

Article 14 of the constitution also prohibits discriminating because of race, creed, social status and family origin. Other types of discrimination such as discrimination on the basis of religion, age, color, marital status, politics, ethnicity and nationality are less pervasive. However, few cases of discrimination based on race, color and nationality have been reported. Hanami feels discrimination because of race and nationality may present a greater problem in the future because of the expected growth in the number of foreign workers due to the increasing internationalization of the Japanese economy.

(b) Part Time Workers

With growing number of workers engaged in service industries, the number of female part timers, particularly housewives participating in the labor force, has been increasing sharply in recent years. Part time employment is able to respond to fluctuating daily or weekly labor demand. Skilled part timers and part timers engaged in specialized work constitute key part of the labor force. Part time workers tend to choose firms and employment conditions, in order to harmonize a career with family duties and therefore, they commute for very short distance.

Part timers work shorter hours than regular full time workers and also do not generally work overtime. In Japan, workers who work less than 35 hours a week are regarded as part timer. A third of part time workers, work over 40% less than full time workers and three-quarters work over 20% less. However, 12% work almost the same number of hours as full-time worker. Part timers generally work on an hourly basis. About 93% of the enterprises surveyed are paid hourly based wages. Three out of every four firms decide on wages, mainly taking into account wage level of part timers of the same category in their regions.

In 1983, the number of part time workers reached 5.03 million of whom 3.52 million were woman accounting for 70% of the total number of part time workers. The most common reasons for hiring part-time workers are: it is to adjust the number of hires according to up and down in production, seasonal rush, it is easy to deal the daily busy periods, to take over before or after regular employee's working hours or during their break periods, personal costs are less expensive, position does not require specialized knowledge or skill and can be filled adequately by a part-timer; it is easy to hire part-timers with required specialized knowledge or skill, re-hiring or retired employees and difficult to hire regular employees (Table 1.8). On many occasions the employer finds problems with part timers such as promotion and advancement, wages, ability to perform duties, job training, personal relationships and adherence ration (Table 1.9).

TABLE 1.8

Ratio of Enterprise—Reasons for Hiring Part-time Workers

(M.A. %)

Enterprise hiring (All Industries)	100.0
Esay to adjust number of hires according to ups and downs in production (sales)	27.1
Seasonal rush	24.5
To deal with daily periods	24.1
To take over before or after regular employee's working hours of during their break periods	5«1
Personnel costs are less expensive	43.4
Position does not require specialized knowledge or skill and can be filled adequately by a part-timer	45.8
Easy to hire part-timers with the required specialized knowledge or skill	3.2
As extended employment or re-hiring of retired employees	6.3
Difficult to hire regular employees	34.5
Others	5.8
Enterprises not replying	0.6

The survey conducted by the Ministry of Labor (1998), found that of the workers Questioned, 80% were regular employees and 16% were non-regular employees. Of the workers employed under other than full time, 62% were part-

TABLE 1.9
Ratio of Enterprise—Problems after Hiring Part-time Workers

	(M.A. %)
Enterprises hiring (All Industries)	100.0
Promotion, advancement	6.0
Wages	16.6
Ability to perform duties Job training	14.0
Personal relationships	16.7
Adherence ratio	25.7
Other	2.0
No particular problems	54.4
Enterprises not replying	9.2

Sources : Year Book of Labour Statistics, 1988.

time, 16% were seasonal or temporary employees, 7.4% were workers employed under contract, and 3.8% were workers dispatched by manpower companies. Non-regular workers made up 61.4% of the total work force in eating establishment, 45.9% in food products distribution, 45.7% in commodities distribution including department stores and super markets, 37.7% in entertainment excluding movies and 35.5% in other services, such as building maintenance and security guards. Furthermore there were part-time worker in 53.7% of the establishments polled, seasonal and temporary workers in 21.3% and workers sent from parent and related firms were 14.1%. Regarding wages total average monthly cash earnings were about 350,000 yen for workers sent from parent or related companies, 190,000 yen for workers employed under contract, 170,000 yen for workers dispatched by manpower companies, 140,000 yen for seasonal or temporary workers and 90,000 yen for part-time as of October 1987.

(c) Senior Workers

In Japan the problem of senior worker is becoming increasingly important and pressing. According to Ministry of

Labor report on employment service (1987) the ratio of job openings to applicant by age was as follows: the total ratio was 0.80, whereas for the age group of 55 years and old it was 0.40 and 0.10 for 60 to 65 years. By 2000 the proportion of workers aged 55 and older in the total labor force is estimated at 23% and sharp increase from 18% in 1985. The percentage of full time employment among older persons is higher than part-time.

Due to shortage of labor, government has to increase mandatory retirement age to 60 years. The law concerning the stabilization of aged workers' employment was enacted and comprehensive employment measure based on this law is being promoted in response to various needs of older people with emphasis on the following points:

1. The encouragement of a continuous employment relationship with the same enterprise or it's affiliated companies until about 65 years old, on the basis of mandatory retirement system at the age of 60.
2. The promotion of early re-entry of the older unemployed who want to be re-employed.
3. The encouragement of temporary and short-term employment for those who leave their job after reaching the mandatory retirement age.

The government also requests the enterprise to extend mandatory retirement age, put up an effective placement service through employment counseling office for aged workers and extends assistance to organizations such as The Association of Employment Development for senior workers.

Many Japanese workers continue to work after they reached the retirement age. Economic difficulty and workaholic attitude are not the major reasons. According to Kawakita Takashi, the most important reasons, why they continue to work, based on his survey are:

1. To make a living (21%)
2. To stay healthy (21%)
3. To supplement the family income (10.7%)
4. To earn the pocket money (4.2%)
5. Love for current job

6. To do something useful in the society
7. The company needs (1.6%)
8. May feel bored with nothing to do ((1.6%)
9. Want friends (0.4%)
10. May feel humiliated without job (0.2%)
11. Most of my former co-workers continue to work (0.2%)
12. Other reasons (1.7%)

From the enterprise point of view the ıeasons for increasing of older persons are for work:

1. Use of the aged peoples' experience and ability
2. They are fit for work
3. Public opinion (good)
4. Difficulty of recruiting young and middle aged persons
5. Work for all ages (available)
6. Continue to work and cheap cost payment

However, there are people who do not wish to take up employment after 55 year because:

1. Live on pension or retirement allowance
2. Have a income from property
3. Take care of children
4. For health reasons
5. Hard physical work
6. Old skills or experiences are useless
7. Not able to find favorable job and wish to attend to hobby or social activities

(d) Child Labor

Child labor was one of the first fields in which standards were adopted by the world community. In Japan minors less than 20 years of age can only conclude any kind of contract with the permission of their parents or guardians. The Labor Standard Law, provides that parent or guardian cannot conclude an employment contract in the place of the minor and also that the minor has the right to receive wages independently and the parent or guardian may not receive the minors' wages by proxy. With the permission of Labor Standard Office, children less than 15 years age but over 12 can work, which does not harm their health or welfare, after school hours. For those under 15 years old who are only permitted to work in specified industries, the maximum is 7 hours a day, 42 yours a week (including school hours). For those more than 15 years old, but less than 18 years old, working time may be extended to 10 hours a day, the total for the week are prohibited for minors under 18 years old. Night work is also prohibited, except for those over 16 years of age who are working on shifts. Minor under 18 years of age are also prohibited from working in the dangerous and harmful jobs specified by an ordinance of the Labor Ministry.

(e) Foreign Workers

The issue of foreign workers has been receiving constant media coverage, discussed at various levels and drawn public attention in Japan in recent years. There are two reasons for such an attention. 1. Internationalization of Japanese economy and society. 2. The number of foreigners who are legally qualified to work in Japan are (termed illegal foreign workers) increasing rapidly.

Japan has a very restrictive policy towards the introduction of foreign workers into Japan. Foreigners coming to Japan can not get visa with a work-permit, except when special abilities are needed.

In 1988 there were 2,44,447 foreigners in Japan, among them large number (1,727,200) were for short-term stay. South Korea constitutes 677,140 out of total classified by nationality. According to figures released by the Ministry of Agriculture, Forestry and Fisheries in November 1989, twenty out of twenty-five major restaurant chain (those with 200 or more employees) were hiring foreign nationals. The number of restaurants employing foreign nationals in this way is increasing. With the globalization of Japanese corporations, there are also increasing examples of foreign national being promoted to executive post at headquarter offices.

The views and opinions are varied among the government and industry circles concerning acceptance of foreign workers.

The chairman of the Japan Chambers of Commerce said, that Japan should sign an agreement with the nations involved under which a system should be devised for accepting foreign workers for a limited period and repatriating them after the period elapses. The Kansai Employer's Association, feels Japan should not rush in releasing regulation of employment for foreign worker but allow foreign workers engaged in professional job and skilled workers to be employed in Japan.

In Japan the Employment Security Authority will handle foreign workers issue with following three pillars: giving guidance on the issue of foreign workers to the employer, coping effectively with illegal work and responding appropriately to foreign job-seekers.

Hanami, says since the number of foreign workers is so low, Japan has no practical problem with such workers and for having kept homogeneous quality of her own workers and avoid the trouble and unrest caused by guest workers both in industrial relations and in society in general. However, the government is worried that if no measures are taken, the situation will likely seriously affect domestic employment and working conditions. The government is of the opinion that in order to contribute, to a solution of the unemployment problems in the neighboring developing countries, it is more effective to extend economic assistance to increase employment opportunities within those countries than to offer limited employment opportunities in Japan.[9]

In Japan the rate of gainfully employed persons tended to decrease on the whole and this tendency was particularly true among young and older male workers. Among female worker, on the other hand, the rate of gainfully employed workers tended to increase, in all age groups except for the age group of 15-16, in particular. This implies that newly hired female workers increased in number. Looking at the relationship between the distributions of the gainfully employed was that the proportion of young workers was high, in high productivity industries or occupations. While the portion of middle-aged and older workers as high in low-productivity sectors. Furthermore the higher the level of educational background, the more conspicuous was the tendency for those gainfully employed to be engaged in the first or second occupational group.

(f) Japanese Job-Seekers

Japanese labor market today is facing with serious problems like: shortage of labor, aging labor force and changing values of younger generations. There is a marked decline in worker's participation rate among young, because of higher education and recent demographic changes. According to this survey more than 80% of high school graduates wish to go for higher studies. In 1988 the employment situation continued to improve. The ratio of effective job openings to applicants continued to climb steadily. In mid-1988 this ratio topped for the first time since 1975, representing an overall excess of job openings over applicants. The marked rise in job openings is largely responsible for the increase in the job openings-to-applicant ratio, while on the other hand, a share drop in job applicants has also contributed to the increased ratio. The ratio of job offers to part-time job-seekers showed particularly marked increase.

The brisk growth of Japanese economy today and tomorrow will depend much upon young Japanese. At a time when Japanese companies look for young job-seekers, the Japanese virtues of hard work, growth-conducive attitude of labor, self-discipline, being content with simple life and sensitivity to others are changing drastically.

There is growing tendency of Japanese companies recruiting young workers today. Why are they recruiting young workers? The important considerations for hiring young workers are: labor shortage, aging labor force, preparing youth for new technology and business expansion and high school career employees to manual section. Takashi Kawakita highlighted six reasons why today young workers are wanted by Japanese companies:

1. An increase in many new jobs due to expanded economy,
2. Young worker respond flexibly to the restructuring of firm,
3. Young workers are paid lower average wages than older workers,

4. Demographic pattern will result in a decline in the young working population in years to come,
5. Young workers will have increasing job mobility, and
6. Expanding demand for highly educated persons among new university graduates.

Large companies always compete with each other in attracting good young workers by providing them education and training programs, sometimes with gifts, trips and parties.

The growing desire of companies to employ young and the disparate labor condition have prompted the Japanese companies to discover very unique recruitment tactics. Unlike in most countries Japanese recruitment practice is very interesting and unique. The recruitment pattern varies by the size of enterprise and the type of occupation. However, the following channels are used for mid-career and part-time workers: public sector employment referral offices, head hunter, introduced by customers or affiliated company, introduced by economic or industrial organization with which the enterprise has relations, introduced by university or research institute professor, personal relationship (friend or acquaintance of employee), want-advertisement, flyer, posted notice, etc. The most common forms of recruitment are: asking graduating of university to invite students of their alma mater at seminar courses and clubs to join their companies, asking professors to recommend their students, sending books and magazines offering jobs to students, conducting recruitment briefings for college students, posting job notice at college and university placement offices, putting want advertisements in news papers, recruitment potential graduates through recruitment counseling centers established by local government, conducting short-term vocational training and study meetings for potential graduates so as to employ them later, employing as regular workers potential graduates who once worked temporarily and lastly employing potential recruits through personal connection.

While hiring new workers, most Japanese companies consider—scholastic record, specialized knowledge or skill, general accomplishment, ability of language, ability to understand and decide, zeal and volition, creativity and ability to plan, cooperativity and health and physical strength. Once a young man is recruited to a large firm, he will be provided job training, which plays the major role in worker's skill acquisition and development and he is expected to remain with the same company till the retirement.

3. CHANGING TRENDS IN JAPANESE WORKER AND MANAGEMENT

(a) Characteristics of Japanese Work

It is accepted that Japanese workers perform much better than their counterpart in other countries today. Kazutoshi Koshiro on the basis of his case study found that attendance rate of workers at large plants of major industries ranged between 90 to 96% and labor turnover was very low. By this he means that the institutional and organizational arrangements in large Japanese firms not only keep the worker's motivation and productivity at high level, but at the same time provide them with a high degree of satisfaction and sense of security.

It is worth noting the general characteristics of Japanese people.[10] Hayashi Chikio (1970) in his survey gave list of adjectives and asked to choose, which they (respondents) felt appropriate Characteristics of Japanese People. The adjectives they choose from the list in order of frequency were: Diligent (16%), persistent capable of 'sticking it out' (58%), Polite (47%), kind (45%), idealistic (23%), cheerful (13%), open (13%), respectful of freedom (12%), national (11%), and creative (8%), while from the list of boo-words, they chose short-tempered (49%), quiet to enthuse, quick to cool off (47%), insular (39%), imitative (27%), vindictive (26%), stingy (20%), cunning (19%), arrogant (9%), insincere (9%) and cruel (5%).

Due to rapid economic growth the living standard of every Japanese worker has been constantly improving, along with changes in their attitude towards living, work and social problems. The Labor Ministry's survey of worker's attitudes show that more than 71% of those who replied were 'generally satisfied' with their dietary standards while 17% answered 'slightly dissatisfied' and only 6% said they were 'very dissatisfied'. Over 60% of the respondents said they were 'generally satisfied' with their standards of clothing, with the 'slightly dissatisfied' and 'very dissatisfied' groups totaling only 23% and 5% respectively. In the case of housing however, 45 answered 'very dissatisfied', while 41% said 'generally satisfied. The study as a whole indicated general stability in worker living conditions. The White paper (1971) on labor found that the percentage of those going on to high school and university has also sharply risen. Sudden development of labor mobility and employment and promotions are more and more based on ability. A new urban middle class has grown where traditional social class consciousness has weakened.

The Ministry of Labor, in nationwide attitude survey attempted to compare attitude of workers in large and small companies. One of the questions had to do with, whether or not they wished to improve their skill and knowledge. An overwhelming majority responded that they did, a negligible number gave negative answers. Only among blue-collar workers there was a slight difference in the level of aspirations, with employees of small firms expressing slightly lower aspirations than did workers employed by large enterprises. This difference might be attributed in the past to the less developed career patterns in small firms. There was no difference in the level of aspirations among white-collar workers by size of the firm.[11]

The Ministry of Labor also points out that the change in workers attitude also gives rise to new desires and discontents. According to the white paper, younger employees seek higher wages more for 'leisure', while middle-age employees are more concerned with 'better housing' and older people want higher wages for 'stability in old-age living standards'. The attitudes of each group reflect its own conditions and, as incomes rise, so do desires. This will no doubt be a continuing phenomenon. Traditional Japanese employee is 'work-centered' or 'industrious' and while this feeling remains strong more and more Japanese consider home life. Japanese workers' values are changing; they feel that they need 'privacy'. Dore says more popular recent coinage in mai-homu-shugi or 'my-house-ism'. This refers to 'privatized' concerns of the man of small ambition—chiefly concerned to get a pretty little house and a pretty little wife and two model children, to have a color TV and a cooler and to join the ranks of maikaa-zoku, the 'my car tribe'.

The Prime Minister's Office, opinion study shows differences in attitudes by age group. While only 56% of employees between 16 and 29 place 'very strong' or 'considerable' emphasis upon their work, 77% in the 30-49 group feel also they way. Interestingly enough, demands of home life are not seen as conflicting with job responsibility, 64% of the above 30-49 group also place the same emphasis on their home life. The survey also indicated that 37% of all Japanese workers to-day find greatest satisfaction in their lives when absorbed in their work, 21% when at home with their families and another 21% when taking part in leisure activities. As could be expected, younger age group enjoy leisure activities more, while middle age group enjoy work more. In the older age groups, the stress is on family life.

The old tight bonds, between employee and employer are deteriorating these days, now more value generally is put on 'loyalty for the minute' than on a commitment 'to live and die with his place', says David Shanks. The pre-requisites where responsible—'ethics of work excellence', 'ethics of duty' and 'ethics of cooperation' are also changing.[12]

The number of employees who feel that work is a human duty is decreasing, comments such as 'work is but one part of life' or I enjoy my work, but 'rest and recreation are also necessary', are being heard more frequently. This means that Japan is leaving the period in which all took life in relation to the individual work and moving into an age where more concern is given to the larger aspect of life than mere work. The Ministry of Labor also found that 34% of all males interviewed gave either the nature of the work or their own suitability to the kind of work offered foremost consideration when deciding to accept employment. Among Japanese workers discontent is becoming common. The Ministry of labor study shows that 66% complain of mental fatigue—a number greater than 42% who object to the physical fatigue of their work. About 20% complained that 'the work is monotonous' or I can't use my 'skill and abilities'. Such discontent is strong among 20-24 age groups, where 28% complained they lacked the chance to use their abilities and 37% considered their work monotonous.[13]

The above findings indicate that work and living attitudes vary widely from generation to generation. One study pointed out that earlier most young Japanese felt they should live 'purely and honestly resisting the evils of the world' or 'without thinking of oneself, offer everything for the public good', but lately young Japanese worker favor living 'according to one's own taste, disregarding money or position' or 'living easily day to day, without worrying'. Even among workers in their 50's do not think completely in pre-war terms, in this group too, selflessness for common good has in many cases given way to desire for a life of greater personal satisfaction.[14]

(b) Labor-Management Relations

The characteristics of Japanese harmonious labor-management relations have drawn considerable international interest to-day. Japan's unique system of life time employment, enterprise union, stable labor-management relations, seniority wage and 'shunto' (spring offensive) have increased the degree of attention and interest among industrialized and developing countries.

Japanese labor-management relations have been extremely stable but in recent years there have been only few cases of strikes for an extended period. The stability of Japan's labor-management relationships achieved as a result of:[15]

1. In a particular enterprise, class-consciousness is not pronounced; therefore, work community is homogeneous rather than heterogeneous.
2. The Japanese workers attach great importance to the employment stability, the seniority wage system and the improvement of working conditions within enterprise. Management also regards worker as an essential partner.
3. Japanese trade union, especially larger trade unions in the private sector, tends to decide their positions taking largely into account the situation of the national economy.

The Constitution of Japan guarantees in its Article 28 that workers have the right to organize, bargain collectively and strike. Trade Union Law supports this constitutional provision.

Japanese trade unions are organized at enterprise level and working conditions including wages are determined by collective bargaining in between the enterprise union and individual employer. At present most trade unions are organized at the level of the enterprise. Of all trade unions, 94.2% are enterprise unions and they comprise 91.1% of all organized workers. Most of these unions are affiliated to industrial and/or regional federation but these federations have limited control. The federations deal with political and institutional problem, which are beyond the scope of enterprise union. The enterprise unions enjoy complete autonomy including finance. I will deal more about enterprise-based trade union later in Chapter 3.

In Japan wages are negotiated between labor and management every spring (March and April). This negotiation is called 'shunto' (the Spring Offensive). Shunto is a bargaining process in which individual enterprise unions simultaneously submit their demand for wage increases, and negotiate with their respective employers under the direction and coordination of national centers and industrial federations. Shunto has become the major wage determination process, unique in the world. The Japan Federation of Employer Association has put forward the principle whereby wage should follow productivity increases. It seems, however, that its main purpose is not to control wages but rather prices. I will have more to say about wages later.

Labor disputes in Japan are settled autonomously in principle, by labor and management. Whenever, labor-management fails to reach an amicable settlement, Labor Relations Commission (LRC) under the Labor Relations Adjustment Law, provides conciliation, mediation and arbitration machinery to settle the labor disputes. Conciliation is the most popular, moderate and simple method.

"In conciliation, a conciliator appointed by the chairman of the LRC, works to resolve a labor dispute by confirming claims of both-sides, holding adjustment and coordination in order to reach agreement through autonomous compromise".

"In mediation, a mediation committee composed of representatives of public, union and management hears both sides' claims, prepares a mediation plan to settle the disputes, and recommends that labor and management accept the proposal".

"In arbitration, an arbitration committee composed of three independent arbitrators decides of a fair and reasonable proposal for settling the dispute and thus arbitration award, having the same effect as collective agreements, binds both sides and brings the dispute to a final settlement".

Most labor disputes were settled by negotiations between labor and management. More than 80% of the settlements involving a third party were reached through conciliation. I will discuss the question of labor disputes and the settlement machinery later in Chapter 6.

(c) Rights and Duties of Employee and Employer

In Japan the rights and duties of the employee and employer are not so much specified in labor contract, because they are provided by collective agreement rules of employment and labor law. The rights of (right to organize unions, right to bargain collectively and right to act collectively) wage earners and salaried employees are enumerated in Article 28 of the constitution.

(i) Employee's Duties

The duties of an employee can be classified as: (i) the duty to work, (ii) the duty to respect professional secrets. The employee has an obligation to do work under the command, authority and control of the employer and to obey his orders. This includes obeying provisions of the work rules and the order of his superiors and generally to do the work required of his during working time at the designated working place with dedication. Japanese employees are required to be devoted to the company's cause even outside the working hours. The employee is obligated to work in the place designated by the employer. Japanese labor is not narrowly specialized in a particular job, but multi-skilled and experienced due to life time employment system and the training on-the-job. Workers expect to be transferred during their lifetime employment, when collective agreement or rules of employment stipulates.

However, recently numbers of cases concerning transfers are brought to the court. The court declares the order of transfer null and void as 'abuse of right' if it finds that the transfer has caused serious difficulties or disadvantages for the employee.[16]

There are two kinds of framing-out (shukko) systems. One is the framing-out in which workers work on a regular basis at another enterprise, under the direction of that employer, while maintaining the status as an employee at the enterprise where he was formerly engaged in work. Another is the framing-out in which workers lose the status as an employee at an enterprise and take employment in another enterprise, which is often an enterprise related to the first one. Framing-out is different from transfer, because framing-out involves a change in the party, which directs the employee. This is a reflection of the principle that rights and obligations concerning provision of labor are not assignable (Civil Code Art. 625). Therefore, framing-outs are impermissible unless the employee consents, even if there is a provision in the rules of employment or collective agreement, that the company sometime orders framing-out in case when there is operational necessity.

Though legally speaking the nature and extent of the duty to respect professional secrets is not so clear, ethically speaking the employee's loyalty to the enterprise is expected by not disclosing his employer's trade secrets or confidential information. The disclosure of information in Japan, is recognized as matter of betrayal as breach of specific obligation.

In Japan, rules of employment often provide for disciplinary action where an employee commits a crime or engage in other conduct outside the enterprise, which harms the credit of the enterprise.

(ii) Employer's Duties

Employer's duty consists of: (1) To provide work, (2) To pay wage, (3) To provide decent working conditions, and (4) Duty at the end of labor contract.

Labor legislations in Japan requires, that the employer takes a number of steps in order to employ an employee, such as: obtaining various required documents and reporting, notifying or registering with government office, details about condition of work, accidents, the employment of certain categories of employees, social insurance, the introduction of certain machinery, equipment or facilities and so on. He must introduce measures to protect his employee's health and to ensure the safety of the plant.

Duty to provide work or use of the worker by an employer is the point of controversy. Such questions are raised when an employer refuses employee to work, after the dismissal is declared null and void by the court and while the employer is paying wages to the employee. The general tendency of the theories and cases, are to answer this question in affirmative because:[17]

> (1) The employee's interest in the actual work should be admitted, since the work itself has a meaning in terms of his won personal dignity, (2) Especially if an unfair labor practice by the employer is involved, the employee's interest in having access to the work place is vital, because of the importance of union activity at the enterprise unaer the Japanese conditions of enterprise unionism, and (3) It is an established legal precedent that the courts will order the employer to accept the right of the employee to work at his former work place if they find that his transfer was illegal.

The Labor Standard Act (Art.11) defines 'wage remuneration of labor when they are called wages, salaries, allowances, bonuses or whatever, but they are not regarded as wages if they form a part of welfare facilities provided by an employer'. Retirement benefits are paid in a single lump sum and regarded as an act of grace by an employer. Under Article 24 (L.S. Act), employer must pay wages in cash and in full directly to the worker at least once a month or on a specified date, except extraordinary wages and bonuses. Payment other than in currency may be permitted by statute or administrative order or collective agreement. Payment by bank transfer of funds into account of an employee is permissible, but the payment by check is not lawful in Japan because of the danger of dishonor. The delayed payment of wages can be punished by a fine. The Security of Wage Payment Act, 1975 was enacted to secure the payment of wages and other monetary interest of employees in the case of their employer's insolvency. Payment to the parents or guardian of a minor or to a representative who has received a mandate from an employee is prohibited. Article 25 (L.S. Act) demands the employer to pay all wages which the employer has already earned, when employee demand payment in order to meet expenses of an emergency, such as child birth, disease, accident, marriage or death of some one who is supported by the employee.

Deductions from the wages may be permitted by statute or administrative order or a written agreement with the majority union or with the representative of the majority of employees if there is no majority union.

The Minimum Wages Act has been passed in 1959. Minimum wages are determined by the Labor Minister or Chief of the Prefecture Labor Standards Bureau. The L.S. Act (Art. 26) stipulates that when the employer is responsible for causing the rest day, the employer shall pay allowance equivalent to not less than 60% of the worker's average wage. This allowance is compulsory in the sense that it is enforced by a fine. Under Civil Code (Art. 536, Sec. 2) the employer is liable to pay the full wage if the performance of the employee becomes impossible for a cause for which the employer is responsible. At least 60% of the wage is secured by the threat of criminal penalties under the L.S. Act. Article 4, demand that the employer shall not discriminate women against men concerning wage by reason of the worker being a woman. However, it is not a violation of the Act to establish wage differentials on the basis of efficiency or technical skills.

Article 1, section 1 of the L.S. Act, provides that working conditions must be such, as will meet the needs of the worker who lives a life worthy of a human being, Article 1 section 2 (L.S. Act), requires the employer that he not only observes the various protection labor law provisions governing safety, hygiene and other working condition, but also to endeavor to promote the raising of standards above the minimum laid down by the legislation. The employer is obligated to allow his employees the necessary time-off to exercise their right to vote and other civil rights and to carry out their public duties.

As per L.S. Act (Arts. 89 and 90) the employer who employs more than ten employees continuously, must draw up employment rules and submit them to the L.S. Inspectors' Office. The employer is required to take the opinion of majority union, or the representative of the majority of employee, before he draws up employment rules or changes them. The employer is also required to make employment rules known to the employees by posting or affixing them in a place where they can easily be seen. The working conditions must be laid down in the employment rules. The Supreme Court has said that in principle as employer can not unilaterally deprive employees' rights which they have already obtained or changing working conditions in a disadvantageous way by changing employment rules, but the revised rules are valid so long as the changes are reasonable, even if each individual employee does not consent to the change, because the employment rules represent uniform determination and collective treatment of terms and condition of employment.

The employer shall provide (Art. 22) the retiring or dismissed worker a certificate stating the period of employment, the type of work done, his position in the enterprise and his wages. Employer shall not include what worker does not ask for and shall not send or circulate information about the nationality, creed, social status or union activities nor make any secret mark on the certificate. The employer must make full payment of wages; return any reserves, bonds, savings or other funds a valuable belonging to the employee within 7 days of his retirement, dismissal or death. The employer must pay the necessary travel expenses of the worker when returns home within the days of the cancellation of the contract, if the worker has cancelled it because the real working conditions were different from those which were specified before the contract, the rights and obligations of both employer and employee terminates.

Since every union has legal status, Japanese employer will have to bargain with every union, which demands to bargain, thus finds difficulty. Obligation to bargain does not mean (employer) to reach an agreement however; employer has to try in good faith to reach an agreement. Collective bargaining is used for matters such as working conditions, while consultation will be used to deal with problems which are not to be suitable for bargaining—dismissal, transfer, promotion change in production, sales or their management policies, the introduction of new methods technology or facilities, the abolition of certain plants or work division, etc. Matters which are regarded as matters of managerial prerogative by the management side are certainly not suitable for collective bargaining. Theoretically, it is generally admitted that the employer has an obligation to bargain about all aspects of managerial decisions if they affect working conditions.

As the constitution guarantees the right to act collectively only to workers, the employer's right to lock-out is recognized or not, is real problem in Japan. The majority admits the right of employers to lock workers out of 'balance or fairness' between employer and worker, but minority do not agree.

(iii) Employee's Rights

The Articles 27 and 28 of the constitution of Japan, are regarded as being the most fundamental legal sources of labor law. Article 27 section 1 provides for the 'right to work', section 2 provides a 'basis of protective labor law' and section 3 'prohibits the exploitation of children'. Article 28 guarantees the 'right of workers to organize, bargain and act collectively'. Thus government has a political obligation to try and provide jobs for all those who are willing to work, with regard to those who do not want to work; government has no obligation to assure them of the wholesome and cultured life. Legally the right to organize, to bargain and to act collectively has been provided by the constitution as human rights. This Constitutional guarantee of workers' rights, including right to bargain, is almost unknown in other countries.[18] In fact, the constitution has given too much protection to the employee and his union. The right to organize is guaranteed for all workers, in terms of the type of organization, organizational principles and policies. Every enterprise in Japan has right to organize union and bargain collectively (even minority union). In 1982 some 9 million employees, which is nearly 90% of the organized labor force, except government employees who are not eligible to bargain collectively, were covered by collective agreements.

(iv) Employer's Rights

The employer has a power as per work rules or on the basis of contract for disciplinary action—warning, reduction in wages, suspension, demotion and discharge, for violations of management rules and orders. Among various kinds of disciplinary actions, discharge is most severe. In Japanese legal theory and in practice a wide range of issues are susceptible to collective bargaining, in fact almost all the issues over which the employer has control are regarded as coming within the scope of bargaining. The argument of the 'management prerogative' has rarely been accepted—except by management ideologies. Article 8 of PCNELR law excludes matters which affect the management and operation of public corporation and national enterprises from collective bargaining.

4. WORKING CONDITIONS

The Constitution[19] provides that standards of working conditions should be fixed by law and proclaims the principle of welfare-state, obliging the government to guarantee a certain standards for the workers. Labor Law aims to protect workers with regard to their working conditions.

Most of the provisions of the L.S. Act of 1947 provide minimum standards for working conditions. Article 1 and section 2 fixes minimum standard working conditions. Therefore, parties of labor relations much not reduce working condition with excuse of this standard and instead, should endeavor to raise the working condition. Working conditions should be decided by the worker and employer on equal basis. The worker and employer must abide by the labor agreement, rule of employment and labor contract; and must discharge their respective duties faithfully.

Under life time employment system, employees prefer to be protected by enterprise union which bargains with the employer about working conditions. The job of Japanese trade union is to decide, control and improve the working condition in an enterprise. Most of the working conditions except wages are decided exclusively by collective bargaining within each enterprise. The employer has an obligation to bargain about all aspect of managerial decisions if they affect working conditions. Any provision in an individual contract which contravenes the standard of working conditions and other treatment provided for workers in a collective agreement shall be null and void, and that invalidated part of the individual contract shall be replaced by the appropriate provision in the collective agreement, since the main purpose of the collective agreement is certainly to improve the working conditions and the general treatment of the workers at that work place. The coverage of collective agreement is limited to the working conditions of member of the union which is a party to the agreement although the same working conditions are in fact also provided for any unorganized employees in the enterprise. The improved conditions whether gained by individual bargaining or brought in voluntarily by the employer, should not be denied of their legality just because a collective agreement has provided for a lower standard. The working conditions specified by the former collective agreement will remain binding on the employer and on the workers, who are union members only until new collective agreements or new individual contracts have been drawn. The L.S. Act requires the employer to clarify the wages, hours of work and other working condition for the workers when they conclude contract. If the real working conditions are different from those stated, the worker is entitled to cancel the contract and the employer must pay the traveling expenses incurred by the worker who has changed is residence to take up the work if he returns home within 14 days of cancellation. According to Article 13 of the L.S. Act, when a contract provides for working conditions inferior to the standards set by the law, only those conditions are invalid and they are replaced by the conditions stipulated in the law.

Article I, section 1 of the L.S. Act, provides that working conditions must be such, as will meet the needs of the worker who lives a life worthy of a human being. The Article I section 2, of the L.S. Act, Law requires that employer not only observes the various protective labor law provisions governing safety, hygiene and other working conditions, but also the endeavor to promote the raising of standards above the minimum laid down by the legislation. The employer will be obligated to secure the decent and humane treatment of workers and raise welfare of his employees. As per L.S. Act, an employer is required to pay the transport cost not only to female employee and employee less than 18 years, but also to those who terminate their contracts because they have found the actual conditions to be different from what was stated before the contracts were concluded. The employer also has to provide time to exercise employee his rights to vote, other civil rights and to carry out his public utilities.

The employer who employs more than ten employees continuously must draw his work rules and submit to the Labor Standard Office, after obtaining the opinion of the majority union (in the absence of majority union, the opinion of the representative of the majority of employees). The following working conditions must always be laid down in the work rulers.[20]

1. Hours of work, rest hours, holidays, vacations and shifts;
2. Wages—methods of deciding, computation and date of payment, promotion and so on; and
3. Matters concerning retirement and dismissal.

If there are any of the following benefits, system or measures the employer must also stipulate them in the work rules.

1. Retirement allowances, bonuses, minimum wage and so on,
2. The cost charged to the employees for food, equipment and other expenses,
3. Regulations covering safety, sanitation and related matter,
4. Regulations about vocational training,
5. Regulations governing accident compensation and relief for injury and illness sustained outside work,
6. Official commendation or sanctions (disciplinary measure), and
7. Other stipulations applicable to all employees.

The employer has to inform his employees of the work

rules and also of the gist of the Labor Standard Act and its by-laws by displaying or posting them in places accessible to all employees.

Though the Ministry of Labor, acknowledges that the improvement in working condition has to be achieved through voluntary discussion between labor and management, it provides various guidance and subsidies in order to ensure and improve the working condition especially to small and medium enterprises.

Working conditions of public servants can be adjusted whenever necessary by Diet, in order to adapt to changes in social circumstances especially changes in working conditions of private sector workers under the Article 28 of national Public Service Law. In case of local public servants in the non-operational sector, their working conditions are determined by the law of local assembly. Regarding personnel of national enterprises and local public enterprises, their working conditions are negotiated through collective bargaining.

(a) Working Hours

"Legal working hours means the period in which the employer has the employee under his direction, including the time when the employee does not actually work but his waiting in a state where he can begin to work at any time". There are no legal provisions about how working hours are calculated. Does it start when the employee enters the gate and continue until he leaves, or does it start only when he makes himself ready to begin work and end when he finishes working? For ordinary work this will be a matter to be decided by agreement or in the work rules. In the absence of any stipulation or established practice, the courts have laid down that it should be calculated from gate to gate. The Labor Standard Act, only stipulates for underground work, the hours of work include the whole period from pit-head to pit-head including recesses. Rest time is not working time, because the employee is not under the direction of the employer during the rest time.

The average actual working hours per year in Japan is over two thousand and one hundred hours per worker. This is much compared to other industrialized countries. According to

Nakamura Tadashi, the working hours in Japan are longer due to:

1. The number of enterprises taking the five-day work-week are relatively small;
2. There is no practice of taking long paid annual leave;
3. Under the life time employment practice adjustments to production level are often implemented by means of overtime working hours rather than employment adjustment, so that overtime working hours may become numerous; and
4. There is very little absenteeism in Japan compared with other countries.

Japanese long working hours are criticized by American and European countries since they unfavorably affect their balance of trade. Japanese workers gradually want shorter working hours, enjoy free time for refreshment rather than wage increase.

The Labor Standard Act lays down the principle of 40 working hours per week and eight hours per day. However, this is a target to be achieved during the first half of the 1990's. Normal working hours per week were established at 46 hours from April 1988 under an amendment to the Labor Standard Act. From April 1991 and the limit is 44 hours per week. Small enterprises, however allowed working 46 hours a week until March 1993. Further 48 hours work per week is permissible in small establishment employing less than nine workers continuously engaging in commerce, entertainment and health and sanitation. In Japan employee and employer upon agreement follow flexible working hours.

Night work is defined by the Labor Standard Act, as the work done between 10 pm to 5 am and it can be changed to that done between 11 pm to 6 pm. A male worker would receive at least 25% increased wage (above nominal wage) for night work. So Japan has very complex legal work hour's system. Working hours per week for the manufacturing sector in various countries is shown in Chart 1.5. Japanese working hours per week (40.0) in 1988 was more than USA (34.7), France (38.9) and West Germany (40.2) and less than UK (43.5) and Korea (51.9).

CHART 1.5

International Comparison of Working hours (Estimated Values for 1987, Limited Primarily to Workers in Manufacturing and Production Industries)

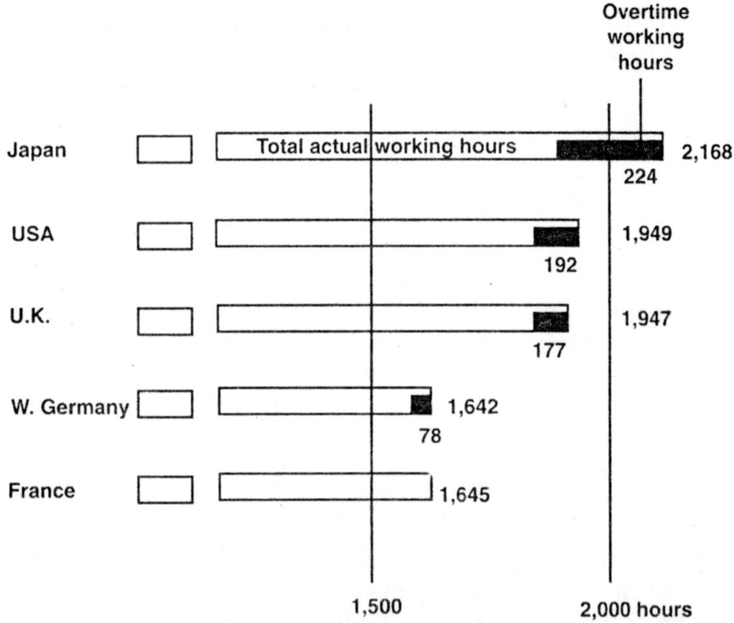

Note : Company scale : those with 5 members or more (Japan)
All companies (USA) those with 10 employees or more (others)
Includes regular part time workers.
Overtime working hours of France not known.

Source : 1988 White Paper on Labour.

(b) Over Time

Over time means work done outside normal working hours and on holidays. The Labor Standard Act, under Article 36 states, overtime work or work on vacation days, is allowed fewer than two conditions; one, condition is that there is agreement with the majority union or with representative of the majority of the employees, in the absence of the majority and second, condition is submission of the agreement to the Labor Standard Inspection Office. Chart 1.5 shows international comparison of actual working hours and overtime working hours. Total actual working hours in Japanese manufacturing and production industries is 2,168 hours more than USA (1,949), UK (1,947) West Germany (1,642), and France (1,645). Over time working hours in Japan which is about 224 hours, are also again more than USA (192), UK (177) and West Germany (78). Due to favorable economic environment and positive policy response of the government and labor unions, short working hours has promising beginning; however, several important challenges must be met for the promotion of shorter working hours. According to Shimada:

1. The rationalization and modernization efforts of small business,
2. Structural reforms for growth in Japanese workers real income, and
3. The people's awareness of the value of leisure time.

He also feels high prices mean low standard of living, which will push Japanese worker for long hours of work. Thus the people sacrifice their most precious free time to accept long hours of labor. It is true only when these challenges are met will Japanese industrial society to truly reorient toward shorter working hours.

The legal approach to overtime has been criticized on the grounds that employees may well be willing to work for longer if they are guaranteed higher wages, and so the employers will have no trouble getting their agreement. This means there is no really limitation on the length of overtime, except for underground and other specified types of work. This is one reason in Japan today for longer working hours. A number of unions lately has endeavored to set some maximum of the number of overtime hours available to each worker each month. For example, 191 unions surveyed by Domei in July 1973, has set 32.9 hours as the average monthly maximum of overtime per worker.[21] The government of Japan itself is now eager to implement shorter hours and a five-day workweek widely. Government considers that the fruits of the economic growth and technological innovation should be appropriately distributed between wage increase and reduction in working hours.

For adult male and female workers in supervisory or managerial position or in jobs requiring expertise or specialized or technical knowledge, there is no legal limit to the amount of work and work on vacation days. The only limit is that in case of underground labor or other jobs injurious to health as specified by ordinance, the maximum overtime shall not exceed two hours per day. The Labor Ministry has made administrative guidance on maximum hours of overtime work to reduce working hours as follows:

15 hours per week/28 hours per two weeks/39 hours per three weeks/48 hours per four weeks/50 hours per one month/95 hours per two months/140 hours per three months/450 hours per year.

As per Labor Standard Act, Article 33, section I, the employer with the permission of the Chief Prefecture Labor Standard Inspection Office, may temporarily extend working hours and order work on rest days in case of accidents and unavoidable temporary needs. Under Article 37, the employer must pay at least 25% increase wage of the nominal wage for overtime.

For example at Toyota the rate of premium payments includes:

Over time—weekdays	— 130%
Holidays	— 140%
Night work	— 30%
Shift work	— 25 or 12.5%
Staggered work	— 25%

The standard wages upon which premium payments are calculated include basic wage, productivity allowance, grade allowance, age allowance, job title allowance, service area allowance and meal allowance.

(c) Rest Period

According to Article 34 (L.S. Act), the employer must in the way of the working hours provide rest periods totaling to at least 45 minutes for those who have worked more than 6 hours and at least one hour for those who have worked more than 8 hours. The rest period must be given to all employees at once, except when the employer has obtained permission to alter working hours from the Prefecture Labor Standard Inspection Office. The employer shall allow the workers to use rest periods as they like. The Supreme Court has stated, '"that a prohibition upon political activity on the premises of an enterprise to maintain order is reasonable and that an authorization system of political activity on the premises of an enterprise during rest periods is not a violation of the principle of free use of the rest period". The only leave of absence to which the employee is legally entitled is time-off work to carry out official duties and to exercise his franchise and other civil rights and to execute his public duties. This time-off is not necessarily with pay but wages are some times paid depending on the length of absence.

(d) Holidays

Under Article 35 (L.S. Act), the employer must provide at least one holiday per week. Holiday means a calendar day from midnight to midnight. The employer can follow a modified weekly holiday's system, in which instead of giving one holiday per week, the employer can provide four or more holidays during four weeks. Though private sector is not obliged to give national holidays (12 days) but most factories and office give national holidays.

The adoption of the five-day work week, 52.7% of all companies and 79.9% of workers were under the system, including those adapting from the system to a modest extent (once, twice or thrice a month). A 5 day working week is becoming popular; however the Ministry of Labor in 1987 found that only 28.5% of the workers enjoy a five-day work week, 12.5% six days off per four week and 15.6% five days off per four weeks. About 21.5% of Japanese workers still have a six days work week. For example, Toyota's holidays include: Saturday and Sunday, public holidays and other specific holidays. The company appoints another day or days as a holiday or holidays in lieu of any one or more public holidays.

Its total working days in 1990 were 246 days and holidays 119 days.

On some occasions the unions may order all or most of their member to take their annual holidays on the same day, which will have same effect as going on strike. This type of act of dispute was originally started in the public sector where acts of dispute are prohibited.

Working time in Japan is said to be some 200 to 500 hours longer actually than in Europe or the United States. Within its "Economic Five Year Plan" issued in May 1988, the government established the goal of reducing annual working time to 1,800 hours by FY 1992 working time in FY 1988 due to the economic but little reduction is expected in FY 1989 due to the economic upturn and a labor shortage, placing the 1992 goal in jeopardy. Long working hours has been responsible for less vacation days.

(e) Annual Vacation with Pay

According to the Labor Standard Act, the number of annual holidays should be 10 to 20 days depending on the length of service. An employee who has worked continuously for one year and who reported for work at least 80% of the working days in that year, will be entitled to 10 days of annual vacation, and with an increase in the length of service, the number of annual vacations will increase by one day each year up to 20 days. Middle and small sized enterprises with less than 300 employees are allowed to give 6 paid annual holidays until March 31, 1991, 8 annual holidays until March 31, 1994 and 10 annual holidays after April 1998. Part time workers who work for more than 5 days or totally more than 35 hours per week can get the same number of paid holidays as a permanent employee. The other part-time workers working less than the above days or hours have paid holidays in proportion with working days or hours. Average number of authorized paid vacation utilization per worker is highlighted in Chart 1.6. In 1988 authorized paid vacation days were 15.3 while vacation days actually taken was only 7.6, thus rate of vacation utilization was 50%. Rate of vacation utilization has been decreased from 61% (1980) to 50% (1988). Authorized paid

CHART 1.6
Average Number of Authorized Paid Vacation days per Year, Vacation days Actually taken, and Rate of Vacation Utilization (for workers)

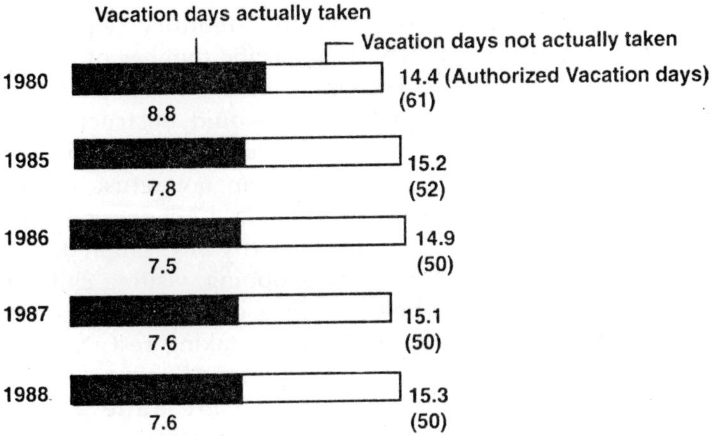

Figures in parentheses indicate rate of vacation utilization.
Source : Ministry of Labours.

vacation days, vacation days actually taken and rate of vacation utilization decreases from bigger companies to small enterprise.

The numbers of paid annual holidays are determined according to the employee's length of service. For example, Toyota's paid annual holidays scheme is as follows:

TABLE 1.10

Length of Service year	1	2	3	4	5	6	7	8	9	10
Number of Paid annual	*	12	13	14	15	16	17	18	19	20
Holidays Since 1991	*	15	16	17	18	19			20	

Note : * = 12 month first employed paid annual holidays may be carried and accumulated to next year. But carry over is limited to two years from the year in which days are originally given.

Apart from these holidays Toyota employee is also eligible for special leaves of absence which are paid: marriage leave—5 days, funeral leave; parent—1 week, parent in-law—3 days; relocation caused job rotation, inter prefecture—1 week, within prefecture—days. (Table 1.10)

An employee who satisfies the statutory requirement acquires as a matter of right to a specific number of vacation days with pay each year. The employer can exercise a right to change the period designated if it would obstruct normal operation of business. The employee is free to select the objective of vacation and employer can not refuse to grant annual vacation because the Labor Standard Act does not define objectives of annual vacation. The majority of vacation days are used for various matters such as: shopping, visiting children's school, going to city or municipal office, going to home country, when employee is unwell or feels like taking rest. Normally employees take one or two days of vacation at a time. Vacations for a long time like a week or two are quite a recent phenomenon in Japanese society and so often some of the vacation days to which employees are entitled are left unused at the end of a year. About 42% of total entitled vacations were not used in 1982 and they are paid off by the employer although such payment-off is deemed to be illegal. On many occasions the vacation days are left unused at the end of the year. Kozo Kagawa, found that only 60.8% of vacation holidays are used by workers among enterprises with 300 employees or more. During the vacations the employer must pay the employees his average or nominal wage.

The quality of working life of employees of large Japanese firms is much better than other industrialized countries today, may be due to better working conditions. Working conditions in Japan differ including wages, according to size of the enterprise. However, working conditions in the smaller enterprise have improved in recent days due to the shortage of labor. Temporary workers are normally denied the better working conditions recognized for permanent worker.

Japan is now placed among countries with shortest work-week, as for the average number of hours worked weekly in manufacturing industries, according to the ILO. The decline in the number of hours worked and the rate of decrease between

1965 and 1975 were most remarkable for Japan as compared the other countries. The reduction in the length of the work-week can not be attributed only to the unions demand and their strength, rather it should be pointed out that the achievements of the Japanese labor movement in terms of the five days week as well as of extended paid vacations are poorer than those achieved by unions in other industrialized countries. This explains why total annual hours of work of Japanese workers are far greater, about 200 more than those workers in other highly industrialized western countries. The Ministry of Labor in 1977, found only 23.1% workers enjoyed a five-day work week, although 48.8% have five day week one to three times a month. Few collective agreements gave workers longer paid vacations than the legal minimum requirement of 20 days for those with 15 years or more service. Japanese workers in general are less concerned about fewer hours and longer vacations than about wages. Most adult male workers would not take the full vacation to which they are entitled, despite the urging of their unions to do so. This attitude toward leisure is due in past to the traditional work-oriented value system but largely to the high cost of leisure, the poor condition of housing, the needs of their children for higher education and insufficient manning at the work place.[22] Japanese workers are not necessarily "workaholics" as western often claim, rather they are exhibiting behaviors patterns similar to those of Americans but under more difficult living conditions characterized by higher costs for housing, sport facilities and most agricultural products.[23]

(f) Education and Training

Education experts from US Department of Education, feel Japanese educational system is more effective, partly because of students have high expectations for achievement and Japanese students study longer and harder than American. However, lately Japanese youth are not taking studies and work seriously. Continuing education and training is an integral part of Japanese employment system, beneficial to the employee, employer and the development of nation as a whole. The relationship between employee and employer goes beyond a mere exchange of labor wages. Traditionally vocational training of employee is taken up by the employer or company in whom the employee works. Most of the employees are recruited when they are fresh from schools and colleges. Japanese enterprises are more prone to recruit youngsters because they provide necessary training anyway. The enterprise will train its labor force according to her needs, in its own training school or on the job, since Japanese educational system is more oriented toward general education than vocational training. They are 381 public vocational training facilities which have been established. There are Vocational training centers—288, vocational training colleges—14, skill development centers—60 and vocational training center for physically handicaps—19.

Education and training within enterprise is widely developed in Japan. The enterprises run training programs for the newly recruited employees to raise their consciousness as a member of the enterprise and also endeavor to update continuously worker's sills through on-the-job training, group training programs and job rotation. According to Ministry of Labor survey 1987, approximately 80% of those establishments polled offered education and training and 90% had organizations which plan and promote education and training programs. The highest 95.4% of those who underwent education and training were new college graduates, followed by those in supervisory posts, who's in managerial posts and those engaged in technological work. Furthermore 80% of establishments surveyed implemented education and training for workers in mid-career. To conducts education and training, the largest number of establishment surveyed used their own facilities, correspondence courses and public vocational training facilities.

In almost all areas of Japanese industry, vocational training opportunities are widespread and extensive. The assumption underlying the training program in Japan is that the firm trains men who afterwards use their skills in the firm. The return on the investment is direct. The object of education and training is to improve enthusiasm to work and morale for new hires and workers in mid-career, improvement in leaderships, for those in managerial and supervisory positions, improvement in professional knowledge for those engaged in technological and clerical work and business operations and sales and improvement skills for those in skilled work. Individual workers are also quite eager to receive vocational training, since it enables them to acquire new skill and it gives them more opportunities for career development within the enterprise.

For example, Toyota believes that its employees are the greatest assets and so places great importance to the long-term development of each and every employee. Its purpose of education and training is: firstly, to strengthen employee-management trust and promote a spirit of corporate involvement through communication, team work and the 3 C's—Creativity, Challenge and Courage; secondly, to develop individuals who can make the most of their own potential. Its education and training program involve three avenues for capability-development i.e., on-the-job-training, collective education and voluntary activities. Collective education includes: education by level of job responsibility and education by job function. It is necessary to see the education and training program of large firm in Japan which includes every aspect of education and training that an employee requires to know.

In-company job training is viewed in relation to overall labor-management, a unique Japanese feature. In-company job training has been developed so well in Japan, because of firm's productivity, managerial control and life time employment. Normally more or less unskilled employees are hired as regular employees, and then they receive training and become full-fledged members of the company "family" and eventually rise to responsible and creative positions in company. In this way life time employment and in-company training complement each other in all major Japanese enterprises.[24]

Frequent transfer is one of the characteristics of the Japanese employer-employee relationship. It gives the enterprise greater flexibility to cope with technological changes, the introduction of new products, and the expansion of the scope of business and the opening of new plant (scrap-and-build) because of innovations and changing business condition. Dore, points out that the high degree of job interchangeability in the Japanese factory is when "workers can be 'posted' within the firm from one factory to another for months or years at a time, much as soldiers are posted to a new station". Although young Japanese workers have high turnover rates, after they are in the mid-twenties they settle in their working career due to intensive and successive on-the-job training.

Japanese enterprises provide variety of courses and run adult education programs. For example in steel plant in 1977 there were 574 courses for worker development listed.[25] Education within the enterprise has two aspects, technological and ideological and one should not underestimate the importance of the latter. The worker development training courses, consist of general training and technical training for middle management, foremen and sub-foremen, ordinary blue-collar workers and shop-trainees as a whole. The percentage of technical training is more than general training expect in case of foreman and sub-foremen. The large percentage of training given for ordinary blue-collar workers and middle management is higher, i.e. 66.5%, while it is only 16.9% foremen and sub-foremen, and 16.6% for shop-trainees as a whole. The percentage of all sections which were selected like engineering and technical subjects was higher (82.5%) than other courses. This brings out a most notable feature of Japanese enterprise participation in technical training and quality control.

The training courses aim also to impart attitudes and moral principles of the enterprise concern. The training not only includes the process of getting to know one's way around the firm, but more particularly with related process of being socialized into the enterprise community. The courses are designed to enable new graduates to grasp the history of the company and of its separate establishments. Further, it seeks to develop within them the spirit and attitudes appropriate to comapny men and while imparting certain basic knowledge and skills relevant to their professional statue as technologists and mangers, to promote the development of character and of their general education.

Internal training in small firms might differ from large enterprise. The survey indicated that the larger the firm, the higher the quality of training, thus the wages of workers in small firms increases very little than larger firms.[26]

According to the Nihon Keizai Shinbun (*Japanese Economic Journal*), the number of new recruits to be employed by the companies polled rise by 18.2% for college, junior college, technical high and senior high school graduates for 1990. Among other findings the number of college or university graduates to be recruited will increase by 27.8% while the number of recruits among high school graduate will increase by 15.8%. In addition, the number of new recruits for clerical and administrative jobs and for engineering work will increase sharply by 30.7% and 31.9% respectively. The number of new recruits among junior college and technical high school graduate will rise by 6.8% but those to be recruited for engineering work will rise sharply by 29.2%. By industry there was notable growth in demand for new recruits in the Steel industry (40.3% increase) in Auto-parts (38.7% increase) and Information and software engineering (30.2%). Table 1.11 highlights the trends among new graduates by education level and their future plan.

Table 1.11

New Graduates, by Educational Level and their Future Plan, 1988

(in persons and %)

Division	*Junior High School leavers*	*Senior High School leavers*	*Junior College leavers*	*College University leavers*	*Graduate School leavers*
A Total	2044 923	1653 156	196 110	382 828	23 779
B Persons going to higher grade of school	1907 358	560 860	5 883	24 779	3 865
C Persons entering working force	44 615	578 073	160 718	297 995	16 778
D Persons working and going to higher grade of school	16 446	3 939	163	34	13
E Interns	—	—	—	7 025	—
Persons entering special training school etc., and	48 073	461 857	—	—	—
Working persons	624	12 205	—	—	—
Without occupations	18 821	100 372	21 788	31 265	1 996
Others	359	1 363	4 216	17 151	1 127
B+D/A×100	94.1	30.9	3.1	6.5	16.3
C+D+E/A×100	3.0	35.9	82.0	77.8	70.6

Source : Year Book of Labour Statistics, 1988.

Increasing number of college and university students majoring in Software engineering are finding work in non-manufacturing. The study group of the Ministry of International Trade and Industry has compiled a report on policy for revitalizing the manufacturing sector. The study group in its report noted the need for correction of the image of de-industrialization of society as well as the need for improved treatment of workers citing as gap in wages between manufacturing and financial sectors as the major reason for the sudden increase in science and engineering graduates 'moving away from manufacturing'. The cause of the problem is the difference in wages and restrictions and competition between the financial and the manufacturing sector.

According to a survey conducted by the Tokyo Keizai Shimpo (The Oriental Economist), of male graduates who joined the work force in 1985. 6.5% left their jobs in the 1988 but in 1989's survey 9.7%, left work. Of those who joined the labor force during the 1986-88 periods, 5.7% left work within three years after they entered firms. The figure was 1.2% points up from the 4.6% of those who joined the work force during the 1985-87 period and left employment within three years.

There is dissatisfaction with company training program, which is proved by the ministry of labor. Nearly 80% companies in the sample were not satisfied with their training program. Some important reasons are: training only for the present job, no systematic training to attend after working hours and on holiday's limited number of trainees, limited class of trainees (Table 1.12 and Chart 1.7). Natoto Sasaki says both employees and companies seem to be less eager for individual than for organizational development. The system of management development and training in Japan is geared to produce general managers rather than functional specialists. The Chart 1.7 shows the pattern of training needed according to top executive, managers, specialists and rank and files.

(g) Promotion

The status of the Japanese employee in his company is based on the seniority system.[27] This determines not only his wages but also the timing of his promotion and retirement

TABLE 1.12
Reasons for the Dissatisfaction with the Training Programmes

Reasons for the dissatisfaction	*Technical Specialists Researchers Managers (%)*	*Office Workers*	*Foremen and Supervisor (%)*	*Skilled workers (%)*	*Ordinary workers (%)*	*Others (%)*
Training only for the present job	15.7	19.6	19.2	35.2	38.8	38.1
No systematic training	61.4	54	51.5	36.3	37.3	47.6
To atted after working hours and on holidays	9.0	4.1	7.1	10.4	7.9	14.3
Limited number of trainees	7.1	7.4	10.1	12.6	11.3	—
Limited Class of trainees	17.6	25.7	21.2	30.8	35.4	19.0
Others	16.7	8.8	13.1	6.0	13.8	28.6

CHART 1.7
Ratio of Employees' Dissatisfied with the Company Training Programme

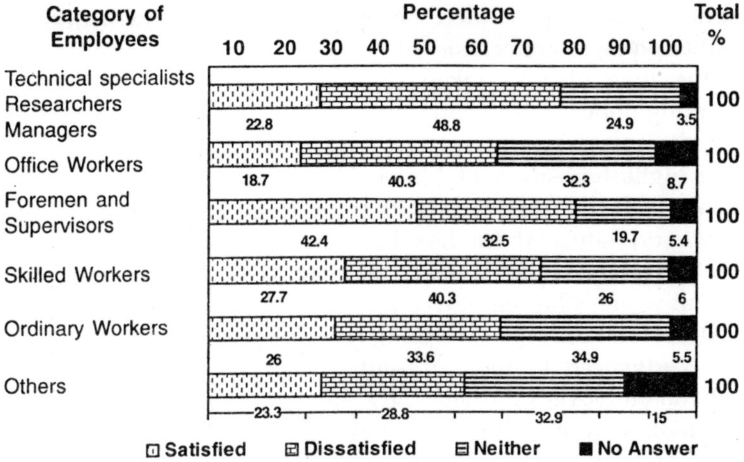

Source : dosha-no Kyoiku-kuren-ni kansuru Ishiki Chosa (A research on Consciousness of Employees concerning Education and Training), Ministry of Labour, 1972.

CHART 1.8
Pattern of Training Desired

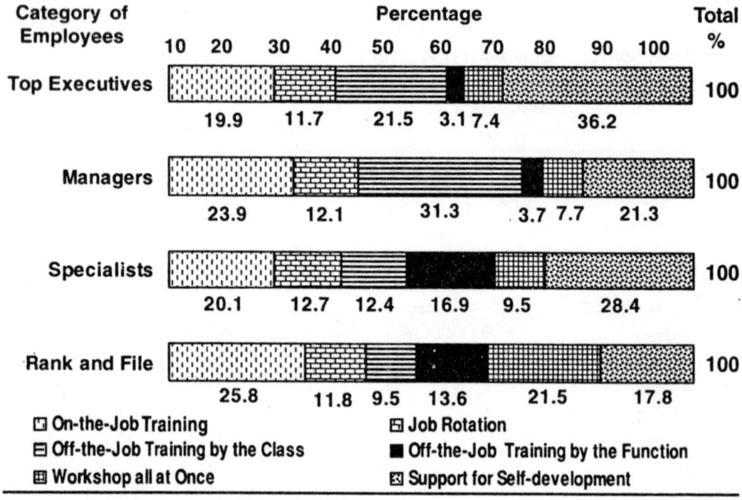

Source : Kigyo-in Kyoiku no Kihonteki vision (Fundamental Vision of Management Education), Institute of Business Administration and Management, Tokyo, 1974.

allowances. As the years pass, however, an able and industrious person can be promoted faster than older fellow workers. Although there are occasional cases of demotions in position or status, they are rare. Likewise, it is rare to find an employee working under another employee with less seniority, in terms of length of service, if both have similar educational background. The highest position of blue-collar employee could hope to attain before retiring was that of foreman or supervisor, however, lately there has been an increasing number of companies which are opening the door to managerial positions. About white-collar employee promotion are often accompanied by transfers. An over-whelming majority of Japanese managers have advanced to their present positions from the ranks of general employees through the system of internal promotion or 'promotion from within' the particular company. Ninety-one percent of full time directors of 134 firms surveyed were promoted from within their companies. Thus it is clear that internal promotion system is a basic and important characteristic of Japanese management. Shirai found in his survey that both blue and white-collar employees of a Japanese company belong to the same enterprise union and those employees who demonstrate competence and leadership abilities had good prospects being promoted to top management positions under the internal promotion system.

Most promotions are based on individual appraisal. The purpose of appraisal is to ensure that each employee's ability and performance is reflected in his wages, bound and promotions. Normally in large companies appraisals are done three times a year-pay revision time, summer bonus time and winter bonus time. The companies also take periodical performance appraisals to evaluate each employee's performance during a specific period. This evaluation will be without regard to service period. This evaluation will be without regard to service and previous performance. Such appraisal results will reflect on grade allowance and bonus. The ability appraisals will reflect on basic wage and in promotion decision.

In Japanese companies promotion is determined in accordance with both his records under appraisal system and length of service.

The key clues of the mystery of Japanese efficiency is the promotion system, since workers expect to stay in the same enterprise of their entire working lives, there is very keen competition of higher positions within the enterprise. The national Civil Service Law (Article 37) originally was conducting competitive examinations to determine who would be eligible for promotion. This competitive system turned out to be very unpopular among civil service employee, they found strange when they compared it with the seniority wage system in private enterprise, where promotion was decided mainly by length of service. Now competitive examinations used for promotion are extremely rare, however with few exceptions.[28]

(h) Retirement

A fixed retirement age of 55 was accepted in the past in Japan, when life expectancies were short and the retirement allowance paid by companies were sufficient to cover expenses.

The improvement in health care, which has extended the active working age, the emergence of the nuclear family, the fact that government old age pensions do not begin until 60 and the labor shortage, have created pressures to extended the fixed retirement age to 60. An early retirement system is some times put into effect very exceptionally, for special categories of employees, particularly for women. Such system is applied regardless of sex, is legal only in so far as it is reasonable because of the nature of work. A number of legal precedents have established the illegality of an earlier retirement age of women and retirement on marriage. Early retirement of women worker has been declared as illegal by Japanese courts.

Chart 1.9 indicate the ratio of enterprise, whether they have retirement system and how this system is determined, i.e. with age limit system and without limit.

CHART 1.9

Ratio of Enteprise, Whether they have a Retirement System and How this System is Determined

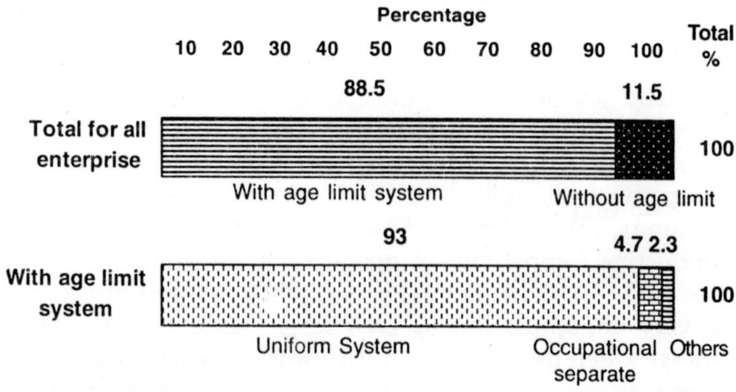

Source : Year Book of Column Statistics—19....

The Japanese worker's wage, promotion and retirement allowance depend upon his length of service in the particular company rather than skill or job evolution. The allowance paid to employees retiring at the prescribed retirement age is particularly generous, thus encouraging employees to stay with the company. Retirement allowance paid in lump sums is often accompanied by pensions, a very important part which may be equal to 25 months wages for those retiring after 30 years of service. The lump-sum retirement benefits are intended to make it possible for a retired employee to buy a small house or start a small business on which he can depend for the rest of life without much worry. Due to high inflation, the retirement sums are no longer sufficient, so lately the public companies have begun to pay pensions to retired workers by the national social security system. The courts held that reducing the retirement allowances was illegal since the provision in the work rules contradicts the provision in the contract.

Most company's work rule lays down that retired employees should not work for other companies and also not make known company secrets acquired during their employment. This provision raises several legal problems. This provision raises several legal problems. According to the courts decision if such knowledge and technique are of a universal and general nature within the particular trade or industry and could be acquire by other employers, then employees should not be prevented from exploiting their accumulated knowledge or grasp of techniques after their retirement.

(i) Dismissal/Lay-Off[29]

In Europe and USA employee dismissal or lay-off are simple and common while in Japan it is very difficult because of life time employment system. There is no legal restriction on the right of an employer to discharge an employee (Articles 627 and 628 of Civil Code). An employer finds it extremely difficult to discharge an employee without a serious and justifiable reason, because of financial burden. Despite business fluctuations in Japan, the employer avoids even vacations for the fear of damaging his close relations of trust with employees.

Labor Standard Act (Article 19 and 20) allows dismissal with 30 days notice in serious situations (inevitable cause) and a temporary paid vacation at 60% of normal salary. An employer can give an oral or written notice, however in order to avoid trouble, employers always give notice in writing. The period of notices (30 days) can be reduced by paying an equivalent amount of wages. Labor Standard Act, does not require any reason to be given for dismissal with 30 days notice, however, legal precedent has established a rather strict rule concerning the reasons for dismissal, regardless of whether or not notice has been given. The employer must first obtain the approval of the Labor Standard Office, this approval does not necessarily guarantee the legality of the dismissal, but dismissal without approval is null and void. The legality of a dismissal without notice will be re-evaluated by the courts in the final analysis. In several judicial decisions, employers have been found abusing their rights. Japanese employers are not allowed to dismiss workers just because of their inefficiency, laziness or any minor misconduct.

American style of 'lay-off', temporary dismissal accompanied by automatic re-employment as soon as conditions permit, also proved to be difficult. The problem would be psychological. Employee would worry about the possibility of permanent dismissal. For employer too, there would always be the danger that capable workers could find other employment in the interim period and then refuse to return when needed. Katsumi Yakabe, feels a desirable alternate, is 'work reduction allowances' or 'short hour allowances'. If such system were officially established and compel a company-paid allowance, temporary employment adjustment, could be smoothly carried out without undue financial burdens on the company or anxieties on the part of employee and employer.

In Japan the Employment Stabilization Fund system, consists the Employment Stabilization Service and the Employment Stabilizations Fund. The former aims to prevent unemployment and to stabilize employment by subsidizing such employment adjustment measures as temporary lay-off, education, training and others. The Employment Stabilization Fund provides the funds for the effective operation of the above services. Employment Stabilization Service includes[30]:

1. Employment Adjustment service in the case of Business fluctuations:

   (a) Employment Adjustment Grant,
   (b) Training Adjustment Grant, and

(c) Subsidy for Training Adjustment Expenses.

2. Employment Adjustment Service in the case of Business conversions:

   (a) Training Grant in the case of Business conversion,
   (b) Subsidy for training expenses in the case of Business conversion,
   (c) Non-duty Grant in the case of Business conversion, and
   (d) Transfer Grant in the case of Business conversion.

When these measures are not sufficient to find new employment for unemployed workers, the following measures are available:

1. Employment creation grant of middle-aged and older workers.
2. Employment Promotion Subsidy scheme.

   (a) Subsidy based on the Employment Structure Improvement Service under the Employment Insurance System,
   (b) Employment Promotion Subsidies on the Employment Measures Law of 1966, and
   (c) Employment Promotion Subsidies based of the law concerning Temporary Measures of Displaced Coal Miner of 1959.

(j) Accident

The frequency and severity of industrial accidents have been decreasing in all industries, including the manufacturing in Japan. Employers have to improve working conditions and to reduce industrial accidents by introducing improved methods of performing work. Trade unions have to tackle this problem, not only at the national level but also at the industry and plant levels.[31] Article 19 of Labor Standard Act, says the employer shall not dismiss a worker injured or taken ill while on duty, during the period of medical treatment and 30 days thereafter, nor shall discharge a pregnant woman or who has given child birth during the period of vacation under provision of article 65 and for 30 days thereafter. During a period of incapacity for work due to accident or occupational disease, the employer must pay the employee 60% of average wage as non-work compensation. Failure to pay this allowance brings the threat of punishment by imprisonment or fine, although in fact it is actually paid as a benefit under the workmen's Compensation Insurance Act, 1947, which covers all employees. If the employer is found to be liable for the accident under the civil law, the employee is entitled to claim the difference between his full wages and the amount of compensation.

The government has established the Seventh Industrial Injury Prevention Program (from 1988 to 1992) to prevent and reduce industrial injuries and diseases and coping with such a changing environment. This program emphasizes on the following issues:[32]

1. Advance assessment of industrial safety and health.
2. Workers health including mental health.
3. Working environment measures for air pollution etc.
4. Safety installation of production equipment etc.
5. Safety and health of workers in small and medium enterprises.

(k) Labor Mobility

The Ministry of labor released the report (1986) of a survey on employment trends. The survey outcome found that the labor mobility rate for 1986 was 21.5% down 0.6% points from the year before, thus showing a decrease for the first time in three years since 1983. The report further found, the reasons for leaving work, the highest percentage of those surveyed cited 'one's discretion' followed by 'employers' discretion', 'termination of contract', 'mandatory retirement age' and 'one's own misdeeds'. In total 344,000 workers, up 27.7% from previous year, left work due to 'employees' discretion'. Thus reduction in the work force in mining, raw-materials and machinery-related manufacturing industries, progressed greatly amidst restructuring of the Japanese economy, representing the second largest personnel curtailment following only that of 1975 after the out-break of the first oil crisis.

The survey report further pointed by age, separated workers aged 45 to 54 rose 3.1% over the year before, and those aged 55 and over, increased 8.1% over a year earlier, reflecting the severe employment situation for middle-aged and older workers. On the other hand, the number of those shifted from secondary to territory industry was approximately 218,000 and that of those from tertiary to secondary higher mobility rate from secondary to tertiary than in the year before.

(I) Working Conditions in Public Sector

Without understanding the problems and characteristics of labor-management relations in public sector, one can not understand industrial relations of Japan.

Public sector employee's rights such as right to organize; right to conclude collective agreement and right to strike has been restricted because of their nature of service. They are governed by special machinery. They are National Personnel Authority and National Enterprise Labor Relations Commission, at the central level and the personnel commissions at the local level, which are playing an important role in deciding the working condition including wages. The National Personnel Authority was set-up with special intention to compensate the restrictions of the basic trade union rights.

Under Article 28 of National Public Service Law, the Diet will adjust the working conditions of public employees whenever necessary especially when working condition in private sector adjusted. The National Personnel Authority which is an independent and neutral body makes recommendations to the Diet and the Cabinet with respect to improvement of wages and other working conditions. These recommendations are very important in deciding working conditions and wages of public employees in Japan.

Personnel commissions are set-up at local level on a similar line that of National Personnel Authority. The working conditions of local public employees in non-operational sector are determined by the Local Assemblies. The working conditions of National Enterprises and Local Public Enterprises, can be negotiated through collective bargaining however, strike action is prohibited. In order to settle possible deadlocks, a compulsory arbitration system under National Enterprise Labor Relations Commission (now merged into Labor Relations Commission) and the Prefecture Labor Relations Commissions, have been established.[33]

According to Article 96 of the National Civil Service Law, any employee in the civil service shall attend to his duties in the interest of public and shall exert his utmost effort in the performance of those duties. The conditions of employment are determined by law. Under the present law a civil servant is allowed to process a grievance or to challenge an unreasonable administrative order in court. Civil servants are employed through entrance examination conducted by the National Personnel Authority. To-day the promotion system based on performance and examination system is discontinued. Civil servants wages and other employment conditions are determined by law. The working hours for a week are 44 hours and twenty days of annual paid vacation. Articles 96 and 101 of National Civil Service Law, prohibits holding more than one position at a time and civil servants are subject to discipline and sanctions for violations of the law or of work rules. The Article 102 of the National Civil Service Law, states that civil servants shall not take part in any political activities except for voting in elections. The government can not dismiss or lay-off civil servants, except on the grounds specified by the National Civil Service and National Personnel Authority Regulations.

5. KEY ASPECTS OF HUMAN RESOURCES MANAGEMENT SYSTEM—THE TOYOTA AS AN EXAMPLE:[34]

It is necessary to know the labor relations of a Japanese company, to get better picture of Japan's industrial relations. In order to realize the basic philosophy of human resources management, Toyota has established the various concepts, to guide the development of human resources management system:

1. Support the Toyota production system,

2. Foster mutual trust between management and union/employees;
3. Ensure fair and respectful treatment.

In order implement Toyota production system, its human resources management includes:

(a) Minimum hiring,
(b) Flexibility to meet production needs,
(c) Kaizen,
(d) Teamwork, and
(e) Role of group/team leaders.

To avoid lay-offs as practically as possible, it keeps hiring of employees to an absolute minimum and it follows flexible worksite practice. For example, flexibility to met production needs include:

1. Overtime work is scheduled flexibly to meet fluctuations in daily production,
2. Holidays work are also arranged as necessary,
3. Broad job classifications—there is no distinction between skilled and unskilled labor,
4. Assistance system—temporary transfer of the work force is arranged as necessary on a group, section, division and plant and or company-wide basis, and
5. Multifunction worker system—the above mentioned broad job classification and assistance system demand flexible or 'multi-function' workers.

At Toyota, employees are encouraged to do KAIZEN—through such activities as the establishment and revision of Standard Work Quality Circle involvement and Suggestion System participation of make safer, smarter and more efficient way of working. These activities also release employees from the continuous repetition of the same work sequences by giving them the chance to use their own creativity.

Responsibility at Toyota is assigned at team level. Within teams members cooperate to fulfil team responsibilities and accomplish team goals regarding production, quality, cost reduction, safety and efficiency. The group and team leaders are responsible for enhancing teamwork and developing good human relationship through fostering own communication in the group-team, apart from the prescribed roles.

In any company maintaining 'mutual trust' between the company and the union and between supervisors and subordinates is very important. In order to foster 'mutual trust', mutual understanding is indispensable. Toyota has various tools for communication, information sharing and problem-solving schemes:

1. Joint meetings,
2. Internal media,
3. Annual supervisor-subordinate consultation, and
4. Other activities.

Joint meetings are conducted through management-union meetings and management-employees. The management-union meeting takes at three stages—Labor-Management Council, Labor-Management Council Specialized Committee and Labor-Management Round-Table Conference. The Management-Union meeting is a place not only for negotiation, but also for each side to present their view of the circumstances which surround the company and for improving communications in general. The basic stance of both parties at the meeting is as follows:

1. Mutual respect of each others view points.
2. Disagreement resolution through discussion (compromise when necessary).
3. Finally, unfailing execution of agreement reached.

The Labor-Management Council deals with wages, bonus and working schedule and meets 10 times a year. Labor-Management Council Specialized Committees include—Joint Wage Committee, Joint Production Committee and Joint Safety; Health and Environment Committee, Joint Benefits Committee and Joint Personnel Committee. The Labor-Management Council Specialized Committees basically deal all working conditions. The Labor-Management Round-Table Conference meets at three levels—company level, plant level and shop level. At company level conference, all management directors (including chairman and president) an all union executive committee members attend. They deal with very important issues such as management policies (investment, production and hiring), economics circumstances, union policies and union activities. This conference meets 3 times a year. Plant level conference includes plant manager, general manager and deputy general managers from management side and from union side top officers' in-charge of the plant, plant director and chief shop stewards. They deal with mainly plant level issues regarding production, safety, health and working environment and meets 4 time a year. Shop level conference is attended by general managers, deputy general managers and managers (management side) plant, chief shop, steward, councilors and shop stewards (union side). They deal only issues regarding working environment and meets once a month.

Management-employee meetings are held regularly at the division, department, and section and group level. The main aim of these meetings include: firstly, to share information regarding corporate circumstances, policies of each level, production schedule, market situation, the course and the results of the company-union discussions, changes in rules and regulations, etc.; secondly, to promote open communication for mutual understanding, here supervisors listen to subordinates.

To foster mutual trust between employee and management, Toyota constantly strives to enhance communication with employees through her various publications. Here every employee has a formal occasion to consult with his supervisor at least once a year. During such discussions, the subordinate voices his concerns and requests on off-the-job, while the supervisor speaks frankly and listens careful his fellow employee's wants and concerns. Toyota believes that open communication among employees after working hours is essential for mutual understanding and therefore, mutual trust. In other work communication away from job brings labor a sense of unity between the company and employees. Measures to foster such communication include—new member welcome activity, called F and M (Fresh and Harmony) activity, sporting events, picnic and other get-togathering by group, department, plant or company level association clubs, etc.

Like many Japanese companies, Toyota also believes that 'employees are company's greatest assets' and therefore, all employees deserve 'fair and respectful treatment'. It tries to achieve this goal by:

1. Equal treatment among all employees,
2. Fair appraisal,
3. Fair wage structure, and
4. Excellent benefit programs.

To foster unity and as an art of company's policy of treating all employees fairly, the same benefit systems and rules and regulations are applied to all employees including production, administrative and engineering staff. To ensure fairness and objectivity, the direct supervisor's appraisal is reviewed and revised as deemed necessary by the supervisor's supervise or/and by the Human Resources Division. Under Fair Wage Structure, employees get fixed amount of monthly wages irrespective of the number of operating days of the month. Productivity allowance fluctuates according to the group productivity index of the month. Absence except paid annual holiday is the cause of wage reduction. One can see here. No distinction is made between the wage structure of production, administrative and engineering staff. For fair and respectful treatment and to promote harmonious relations between employee and management, Toyota provides it's employee a very liberal excellent benefit programs, which include:

1. Health care insurance, workers' compensation program, life insurance, company housing—for stable living,
2. Sports center, recreational lodges, membership of resort clubs—for fulfilling life, and
3. Saving plans, house ownership programs, corporate pension plan—for future life.

The latest Toyota's revised Human Resources Management system includes—maximization of each employee's potentiality and encourages individual initiatives. The purpose of restructuring is for more streamlined decision-making and for the best use of each employee's ability. Under new grade system and job titles, promotion and wages of an employee is determined in accordance with his grade. Promotion to a higher grade is made irrespective of the availability of job title. Under appraisal and wages scheme, increased focus will be on each employee's ability and performance. To achieve maximum employee's potentiality Toyota has new jobs rotation system. Under new system, Toyota abolished time-keep or abolished time card system to encourage each employee's autonomous control and the sense of responsibility of his own time management and for administrative, engineering division, it introduced flexile working hours. Its philosophy behind flexible working hours is to:

(a) Encourage each employee to work effectively and creatively,
(b) Allow each employee the opportunity to exercise his own sense of responsibility and time management, and
(c) Through the above two, it tries to revitalize individual employees and the organization as a whole.

Notes and References

1. Japan consists of four main islands and thousands of smaller islands. It covers an area of 377,719 sq km. Japan's total land is about one-twenty-fifth that of USA, one-ninth that of India and one-and-a half times as big as that of UK. Japan occupies less than 0.3% world land. Her mountains cover about 73% of the total land area and the remaining 27% is relatively flat. Thus the arable and habitable land is extremely limited. Japan has about 123 million people and support 1,867 per sq km of cultivable land. Although poor in natural resources, supporting a massive population, forced the people to live simple and hard-working, which today constitute moral features of Japanese people?
2. The emperor who ascended the throne in 1868 at the age of sixteen was a brilliant person. He issued what is known in western history as the charter oath of emperor, consisting of five articles which laid down the guiding principles of government for the new regime in Japan: 1. Assemblies widely convoked shall be held and all important decisions shall be made only after public discussion; 2. the welfare of whole nation shall be promoted by the cabinet efforts of government and the governed; 3. all subjects shall do their best and never grow weary of accomplishing their legitimate purpose; 4. all absurd usages of past shall

be abandoned, Justice and righteousness shall regulate all action; 5. knowledge shall be caught from all over the world and thus the foundation of imperial polity be strengthened.

3. Blanpain, R. (Rd.), *International Encyclopedia for Labor Law and Industrial Relations*, (Japan section written by T.A. Hanami, Kluwer Law and Taxation Publishers, The Netherlands, 1985, p. 16.
4. Kuwahara Yasuo, *International Relations System in Japan—A New Interpretation*, Japanese Industrial Relations, Series No. 16, The Japan Institute of Labor Law, Tokyo, p. 5.
5. *Ibid.*, p. 26.
6. Katsumi Yakabe, *Labour Relations in Japan, Fundamental Characteristics*, International Soceity for Education Information Inc., Japan, 1974, p. 10.
7. According to white paper on working women—1988, Women workers who left work for reasons of marriage and child birth were 16.1% of separated women workers, a decrease from 22%, 10 years ago. Thus the average length of service by full time females reached 7.1 years, compared with 5.5 years to 10 years ago.
8. Hanami, T.A., *Labor Relations in Japan Today*, Kodansha International Ltd., Tokyo, p. 33.
9. Nakamura Tadashi, Labor in Japan (Question and Answers), The Japan Institute of Labor, Tokyo 1988, p. 112.
10. Dore Ronald gives his own characteristics of Japanese and Englishman, while analyzing the general attitude (see British Factory—Japanese Factory, The Origins of National Diversity in Industrial Relations, London, George Allen and Unwin Ltd., Ruskin House Street, 1973).
    The following are the characteristics of Japanese worker:
    1. The Japanese are lesser individualists, are more inclined to submerge their identity in some large groups to which they belong and more likely to be observed by a sense of duty.
    2. The Japanese are less self-confident and more neurotically preoccupied with retaining good opinion of others.
    3. The Japanese are more introverted.
    4. The Japanese are less men of principle than the British.
    5. The Japanese are imitative.
    6. The Japanese are more ambitious.
    7. The Japanese are more submissive to superior.
    8. The Japanese are more slavishly diligent.
    9. The Japanese are careless about what happens outside their groups and have less sense of social responsibility to correct abuses in their own society.
    10. The Japanese are more childishly naïve.
11. Taishiro Shirai (Ed.), *Contemporary Industrial Relations in Japan*, University of Wisconsin Press Ltd, Wisconsin 1983, (article by Koike—Workers in Small Firms), (For male worker's aspiration to improve skill and knowledge, by size of the Firm, age and occupation, All Industries. See also Rodosho, Tokei Johobu, 1972.
12. *Japan Times*, Tokyo, August 20, 1990.
13. Katsumi Yakyo, *op. cit.*, p. 76.
14. *Ibid.*, p. 78.
15. Nakamura Tadashi, *op. cit.*, p. 5.

16. Kagawa Kozo, *Introduction of Japanese Labor Law* (2), p. 6.
17. Blanpain, R. (Ed.), *op. cit.*, p. 64.
18. *Ibid.*, p. 101.
19. Articles 2 and 28 of the constitution are regarded as being the most fundamental legal sources of labor law. Article 2 section 1 provides for the right to work. Section 2 provides for protective labor law in general by requiring the fixing of standards of working conditions by law.
20. Refer for details, *International Encyclopedia for Law and Industrial Relations*, Part I, Chapters 3, 4, 5, 6 and 7 which deal hours of work, overtime and holidays. The protection of Women and Minors, Remuneration of Benefits, the termination of individual labor contracts and covenants of non-competition, invention by employees.
21. Domei (Japanese Confederation of Labor) 1974, *Rodo Joken to Chosa Hokoku Todushu* (special report on working conditions), Shiryo Series No. 22, Tokyo, p. 29.
22. Taishiro Shirai (Ed), *op. cit.*, p. 132.
23. The higher costs are directly attributable to the fact that the amount of inhabitable land per person in Japan is very limited. Japan supports 1,867 persons per sq km of cultivatable land, whereas in Western Europe the number is 310, in North America 110 and in America only 28 (see also Taishiro Shirai (Ed), article by Koshiro)
24. Katsumi Yakabe, *op. cit.*, p. 6.
25. See Koshiro's Article—*The Quality of Working life for 'Continuing Education and Training'* in Taishiro Shirai (Ed.), Contemporary Industrial Relations in Japan, Chapter 3.
26. See Koike's article—*Workers in Small Firms for the career of workers in Small Firms*, where he has discussed questions such as: 1. do workers change their positions within workshops at times or regularly? 2. have the long-service workers had experience in most jobs in their workshop? The answers to both questions show very similar tendencies (Taishiro Shirai (Ed.), Contemporary Industrial Relations, Chapter 4).
27. Dore Ronald, in his research found at Hitachi, promotion from grade to grade simply means more status and higher level of annual salary increase (see British Factory and Japanese Factory, pp. 67-70 and 99). The Hitachi system of career promotion, blending the twin criteria of performance and seniority, ensure that there is not too wide gap between expectation and appointments (see also Koshiro's article—The Quality of Working life, for his description on work life in the Factory—Taishiro Shirai (Ed.), Contemporary Industrial Relations in Japan).
28. See Koichiro Yamaguchi's article—*The Public Sector: Civil servants, for various issues pertaining to civil servants* (Taishiro Shirai (Ed.), Contemporary Industrial Relations in Japan).
29. A discharge most often is a disciplinary sanction, a dismissal may be because of redundancy or business fluctuations.
30. Blanpain, R. (Ed.), *op. cit.*, p. 91.
31. The Enterprise Union at Steel Plant launched a 'Zero accident' movement in 1972, creating union safety organizations at the plants and in small groups at shop-floor level. The tenth of each month is 'safety day', when joint union-management meetings are held to examine the results. Similar activities can be found in each of the other plants.

32. See Nakamura Tadashi—*Labor in Japan*, p. 162 for an explanation—"what are the trends in industrial injuries and the main counter-measurers to prevent them?"
33. Please note the Public Corporation Labor Relations Law, was changed into National Enterprises Labor Relations Law in 1987, because all Public Corporations were privatized. Now there is no Public Corporation in Japan. The Public Corporation Labor Relation, was changed to National Enterprise Labor Relations Commissions in 1987, the same is now merged to Central Labor Commission, 1988. So there is no Public Corporation Labor Relations Commission.
34. Toyota's Human Resource Management system, discussion is based on their literature shared with me and also my personal interviews with staff of Toyota.

2

Basic Characteristics of Japanese Industries Relations : An Empirical Survey

1. LIFE TIME EMPLOYMENT : AN INTRODUCTION

The study of industrial relations consists of two different aspects: management-union relations and employee-employer relations. Many attempts have been made to describe Japanese industrial relations through 'Life Time Employment', the 'Seniority-based Wage' and 'Enterprise Union'. This methodology still seems to be appropriate.

In the last four decades Japanese economy has attained a remarkable growth and the dramatic rise in its exports in manufacturing products. This achievement has been the center of world attention and won the praise, while the advanced industrial nations of the west suffer with economic stagnation. Today Japanese industrial goods have captured world market because of their high quality, but about 20 years ago Japanese goods were generally regarded as being of poor quality. Why such a great change? The answer lies in some fundamental differences between Japanese and western concept of employment, trade union and wage structure in manufacturing industries in Japan (not in the agriculture sector).

Among other factors[1], scholars often pointed out, Japanese industrial relations as a contributing factor for such a success. Yes, because the only asset the Japanese economy has is her human resources and the industrial relations have contributed to the development and utilization of this human resource in most efficient manner. Japanese industrial relations system has increasingly been attracting the attention of western labor specialists, academicians and labor practitioners, while some Japanese scholars look at it negatively. However, majority of labor specialists believe that the principle key for Japanese success is her industrial relations. Some authors even have begun to suggest that American firms borrow Japanese practice in the search for better productivity and enhanced competitiveness[2]. For example, Vogel bluntly recommends that it is now time for America to look to Japan to find out how it can improve the performance of her productive and social organizations. The OECD report, suggests that there are certainly valuable lessons that Western countries can learn from Japanese experience. Dore speculates, though some what wryly, those British industrial relations may well be moving toward a pattern more like the Japanese, which subtly implies that Britain cold get some useful tips in Japan in the prospective course toward convergence.

Many factors are responsible for the success of Japanese industrial relations, Koshiro, mentioned the following 'Holy' secrets for higher productivity of Japanese industries. These have also contributed for the success of Japanese industrial relations too:

1. Trade Union policies toward technological change.
2. Low propensity to strike.
3. Flexible employment adjustments under the system of life time commitment.
4. Low separation rate of employment.

5. Low absenteeism and high worker morale in Japanese factories.

The characteristics of Japanese industrial relations which have drawn considerable international attention can be summarized as "Life Time Employment", "Enterprise Union" and "Seniority Wage System". These terms certainly are convenient in attempting to explain Japan's system, but their meaning changes according to the writer, and their meaning should not be thought of having remained static. A popular publication of the OECD (1977) which attempted an analysis of industrial relations concluded that, Japanese industrial relations has "the fourth Pillar", i.e. the "social norms within the enterprise". I feel that cultural factors play most significant role in formulating the industrial relations system in Japan just as in other countries. It is more in case of Japan because of her homogeneous culture and traditions developed by a single race on isolated island.

All of these distinctive characteristics play a part in promoting the loyalty of employees towards their enterprises, the flexibility of the labor force with regard to technological changes and the cooperation of the unions with the efforts of management. Thus the Japanese industrial relations system has on the whole, had the effect of stimulating economic growth and technological advancement in the post-war period, although it has also allowed some minor problems to arise, particularly in the field of small enterprises, which have been caused mainly by partial recession.

Since it is a complex task to study the whole of industrial relations of Japan, in this part I shall first describe the basic characteristics of Japanese industrial relations then proceed to analyze the Japanese employees views or preferences on the basis of my survey and in conclusion some assessment will be made to find whether these characteristics are really unique?

2. LIFE TIME EMPLOYMENT: NATURE AND PRACTICE

Let us talk specifically about Life Time Employment. In understanding the nature of Japanese Industrial Relations, we must regard a company as a 'community' where members remain in a group for a long period, i.e. "Life Time Employment". Industrial relations in Japan as said earlier are governed by three distinctive characteristics: Life time employment, Enterprise unionism and Seniority wage system. Abbeglen, in his evaluation says, "the system of employment in Japan is highly efficient one, and one that is corresponding with the main values and behaviors patterns of Japanese society. It is in many ways human, less brutal system of employment than the west has developed. It certainly is characterized by less conflict. Both its economic effectiveness and its social value work to maintain the system". Studies show that life time employment, its original form can be seen in the management of large enterprise in 1920's and in the wartime labor administration. It was not until the post-war period that the principle life time employment was extended to include blue-collar workers. Abolition of status differences between blue-collar workers and white-collar workers, i.e. treating blue-collar worker as white-collar—the loyalty of the blue-collar worker' was a fundamental goal of the post-war union movement. The distinction between white and blue collar worker in Japan is fading away. The blue-collar workers in large firms are white—colorized due to wide ranging and flexible mobility of workers within a plant. The most important distinction that prevails in Japan is between permanent and temporary employees.

Permanent employees largely out number temporary employees in most enterprise except in small ones. For example, at Toyota Motor Corporation, only 2.6% employees are temporary while 95% are regular employees. However, the yearly hiring rate of temporary employees is higher than regular employees. The number of new hiring in 1989:

TABLE 2.1

Regular employees	-	2,840 (35.9%)
Sub-employees	-	910 (11.5%)
Contract employees	-	100 (1.3%)
Temporary employees	-	3,850 (48.8%)
Toyota Technical high school students	-	200 (2.5%)

Table 2.2 highlights the number of employees at Toyota as on January 31, 1990:

TABLE 2.2

	Male	*Female*	*Total*
Regular employees	58,060 (91%)	5,640 (9%)	63,690
Office	16,480	5,570	22,050
Plant	41,580	70	41,650
Temporary employees	1,740 (2.7%)	Nil	1,740
Sub-employees	380 (0.5%)	Nil	380
Contact employees	160 (0.2%)	180 (0.2%)	340
Toyota Technical high school students	700 (1.0%)	Nil	740
Total	61,030 (91%)	5,820 (9%)	66,850

Japanese employees in many companies are classified in many categories. For example, at Toyota they are classified as regular employee, sub-employees, contract employee, temporary employee, technical students and part-timers. Sub-employees are production employees recruited on an irregular basis. After certain period, depending upon performance, attendance etc. may become regular employees.

For the last several years temporary employees have amounted to less than 20% of the total. According to the data on the duration of service by age groups, nearly four-tenths of workers 50 to 54 years of age have worked in their present enterprise for more than 25 years. A comparison of different countries concerning how many times, a worker has changed job has shown distinct trends. Employees from smaller enterprises tend to prefer to change job rather than stay in the same enterprise for a long time, since smaller enterprises have relatively weak economic power. As a result of these in smaller enterprises relatively small proportion of workers enjoy life time employment practiced. The larger the employee population the higher the percentage of standard employees, the percentage tends to be higher among white-collar workers. As regards female employees, a large number of them leave their jobs for various reasons; hence only male employees in larger enterprise can enjoy the benefits of the life time employment practice. Table 2.2 shows the percentage of separated employees by gender and reasons for separation. For example, 71.5% in Japan never changed their jobs.

The distinction between permanent and temporary employees is not a legal one, since temporary employees who are employed for indefinite terms are given the same protection regarding dismissal. However, in practice temporary workers are first to be dismissed whenever the enterprise as surplus labor. Permanent workers enjoy job security, guaranteed steady advancement in rank and wages, the required training for job and a generous sum as a retirement allowance. Temporary employees do not usually enjoy such privileges. Though temporary employees are an essential ingredient of the life time employment system but they are 'second-class citizens' compared with regular employees, being the 'last hired and first fired'. Today in Japan in most of the larger enterprises and many of the smaller and medium sized enterprises, the life time employment system has a steady base; but the difference in status and working condition between permanent and temporary employee continues to exist.

Life time employment system can be found in most Japanese enterprise, irrespective of their size. This practice has been established after long efforts and discussions between social partners on the basis of strong demand of workers for employment stability and on the recognition by employers of its necessity and its favorable effect on worker's morale. Life time employment practice is not forced either by labor law or a contract, but widely accepted and applied by employee and management for mutual benefits. Therefore, it is clear that employees can retire voluntarily whenever they wish.

The conditions of demand and supply of the labor market in Japan has changed drastically since 1973. The unemployment rate in Japan is very low due to relatively high economic growth and employment practice. Employees are hired each year when they finish school or university, mostly inexperienced young people through careful selection process. Chart 2.1 indicates the items evaluated at the time of interview. Character and personality are important. After a period of probation, workers gain the status of permanent employee. Labor Standard Act, under article 14 provides "Labor contracts, with the exception of those without any set period, shall not be conclude for a period longer than one year, except in the case of those requiring a definite period for the completion of a project". This means there is no legal obligation for employees to stay in a particular enterprise longer than one year. The employer too has no legal obligation to keep his worker, he may dismiss with or without notice depending on the reason for the dismissal. As per article 20 of Labor Standard Act, the employer must give at least a

CHART 2.1
Employment Structure
A Typical Model of a Large Japanese Company

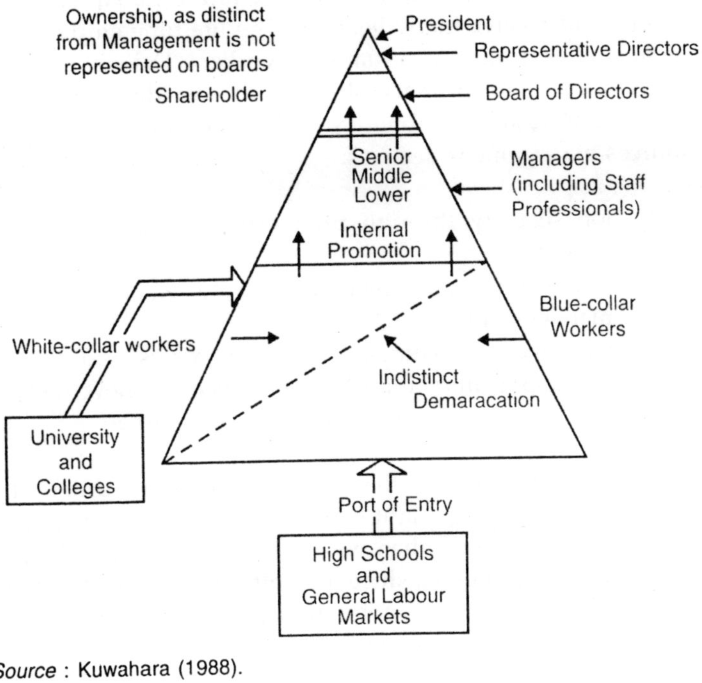

Source : Kuwahara (1988).

thirty days advance notice before dismissal or pay a compensation amounting to thirty days average "except when the continuance of the enterprise is made impossible by reason of some natural calamity or other inevitable cause or when the dismissal is caused by the employee's own behavior". The dismissed employee whenever ordered to be re-instated prefers to claim damages instead, partly because of the life time employment system (under which the second job is usually interior to the first) and partly because of the sentimentality of the employees who neglect their best economic interests in order to save face. In most cases the dismissed employee will seek to go back to his former working place unless the matter has been settled by conciliation. But, quite often, re-instated workers do not remain long in their old jobs because of the damage done to their personal relationship with the management and their former colleagues.

The newly recruited employees are provided with education and training and expected to remain with the same company until they retire. These workers are called 'standard workers' and receive many benefits. The life time employment system applies primarily to standard workers. The management considers it as their primary objective to provide employment security. For example, Toyota's basic philosophy of human resources management declares:

1. job security through prosperity and growth of the company,
2. stable and positive relationship between employee and management,
3. employees are company's greatest assets, and
4. the opportunity for each employee to show his/her 30's spirit, creativity, challenge and courage.

In 1974, for example, the head of a Japanese Union at a camera manufacturing plant agreed to a new contract that permitted lay off. Then, when people actually lost their jobs, he tried to commit suicide, since he felt responsible for their misfortune.[3] Employers are not expected to dismiss permanent employees. Dismissal is rare and can be only as a result of grave misconduct on the part of an employee or of an unusual decline in business. Even during recessions, management will avoid dismissing permanent worker as much as possible by resorting to various employment adjustment mechanisms such as: suspension of new recruitment, decrease in overtime working hours, a temporary rest with and reallocations and transfers of workers. Employment Adjustments are done also through system called 'loaned employee'. When management faces inevitable problem of surplus labor, she will look for volunteers to retire. Management tries also to carry out employment adjustment caused due to introduction of new technology and innovations, without dismissing employee but take up steps such as retraining and reallocating workers within the enterprise.

According to the Ministry of labor, whenever managements are forced to reduce work-force they normally use methods such as transfer to other sections (81.7%), temporary transfer to subsidiary or related company (28.0%), offer of early retirement, dismissal (21.7%) and other (11.4%). In most Japanese companies rotation system and transfer or reassigning workers is followed in order to: apply workers existing skills, knowledge in the new field, use surplus work force practically and main operation can not be left to mid-career new recruits. About 55% of rotations and transfers have favorable effect on business operation and other 35% expect future favorable effect. The Table 2.2 indicates the various reasons for rotation. Seconding or placing workers under different affiliation. Rotation system is used in most Japanese companies due to various reasons. The important reasons for rotation are: Right person for the right job, education of employees, elevation of employee's morale, satisfying employees wish, improvement of human relations and expansion and reduction of particular department (Table 2.3).

By providing employment security the employer acts as a 'father' who recognizes his 'child' as permanent member of his family, in turn the worker offers unlimited commitment and loyalty to his employer.[4] In the west, it is the government's responsibility to take care of the workers who are no longer needed, while in Japan it is the responsibility of private enterprise to assure employment. Companies go to great length

TABLE 2.3
Reasons for Job Rotation %

Number of employees	"The right person for the right job"	Education of the employees	Elevation employees morale	Satisfying employees wish	Improvement of human relations	Expansion and reduction of particular departments
(1)	(2)	(3)	(4)	(5)	(6)	(7)
Over 5,000	92.6	52.4	62.5	60.6	38.7	61.7
1,000-4,000	86.1	28.9	56.2	50.3	,31.3	65.4
500-999	86.1	25.0	49.8	48.2	42.1	57.5
300-499	76.5	18.1	40.5	38.2	36.9	59.9
100-299	66.3	8.5	34.2	31.0	31.4	45.3
50-99	67.6	10.5	33.1	34.6	33.8	41.5
30-49	59.2	5.9	28.9	24.6	30.5	31.0

Note : The main figures mean the ratio which answered in the affirmative to the question.
Source : Koyohanri no Jittai (The Actual State of Employment Management), Rodohorei Kyokai, Tokyo, 1974.

to keep their employees working. The 'traditional' model of Japanese industrial relations does not simply treat the company as a 'market' where labor power as a commodity is bought and sold. A company is a 'community'. In this sense, the 'traditional' model diverges from the neo-classical corporate model. From this point of view, the company is not a property of the stockholders. Capital and management are separate and the management actions are not controlled by stockholders. The company's policies are influenced by company executives rather than shareholders.[5]

'Non-standard workers' are hired to supplement standard work force and these will have lesser benefits and may be laid off if business declines. Often companies hire temporary workers and may utilize the services of outside employees on contract. Fig 2.2 is a diagrammatic representation of the employment structure of a large Japanese firm showing the various types of workers. As long as enterprise is booming temporary employees' contracts are renewed; but employers refuse to renew contracts when it is necessary to cut manpower. In other words, Hanami considers temporary employees are the 'shock absorbers' of business fluctuation in a life time employment system. Due to labor shortage and demand for quality, some enterprises have promoted some of their temporary employees to permanent status. Also often enterprise employs those employees who have been already working in another enterprise as a permanent employee. This is true in larger enterprise however, in smaller and medium sized enterprises the life time employment system has a steady base.

The employees are obligated to work in the place designated by an employer. It means the employer has a right to transfer his employee. In case of permanent employees, their frequent transfer from one job to another and also from one work place to another has been regarded as a matter connected with life time employment system.

Majority of Japanese workers under life time employment, depend on how much they can get from a particular enterprise in which they are employed till their retirement. Working conditions in other enterprises are no concern to them, since they do not expect to move from one enterprise to another. Some times wage level in a certain industry in certain district may concern to those workers who might eventually move within region.

Under life time employment system permanent employee enjoys liberal and generous benefits from the enterprise. Here the permanent employee receives annual wage increase which is given automatically with each year of service, thus the employee's total monthly income depends upon the length of service in the enterprise. Most Japanese enterprise pays bonuses in addition to monthly wages. Often bonuses range from three to six times the average monthly wage. In addition to these retirement allowances are paid in lump sum also depend on the length of service. Employees are encouraged to stay with the company by paying them generous retirement allowances. Apart from liberal and generous benefits a Japanese employee gets from his employer, many companies offer very attractive welfare plans. For example, Matsushita Electric Company, provides monetary, health, welfare and also welfare for better quality of life (Appendix 2.1). Welfare programs aims for better quality of life. The objectives of better quality of life are achieved through various promotion activities by providing variety of facilities'.[4]

3. WORKERS' COMMITMENT

The life time employment practice in Japan has created employee's strong loyalty and identification with their enterprise. Japanese labor works for a company; he is granted life time membership in the company as long as it continues in business and he feels less resistance to changing job. In international comparison too, Japanese worker have a strong sense of common interest with the company he works and believes that expansion of company is linked to the improvement of his own standard of living. Japanese employees may be by mature level to the firm that employs them. On the other hand, loyalty can be nurtured as it is usually the case that the longer a person stays with an organization, the more loyal he becomes. Therefore, under the life time employment system, loyalty is strengthened as one's position rises within an organization. The seniority system, supporting life time employment from inside and the wage system based on seniority are other "closed" system found in Japanese firms. Those in higher positions in an organization are usually older and better paid. This system almost completely eliminates the possibility of labor mobility among firms, it is extremely difficult to find job in other firms with similar, let alone improved terms and condition. The company itself is occupation and life for him. The Japanese worker is a hard worker who devotes heart and soul to the job. He is really the "typical dyed-in-the-wool workaholic, the business warrior!" The commitment of an industrial worker is judged on the values he has—value of performance, value of discipline. A Japanese worker has 'the value of performance and discipline', because he finds satisfaction in performing his role and responsibility well. He does his best in the company he enters, the job he takes up, not because some one wants him to perform well or not even for immediate monetary benefits, but out of his own will. Such values have been inculcated in him from home and school. He is committed to his job.[5]

The Japanese worker's work-role including his values, expectations and commitment are highlighted in Chart 2.2. This model proposes his devotion, commitment and discipline in work performance based on enterprise philosophy and work situation. Block 1 shows the work-role of a Japanese employee, is influenced by family, school and friend circle. His commitment is inculcated at this stage and determines his expectations, i.e. positive expectations such as company's prosperity which determines his future (block 2). His commitment to work and to company is appropriate to the goals of his company (block 3), produce high job performance, discipline and morale (block 4). High job performance and favorable discipline and morale create high motivation (block 5). A person comes to work and develops positive attitude to his work and company for want of better working condition and reward (block 6). His reward and other conditions of work depend upon company's philosophy (block 7). Fortunately, Japanese companies are like family organization, which practice favorable environment (block 8). Japanese worker's expectations further depend on his commitment and favorable environments such as: life time employment, seniority wages system and enterprise union.

CHART 2.2
Work-Role of Japanese Worker

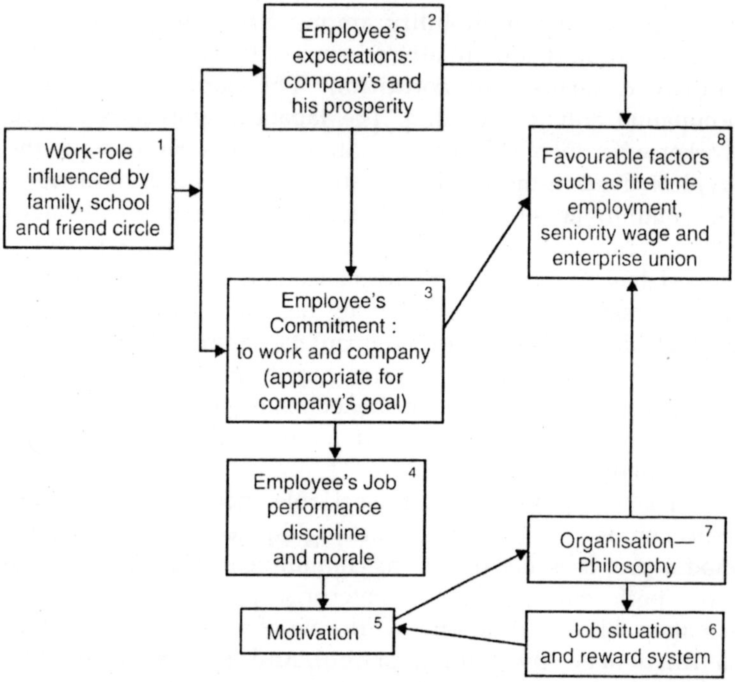

Employee's commitment which need to be appropriate to the goals of company, depends further on life time employment, seniority wage and enterprise union. Japanese worker's performance, discipline, morale and commitment are determined by job satisfaction not due to pressure on them to do well. This model of work-rule applies in the context of industrial employment.

An individual employee is always quite eager to receive vocational training since it enables him to acquire new skills, efficiency and opportunity for promotion within the enterprise. Employers are generally convinced that good returns are gained by providing vocational training within their enterprise and also because the resulting improvement in worker's capacities is expected to become a sources of further development of their enterprise. According to a survey, nearly nine out of ten enterprises carry out training programs and one-third of all employees receive education and training. The larger the enterprises, the higher proportion of them provides internal training and the number of workers participating in training program is high.

As said earlier the mystery of Japanese efficiency is the promotion system. Since workers expect to stay in the same enterprise for their entire working lives, those recruited in the same year compete fiercely with each other. The differences in rank and status result in substantial differences in total wages and in retirement benefits.

Most Japanese enterprises still function like traditional social groups in which members share a strong sense of belonging and exclusiveness. Thus the relationship between employer and employee does not depend only on terms of contract but they are bound as on by fate in conditions which produce a tie between men and man often as firm and close as that between husband and wife.[6] Since employees stay in the same enterprise for their entire working lives, their fate and well-being depend almost entirely on the prosperity of the enterprise. Japanese enterprises are often considered as an "enterprise-family and to employer and employees as family members". Thus enterprise family consciousness produces a total commitment by the employees toward the enterprise.[7]

"Kaizen"—the search for a better way of doing things is a definite policy of many companies. For example, Toyota employees make on an average 1,966,786 suggestions per year (suggestions per employee is 34.8%). Ninety-seven percent of these are adopted. This way companies in Japan show respect for the ideas of its employees.[8]

Under life time employment system Japanese enterprises provide various benefits to its employees. Starting from vocational training it takes care of children's education, provides recreation facilities, arranges transportation and trips, takes interest in personal matters, undertakes social security or social welfare and refrain from dismissing. According to Talcott Parson, Japanese enterprises are good examples of "functional diffusiveness". They should thus be classified as "traditional" rather than "industrial". However, the fact is that the "traditional" features of Japanese enterprises have contributed to business efficiency, technology development and an astonishing expansion of business operation.

4. EMPLOYMENT SYSTEM IN JAPANESE COMPANIES : AN EXAMPLE

Japan is experiencing labor shortage. Every company resorts to various channels to obtain adequate supply of labor. Employment system in Japanese companies is again typical and interesting to foreigner. It is necessary to know here employment system, personnel transfer, corporate evaluation structure, and promotion system and personnel development programs.

For example at Matushita Electric Company the basic concepts to employment are: 1. to ensure the hiring of personnel by fully understanding the type of people by the company, and 2. to be impartial. Company recruits individuals who strive to play an important role in the achievement of the company's goal. (This indicates that Japanese companies give more weight age to worker's commitment and character). To be impartial implies to hire individuals with various characters and dispositions such as outgoing, determined and intellectual type.

In Japan staying with the firm never implies staying on the same job. Instead, flexibility and frequent internal mobility over a wide range of jobs is the rule, thus giving workers an opportunity not only to acquire a range of skills but also to understand the total process. Basically there can be two reasons for transfers. Firstly, organizational needs and secondly, personnel development needs. The organizational needs include corporate revitalization, development prospective workers, dissemination of know-how and shifting of personnel within the company. On many occasions company transfer a worker to develop positive action and broaden individual outlook, for self-improvement and for the recognition and demonstration of aptitude.

Japanese evaluation structure of a worker is broad-based. Generally, criteria for rating followed by large companies are: comprehensive individual ability, job performance, personal conduct and performances. The methods used for evaluating are self-evaluation, development guidance, performance evaluation report for wage increase and performance report for bonus. The evaluation results are used for training, transfer, promotion and for wage determination. Evaluation results are implemented efficiently and quickly.

Large companies also practice programs such as: self-evaluation and counseling program, promotional transfer, job-posting program, personnel transfer, consultation office, internal study program and overseas study program.

Rarely a Japanese worker is confined to one job during his working life with a company. He would have a series of closely related jobs and these series would determine the breadth of his skill, how much his wages should increase and promotion. In all large industries the basic concept of promotion is based on merit and emphasis on promotion of young talents. The procedures used for promotion is selection based on various angels such as evaluation and interview and frequency of promotion is yearly and done by head office of the company. All promotions are based on equivalent rank system. Matsushita classifies three different rank structures: 1. Managerial and supervisor staff, 2. Specialist, and 3. Expert. The managerial and supervisor staff includes: group head, supervisor, manager, general manager and divisional manager. Specialists include: chief engineer and assistant councilors and senior assistant coordinator. All of these ranks have prescribed responsibilities and functions. All large companies have the long-term personnel development policy which includes prescribed objectives, methods, and promotion policy and development organization of personnel development. Japanese companies also have well defined programs for senior employees.

Under life time employment do Japanese workers are workaholics? A European Community Report (1979) commented unkindly that Japan was "lands of workaholics who live in what westerners think are hardly better than rabbit hutches". According to Marilyn Machlowitz, a Manhattan management psychologist, workaholics are "those whose desire to work long and hard is intrinsic and whose work habits almost exceed the prescription of the job they do and the expectations of the people with whom or for whom they work". Vogel, in his book, "Japan as Number 1" remarked that Japanese like to work hard and play hard and zest for carefree relaxation. It is true Japanese workers really work hard. In 19 manufacturing companies, Japanese worker worked an average of 2,168 hours more than USA (1,949) UK (1.947), W. Germany (1,642), and France (1,645). Overtime working hours in Japan is about 224 hours, is again more than USA (192), UK (172) and W. Germany (178). According to Nakamura, as mentioned earlier Japanese worker work hard because: 1. the number of enterprises taking five-day week-work are relatively small 2. there is no practice of taking long paid annual leave, and 3. under the life time employment practice, adjustments to production level are often implemented by means of overtime working hours 4. there is little absenteeism. Japanese labor works hard not only to please a boss, earn promotion, meet targets and meet short range rewards; but for the reward of a full working life, which normally expect to spend in one particular company.[9]

It is necessary here to examine the Japanese system of work organization. Ever since Adam Smith taught the concept of division of labor, it implies an individual's job. The Japanese division of labor goes down to the level of small group only, not to the individual. Divisions of work among the members of small groups it left to the group '"group task". Japanese work organizations are truly collection of groups rather than collection of individuals. Employees are not selected for specific job like in the west but for the organization. Therefore, employee's attitude and character determines his entry to a firm rather than his skill. All new employees in Japanese organizations join as "worker". Everybody is a management trainee and everybody starts career as worker under life time employment practice. All necessary training will be provided by the organization. There is no clear line of demarcation between management and worker since a worker is involved in the management at various levels.

The system of life time employment and communal social spirit of a company are basically the characteristics of large, prestigious and older companies only. Small enterprises are non-unionized and their labor requirements fluctuate according to varying work load. They do not offer job security to their employees. Because of intense free market competition, thousand of such enterprises fail every year. Japanese government does not help them to survive. In Japan the elimination of inefficient firm helps in the relocation of labor to more productive units. This is an example of internalization of productivity norms in Japan. Unemployment and population growth are virtually absent in Japan.[10]

Life time employment in Japan, is quite different from that of America and Europe, where employees not necessarily remain with the same company till they retire. Japanese system is unique and exhibits merits and demerits. For example, it provides strong stability which is more advantageous to the employee and on the other hand it often leads to undesirable rigidity. It is disadvantageous for the employer particularly at times of recession. Yet, the employer is eager to continue this type of employment due to various reasons. The obvious reasons are: it serves as a guarantee against future labor shortages and creates special moral and sentimental relationship between employer and employee. Managements have free hand in reallocations and transfers and can respond easily to the changes in work organization due to technological innovations. Managements put all efforts not to dismiss even when there is a problem of labor surplus. They try to keep permanent employees through reallocations, reduction of overtime working hours, temporary rest with pay and training. Because of such an employment security, workers will be concerned always with well-being and development of their enterprise.

Japanese business leaders and employers have regained confidence in their labor-management policies as a result of their remarkable successful business and economic performance. Though Japanese Industrial Relations is considered by some scholars as a stereotype, but employers have been convinced that their Japanese style labor-management practice is a valuable asset rather than deterrent. Sakurada Takeshi, a former President of Nikkeiren (Japan Federation of Employer's Associations) often remarked that Japanese business enjoyed "three sacred treasures" in its industrial relations system—life time employment, the nenko (length of service reward wage system and enterprise unionism).

Employees too favor life time employment system because they feel confident and trust on enterprise for stability, participation and identity. Under this system employees not only enjoy stability but improve their technical skill, career development plan within the enterprise, get the seniority wage which is often kept in line with the living cost of employees and their families and promotion which are filled internally. Whitehill and Takezawa's survey results indicated that Japanese workers were found to have greater loyalty and commitment to their company, feel greater employment security, and enjoy closer mutual involvement with their fellow worker's, than an American. Such an environment influences worker's motivation.

Under life time employment unskilled laborers are hired and made permanent after constant on-the-job training. In the process of training and employee will become full-fledged member of the company family and will be influenced by the tradition and spirit of the company. In this way life time employment and company-training complement each other in all major Japanese companies. Therefore, the system can be criticized for being over pragmatic, training the man only for his immediate job and for lacking broad social content. Marxists in Japan consider the life time employment and in-plant training system as a capitalist policy designed to subjugate workers by discriminating between the regular and the temporary employees and to prevent free mobility in a modern and open labor market.

Apart from this limitation the life time employment system appears to have significant merits for both worker and employer, thus it would not be wise to predict the decline in the near future. The changes in labor supply and demand do not necessarily determine the future, as long as the management wishes to keep important workers in the company for long period of time and employees regard his company as an important sources of peace and security. In the Japanese labor market too, the flexibility is increasing. There is an increasing number of part time and dispatched workers on the one hand on other hand life time employment has become diversified. More transfers within the related companies are made, so the sphere of life-time employment is expanding. On the whole life time employment practice will continue and maintain unique Japanese labor relations.

Due to recent drastic changes in the socio-economic environment, some important changes are occurring in Japanese-style employment practice. Several research studies which discussed the increasingly flexible Japanese labor market have been publiushed.[11]

According to Economic Planning Agency (1990) more than 20% of all Japanese workers surveyed expressed a strong interest in switching jobs several times during their life time. Approximately 22.4% of the 6000 employees working for nation's top 2000 firms surveyed said they would like to take on a new job after taking some time out from the labor force, in order to focus their energies on broadening their knowledge and or acquiring certain skills. They want the opportunities go through this process a number of times during their lives. The Report feels that the business community and society at large are unable to keep up with the quick pace of change in workers attitude. Adaptability in the work force will vary likely be ensured via the increased of job switchers and the larger market for experienced workers, report predicted. About the time spent on work, leisure and education, about 35.9% said they preferred to learn while holding their job, while about 22.4% said they wished to leave their jobs in order to direct their energies toward their pursuit of leisure and/or self-improvement. Approximately 13.9% said that they wanted to work hard and earn a substantial amount of money while they were young as they would be free to do whatever they want later in their lives. About 13.5% said they wanted to complete their education by about the age of 22, after which they would work until retirement or about the age of 60. Further, the agency found that 10.6% wanted to study or acquire some skills after quitting their jobs between the ages of 45-50 so they would be prepared to embark on a new career during the later part of their lives.

Takeshi Inagami concluded on the basis of his survey that life time employment practice in large companies will be progressively "eroded" in the future, but it would be an exaggeration to say "life time employment practice will collapse". On the whole many small and medium sized firms forecast that the labor force will be stable. Taken as whole, it is thus expected that long-term employment practice will rather be promoted.

The Ministry of Labor, report says that the average length of continuous employment of workers in their early 20's is tending to actually decrease. After the first Oil crisis, due to labor adjustments, the length of service of those in their 40's also declined although more recently it has increased again. As per the Business Policy Form Japan (1986), in companies 1000 or more workers, about 85% of males are 'standard employees', while in companies with 100 to 999 employees the proportion is around 70% and even in companies with 10-99 worker it is greater than 50%. In short, over the past 20 years, an increasing number of workers especially those aged 30 or more have tended to stay on their jobs long-term. This applies regardless of industries, size of firm or sex. The conclusion is that the practice of life time employment in Japan has strengthened.

Life time employment practice can lead to the aging of work-force. According to the 'traditional model' this leads to increased labor costs. So many large companies have started to take measures to tackle age related problems, although these are late to change in market demand and competition and technological changes. As per the Policy Planning and Research Department, Minister's Secretariat, Ministry of Labor (1987), firstly, though companies still prepare to hire new graduates, more are in favor of utilizing part time workers and hiring mid-career workers. Further, large enterprises in particular have been favorably disposed towards using temporary worker agencies, talent scouting and hiring foreign workers. Secondly, a trend towards 'loaning' older employees to other companies and a subsequent switch to permanent transfer is becoming evident. Thirdly, regarding the types of companies that receive loaned workers, many belong to the same enterprise group as the companies banning the workers.

Indeed life time employment system has advantages to the management and worker. In Japan the supply and demand for labor is expected to undergo structural changes in the future. Government will have great task of attaining full employment and build up work-force were worker's abilities are fully developed and utilized by stabilizing working life, in response to changes in the structure of labor supply and demand. Japanese society is finding structural changes as the aging population, people with higher education and participation of the female labor force increasing. It is therefore, important to make worker's occupational career more flexible to the changing circumstances. The key words in today's Japanese industrial relations are "Elasticity" or "Flexibility" in dealing with changes and 'cooperative' relations between labor-management.

5. LIFE TIME EMPLOYMENT: SURVEY INTERPRETATION

It is believed that the changes in the supply of labor has led to gradual alterations in the field of 'life time employment', 'enterprise-based labor union' and 'seniority-based wage' which are considered as the unique pillars of the Japanese industrial relations. The brisk growth of Japanese economy today and tomorrow will mainly depend upon the attitude of employees and mainly job seekers (university and high school graduates) towards these basic features. An interesting question therefore, one has to examine is: firstly, is the attitude of Japanese employee and young job-seeker towards these unique feature changing? Secondly, will the Japanese employment practice, enterprise based labor union and seniority wage system ever change? Several research studies have been made to describe Japanese industrial relations through these aspects. This survey has been taken up with an aim to explore the attitude of Japanese employees and job-seekers and try to see how far their outlook has changed. The results of this survey are more or less in harmony with earlier findings.

Life time employment system can be found in most of the Japanese enterprise, irrespective of their size; and such an employment practice is not forced either by the labor laws or contracts but widely accepted by the employees and managements for their mutual benefits. Due to rapid socio-economic changes in Japan, the Japanese worker's attitude towards their living, work and social problems has started deteriorating today faster than ever. There is rapid change in the outlook especially among young workers. Youth seek higher wages, more leisure and privacy; favor jobs that involve "3 K's"—'kiraku (comfortable), 'kirei' (clean) and 'kyuka' (holidays). They dislike naturally those jobs that involve other "3K's"—'kitanai (dirty), 'kitsui' (hard) and 'kiken' (risky).

Earlier most Japanese felt that they should live "purely and honestly resisting the evils of the world" or "without thinking of oneself, offer everything for the public good"; but lately, Japanese especially the young, favor "living easily day-to-day without worrying". It is no exaggeration therefore, that 59.5% young people prefer leisure and only 38.7% wish to take up work. Among people prefer leisure 55.3% are males and 63.1% are females and of those who wish to take up work, 49.2% are males and 32.2% are females of those who prefer work, 75.0% wish to take up meaningful work and other 23.6% easy work. Male response for meaningful work is 78.2% while female 72.2%. About easy work male response is 20.3%, while female 26.4%. What do university students want most? The priorities are: to travel abroad (27.3%), a girl friend/boy friend (25.0%), pursue language studies (21.5%), a car (21.4%) and to become immersed in something (18.1%). Thus old bonds—'ethics of work excellence'. On an average about 65% responded that they are content to be average, when asked a question "do you wish to work better than the average?" What develops her according to Naoto Saski, "is not individualism with the consciousness of responsibility but selfishness without it the Peter Pan Syndrome"? He further says, as people think their efforts will not be rewarded, so they limit their exertions and hence become themselves "Homomoratorium". In looking at these deteriorating attitudes of Japanese worker, more so the outlook of youth, one would like to get an insight into the Japanese industrial relations future by analyzing the attitude of worker and young job-seekers of tomorrow's work force.

According to some studies although life time employment, enterprise-based labor union and seniority wage system are found to be deteriorating; these will not collapse. Japanese employees by nature are loyal to their firm that employs them. About 71.5% Japanese employees never change their jobs, while for example 56.1% change in F.R. Germany.[12] This is true with this survey also. It should be noted that young job seekers are not receptive to the changes in employment practice and adopt for a new system, however, they are receptive for a change in the criteria of wage determination. It is found that employees and job seekers still prefer life time employment and enterprise based labor union but not equally in favor of seniority wage system. Chart 2.3 indicates the preferences of employees, university and high school job seekers on life time employment, enterprise based labor union. On the whole 62.8% job seekers and 71.1% employees are in favor of life time employment and only small percentage does not prefer. Same with the enterprise-based labor union, where 89.6% employees and 70.1% job-seekers prefer life time employment. Chart 2.4 deals with employees preferences based on nature of employment, i.e. permanent/temporary and white/blue collar. As expected the large percentage of permanent and white collar employees preferred life time employment and enterprise union than temporary and blue collar.

CHART 2.3
Life Time Employment

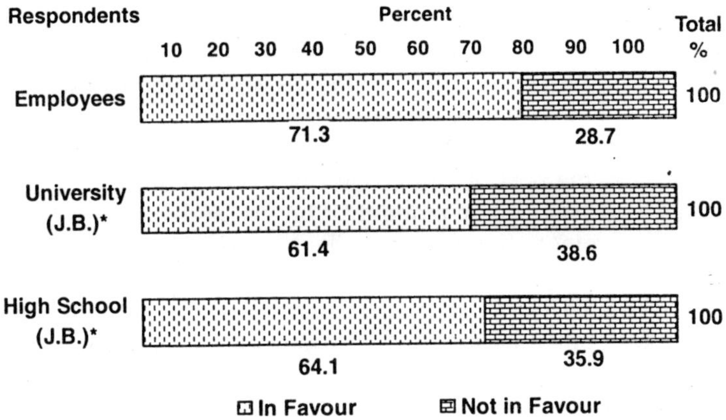

*J.B. = Job Seekers.

Life Time Employment

Why is response for life time employment so favorable? The result shows that Japanese employees and even young job seekers are well aware of the merits of life time employment. They favor life time employment because:

CHART 2.4
Enterprise Union

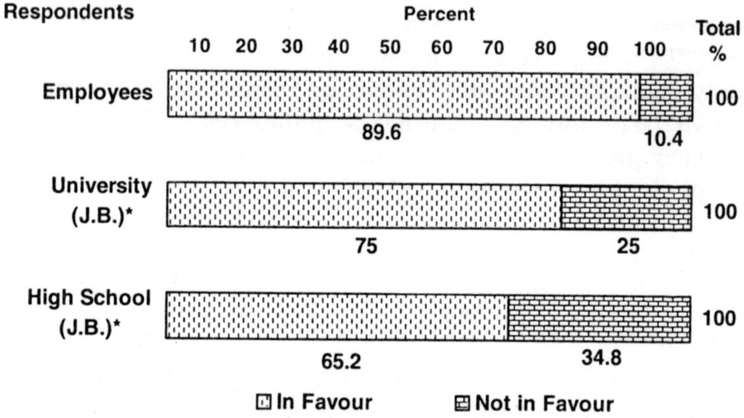

*J.B. = Job Seekers.

1. they feel confident and stability of employment,
2. improve their technical skills and career development plan within enterprise,
3. get seniority wage which is often kept in line with living cost of employees and their families,
4. get handsome amount of bonus, and
5. promotions which are filled internally.

About 68.4% young people prefer work for "stability" and 30.2% for "potential for the development".

Tables 2.4, 2.5 and 2.6 are answers to the question, why life time employment is preferred, (on the basis of preference ranking?). The employee's orders of preference ranking are:

1. Monetary benefits (43.3%),
2. Job security (38.3%),
3. It helps in maintain good employee and employers relations or human relations,
4. Job satisfaction (33.3%),
5. Provides better promotion opportunities (46.6%), and
6. Provides opportunities for personal growth, status and recognition (38.3%).

TABLE 2.4
Employee's Preferences on 'Life Time Employment' (YES)

Preference Ranking	*Reasons*	*Workers Responded (*)*
First	Monetary benefits	43.3
Second	Job Security	38.3
Third	Helps in maintaining good employee and employee's relations	40.0
Fourth	Job Satisfaction	33.3
Fifth	Provides better promotion opportunities	46.6
Sixth	Provides opportunities for personal growth, status and recognition	38.3

TABLE 2.5
University (J.B.)* Preferences on 'Life Time Employment' (YES)

Preference Ranking	*Reasons*	*Workers Responded (*)*
First	Monetary benefits	44.0
Second	Job Security	33.8
Third	Helps in maintaining good employee and employee's relations	37.2
Fourth	Job Satisfaction	28.8
Fifth	Provides better promotion opportunities	30.5
Sixth	Provides opportunities for personal growth, status and recognition	32.2

*J.B. = Job-seekers.

About job-seekers there is not much difference between university and high school, except in case of third and fourth preference. In my personal interviews I found many employees expressing their interest in lifetime employment because of custom, tradition of Japanese society and few said under this system we can be more loyal.

The study found that large percentage of Japanese employees attach great importance to the employment stability and seniority wage, where monetary benefits are very attractive

TABLE 2.6
High School (J.B.)* Preferences on 'Life Time Employment' (YES)

Preference Ranking	*Reasons*	*Workers Responded (*)*
First	Monetary benefits	55.4
Second	Job Security	43.0
Third	Provides better promotion opportunities	29.1
Fourth	Job Satisfaction	24.0
Fifth	Helps in maintaining good employee and employee's relations	28.4
Sixth	Provides opportunities for personal growth, status and recognition	31.3

*J.B. = Job-seekers.

such as annual wage increase, bonus and generous sum as a retirement allowance. Whatever, the purpose of the employer, behind paying such a liberal monetary benefits to his employee, this has proved to be mutually beneficial. One of the reasons why young job-seekers favor lifetime employment, is to receive education and vocational training within the enterprise. Those who favor lifetime employment overlooked the demerits such as: 'monotones work' and 'immobility', because in large firms today, staying with one firm never implies staying on the same job. For example, the Toyota Motor Corporation believes that employees are company's greatest assets, so place great importance in the long-term development of each and every employee through on the job-training, collective education and voluntary education. The flexibility and frequent internal mobility over a wide range of jobs is the rule, thus giving workers an opportunity not only to acquire a wide range of skills but also to understand the total process. Most large companies provide the opportunity for each employee to show his "3 C's" spirit—Creativity, Challenge, and Courage and also conduct job rotation.

Based on age, work experience and income group following interesting findings are found:

1. The largest (42.1%) percentage age-wise, who favored life time employment belong to an age-group of 25-34 years.
2. Further classification of responses indicate that the largest (25.53%) percentage however, belong to a age group 25-29 years, the remaining (16.8%) are from 30-34 years age group.
3. Out of 71.3% those who favored life time employment, the largest percentage (40.9%) employees belong to 1 to 6 years of work experience.
4. As work experience increases the percentage in favor of life time employment decreases.
5. Out of 71.3% in favor life of time employment, the largest percentage (55.4%) employees belong to the income group 100,000 to 300,000 yean.
6. further classification shows that an equal responses of 27.7% from each of the following income group, i.e. 100,000 to 200,000 yean (27.7%) and 200,000 to 300,00 yean.
7. Lower the salary higher the response in favor of life employment.

Life time employment in Japan does exhibit certain limitations also. For example, while providing strong stability it often leads to undesirable rigidity. Some critics earlier believe that Japanese life time employment is too pragmatic, training the young man only for his job and for lacking broad social content. Marxists in Japan consider the life time employment and in-plant training programs are a capitalist policy designed to subjugate workers by discriminating between the regular and temporary employees and prevent their free mobility in a modern and open market.

According to Tables 2.7, 2.8 and 2.9, employees and even job-seekers are well aware of the disadvantages involved with life time employment, even though a small percentage resisted. The reasons for being not favorable according to the employee's preference ranking are:

1. Life time employment is monotonous or uninteresting (33.3%).

TABLE 2.7
Employee's Preferences on 'Life Time Employment' (NO)

Preference Ranking	*Reasons*	*Workers Responded (*)*
First	Monotonous or Uninteresting	33.3
Second	Does not provide fair promotional opportunities	36.3
Third	Makes me immobile	36.3
Fourth	Not monetarily very attractive	27.3
Fifth	Makes me more dependent on employer	30.3
Sixth	Creates commetition among equals	33.3
Seventh	Provides little opportunity to learn other skills	48.4

TABLE 2.8
University (J.B.)* Preferences on 'Life Time Employment' (NO)

Preference Ranking	*Reasons*	*Workers Responded (*)*
First	Monotonous or Uninteresting	45.7
Second	Makes me immobile	31.4
Third	Provides little opportunity to learn other skills	22.8
Fourth	Makes me more dependent on employer	20.0
Fifth	Does not provide fair promotional opportunities	25.7
Sixth	Not monetarily very attractive	22.8
Seventh	Creates commetition among equals	51.4

*J.B. = Job-seekers.

2. Does not provide fair promotional opportunities (36.3%).
3. Makes me immobile (36.3%).
4. Not finally, provides little opportunity to learn other skills (48.4%).

Again the response of university and high school job-seekers is not much different except incase of first, third, fourth and fifth preference, where we find slight variation. It is quite interesting to note the preference rankings of job seekers are not

TABLE 2.9

High School (J.B.)* Preferences on 'Life Time Employment' (NO)

Preference Ranking	*Reasons*	*Workers Responded (*)*
First.	Makes me immobile	45.7
Second	Monotonous or Uninteresting	31.4
Third	Does not provide fair promotional opportunities	
Fourth	Provides little opportunity to learn other skills	22.8
	Makes me more dependent on employer	20.0
		25.7
Sixth	Not monetarily very attractive	22.8
Seventh	Creates commetition among equals	51.4

*J.B. = Job-seekers.

much different from actual employees. It is very interesting to note also that those who are in favor of life time employment gave first preference for monetary benefits.

These days among Japanese employees, discontent about their work is becoming common. The result of this survey is not very different from the Ministry of Labor or Economic Planning Agency's findings, which shows that 66% of employees complain of mental fatigue—a number greater than 42% who object to the physical fatigue of their work. About 33.3% in this survey felt that life time employment is 'monotonous or uninteresting' while Ministry of labor found 20% complained that 'the work is monotonous' or 'I can't use my skills and abilities'. Such discontent is strong among 20-24 age groups, where 28% complained they lack the chance to use their abilities and 37% considered their work is monotonous. The survey also found that overwhelming majority responded that they could like to improve their skills and knowledge and mainly job-seekers expressed to be mobile. Though life time employment in large firms is still strong, employees from smaller enterprises tend to prefer to change jobs rather than stay in the same enterprise for a long time since smaller firms are relatively weak economically.

The study therefore, indicates that though Japanese are generally satisfied with their work but their level of aspiration is changing very rapidly. The large majority express their desire in switching jobs, improving their skills and broadening their knowledge, which means the aspirations are not as weak as generally believed. However, it would not be wise to predict the decline in life time employment, even though there is a change in demand and supply of labor. On the whole the life time employment practice will continue and maintain unique Japanese industrial relations at least in large companies. Indeed it has advantages to the management and workers.

Notes and References

1. The Japanese economy, to which industrialization came late found it necessary to depend on cheap labor, longer working hours, and poor working conditions in order to compete with already developed economies of western world.
2. Daniel Quinn Mills, Labor-Management Relations, McGraw Hill series in Management, New York, 1982, p. 558
3. Richard T. Johnson and William G. Quchi, "Made in America (under Japanese Management)", *Harvard Business Review,* 52:5, Sep.-Oct., 1974, pp. 61-69.
4. See Haruo Shimada's article—"Japanese Industrial Relations—A New General Model? Here he has elaborately discussed Japanese Industrial Relations and its various issues. The classical cultural approach, descriptive institutional approach, functional analysis and new-cultureless synthesis (Taishiro Shirai (Ed), Contemporary Industrial Relations in Japan, Chapter 3).
5. See 1. Takashi Inagami's article, "Japanese work place industrial relations, for commitment: Corporate Community and Private Life" (chapter 3) and "Labor-Management Communication: Cooperative Relations and Participation" (Japanese Industrial Relations, series No. 14, The Japan Institute of Labor, Tokyo); 2. Ken'ichi Odawara, The Competition Principle in Japanese Companies and Labor Union: A Premise, Research in Asian Economic Studies Edited by M. Dutta, Vol. I, 1988, Part B, Greenwich, Connecticut, London, England.
6. Chie Nakane, Japanese Society, Berkely and Los Angles: University of California Press, 1972, p. 14.
7. Hanami Tadashi, Labor Relations in Japan Today, Kodansha International Ltd., Tokyo, p. 8.
   The worker's attitude has its roots in the particular Japanese historical and social background that can be summarized in the terms, "Shudan-Shgi (group collectivism). This group spirit is manifested in such terms as "Kigyo ikka" (one enterprise and one family), "mi-uchi" (insider or "Uchi no Kaisha") my company in the sense of being "my group" (as cited in Katsume Yakabe, Labor Relations in Japan).

8. Punekar V.B., Work Value and Industrial Development: A Comparison of the Indian and the Japanese experience, *Indian Journal of Industrial Relations*, Vol. 24, No. 3, Jan., 1989, p. 255.
9. For more detail, refer "Labor productivity and Recent Employment Adjustment Programs in Japan: Are we Workaholics?" Article by Kazutoshi Koshiro and "Worker Motivation in Japan" by Hanami Tadashi, (Highlights in Japanese Industrial Relations, *The Japan Institute of Labor*, 1983).
10. Rastogi P.N., The Culture of Productivity, *Indian Journal of Industrial Relations*, Vol. 22, No. 2, Oct., 1986, p. 165.
11. Refer Takeshi Inagami's article, "Changing Japanese Style of Employment Practice, *Japan Labor Bulletin*, Oct. 1, 1986, p. 4.
12. Preference for Changing Jobs:

    A = actively searching job for a better job

    B = Not searching for new job, but would change if one with better working condition comes along

    C = Have no intention of changing job, but want to in future

    D = Have no intention of changing job

    E•= Don't know

    F = Unclear

    For more details refer, Ingami Takeshis', "Changing Japanese Style of Employment Practice", Highlights in Japanese Industrial Relations, Vol. II, *The Japan Institute of Labor*, Tokyo, pp. 40-44.

3

Enterprise-based Union

1. NATURE AND CLASSIFICATION

Trade union plays major role in the modern industrial relations. They have born of the necessity to protect workers interest and defend from encroachment, injustice and wrong done to them by the employers and to protect workers in their alienable right to higher and better life. The trade unionism in one country is not comparable to that in another country because of varying approaches, roles and functions assumed by it from time to time.[1]

There are two aspects in industrial relations in every country—cooperation and opposition. One aspect concerns the relationship between management and employees and the other concerns the relationship between management and the labor union. Fujibayashi, called the former "primary relations" and the later "secondary relations". In case of enterprise union in Japan, the boundary between confrontation and cooperation is ambiguous. He further remarks: "The labor-management relations in Japan, especially with regards to that between and enterprise union and the management is often ambiguous.

There are two basic types of relations: antagonistic and non-antagonistic and these primary and secondary relations are undeniably indivisible and peculiarly mingled. It is absolutely impossible in Japan to strictly distinguish between the primary relationship, which assumes, in principle, cooperation between employees and management; and the secondary relationship, which is based on collective bargaining or conflict of interests between both parties, as in the US and European countries. The feature characterize in industrial relations in Japan.[2]

In Japan, labor unions were not legally authorized until the end of World War II. The present model of Japanese industrial relations, which includes enterprise union, only applies to the post war period. Until 1960, industrial relations were characterized more by confrontation rather than cooperation, so the widely-recognized pattern of cooperative industrial relations only took root after the 1960's (Figure 3.1).

FIG. 3.1

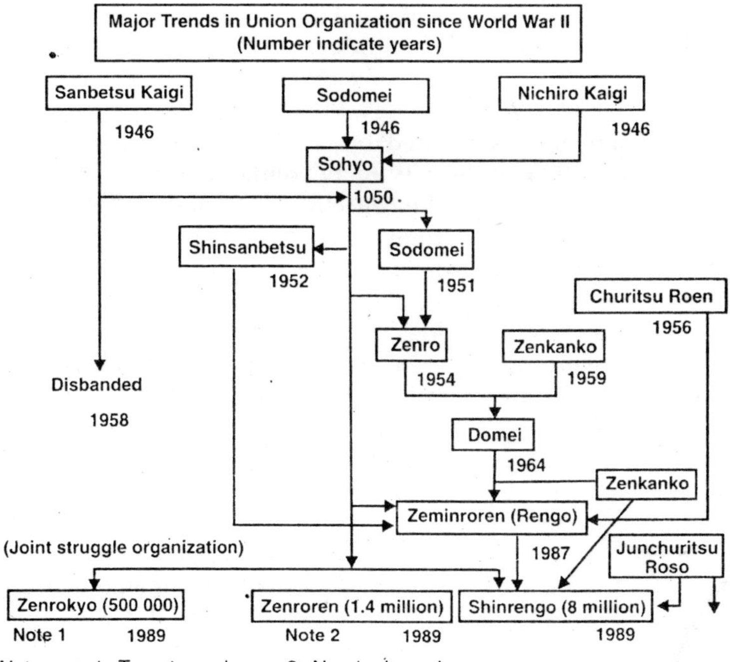

Notes : 1. Target numbers. 2. Nominal numbers.
Source : Nippon Business Facts and Figures, 1990.

The Constitution of Japan under article 28 establishes the foundation of collective labor law, by guaranteeing the right to organize, to bargain collectively and to act collectively for all workers, while Article 27 which requires the fixing of labor standards by law, lays the foundation of protective labor law. Such a constitutional guarantee of the workers' basic rights has provided a strong base for the development and growing influence of the trade union movement.

The Constitutional provision is supported by the trade union law, whose contents are as follows[3]:

1. Workers have the freedom to organize trade union without any permission or notification to the administrative office.
2. Employer's certain conducts towards unions and workers called unfair labor practices are prohibited and specific remedies by the Labor Relations Commission are provided in case of violation.
3. Appropriate acts of trade unions are free from criminal as well as civil liabilities.
4. Individual contract of employment will become void, when it contravenes the provisions of collective agreements reached by unions and employers. The invalidated part is to be replaced by the relevant provision from the collective agreements. In the mean time, under certain conditions, the effect collective agreement is extend to cover similar kinds of workers in the same work place or in the same policy.
5. The labor relations commission provide remedy for unfair labor practice and help to settle labor disputes. The Labor Relations Commission, tripartite Representation from public interest, labor and management has been established by central and local governments.

The law restricts the basic trade union rights such as right to strike. In compensation for these restrictions for employees in public sector, law provides the National Personal Authority at the central level and the personnel commissions at the local level.

Strong unionism was encouraged in Japan by Allied Occupation Forces for two reasons:

1. To counteract and influence big businesses, which together with military leadership, was presumed to have led Japan to war
2. To democratize the Japanese society.

Workers wishing to form unions did not face any objections either from government or from employers who were weak. When there is no resistance to unionization it is quite natural and most convenient for the workers to start their organizing efforts within the enterprises. This is one of the historical reasons why after World War II unions were organized within the enterprise. The economic dilapidation and confusion shortly after the World War II also provided fertile ground for the emergence of unionism. Thus within 10 years of the end of the war, the unions were organizing more than six million workers, the organization rate having reached 35%.[4] A Japanese worker mostly stays with his enterprise till he retires and highly conscious about his enterprise as well as loyal. The Japanese worker is employed as a "total man" or "marugakae". Unions too are organized on the basis of individual enterprise and their members therefore, tend to be markedly enterprise-oriented.

Broadly unions can be classified into two major categories: Reformist and Revolutionary. Revolutionary unions are those unions, who generally seek to destroy capitalistic industry, to abolish the wage system and private property, to put an end to society-based primarily upon competition and individual rights and to substitute some other system. Generally, socialist or communist Japanese union system does not belong to revolutionary type; but we can safely consider it as reformist union, which aims for the preservation of the capitalist society and the maintenance of usual employee-employer relationship and of competitive production. These can be of two types: Business unions and Friendly or uplift unions.

Enterprise union being the most important part of the Japanese industrial relations system, collective bargaining mostly concluded at enterprise level. Enterprise union is a type of union where employees of the same firm, irrespective of whether they are blue or white collar workers are organized together in a single union. Like life time employment, enterprise union also has attracted increasing attention from labor specialists who see it as an important contributor to the remarkable economic growth of Japan. Before the Meiji Restoration, the present form of industrial relations did not exist and industrial relations gradually evolved over the succeeding 120 years of industrial development. The pre-war period saw a series of violent labor disputes and merciless oppression and disputes repeated until the 1960's. These often bloody encounters were far from the ideal of 'cooperative' industrial relatrions[5]. Thus many scholars are confused and surprised to see the transformation in values which took place within only ten years after the oil crisis. Despite the complete destruction of industrial structure during World War II, unionism in Japan was rebuilt from scratch after World War II and spread like wildfire to recover to the pre-war level of organized workers.

In 1947 a Ministry of Labor survey showed that there were four types of labor union units: the "enterprise union" (composed of employees working at a single employer in a single location), the "industrial union" (composed of workers in the same industry, regardless of employer, job location or contents), the "craft unions" (composed of employees in the same trade) and "other unions" (organizations of workers in a particular regions, regardless of employer, industries or occupations).

Broadly Japanese trade unions can be classified as: the enterprise unions, local unions, industrial unions and national unions. The local unions are formed at regional, prefecture and district level. Most of these unions take part in educational, political and cultural activities, improve communication between various unions and they do not play an important role in bargaining. The industrial unions are usually federations of enterprise unions within different industries. The bargaining activities of these unions are virtually the only example of genuine industrial bargaining. On the whole, these unions have not been very successful in bargaining and concluding agreements at the industrial level. There are four (Sohyo, Domei, Churistsuroren and Shensandetsu) national unions. The unification efforts of these national centers are growing stronger year after year, which we will discuss later in this chapter (Table 3.2).

In 1989 the trade union membership in Japan was approximately 12,227,000 with 33,683 unions. The unionization rate was estimated at 25.9% compared to UK and West Germany, the rate is low but higher than of the US (Table 3.3). Most trade unions today are organized at the level of the enterprise. Of all the trade unions, 94.4% are enterprise unions (others are craft and industrial unions) and they comprise more than 91.0% of all organized workers (Table 3.3).[6] Japanese labor union, union members and unionization rate has been highlighted in Table 3.1. The most important reason for an increase in membership is newly employed workers (82.3%) while reason for decrease—moderation in employing workers (44.7%). Table 3.4 explains the ratio of labor unions and reasons

TABLE 3.1

Japanese Labour Unions, Union Members and Unionization Rate (1970-1989)[a]

	1970	*1980*	*1985*	*1989*
No. of Unions	30,058	34,232	34,539	33,683
No. of Union Members (1,000) A	11,605	12,369	12,418	12,227
No. of Employees (1,000) B	32,770	40,120	43,010	47,210
Estimated Unionization Rate (A/B)	35.7	30.8	28.9	25.9

a. Unions are labour unions and not unit unions.
Source : Ministry of Labour, Japan, Labour Union Basic Survey, 1989.

for increase and decrease in union membership. Lately the union density is decreasing due to complex reasons. There are several factors responsible. According to Kuwahara:

1. The management policy to reduce the number of regular employees and fill the gap with temporary workers, part time, etc., who are not union members. In particular the trend to employ more female workers increased.

TABLE 3.2
Japan's Major Labour Federations
(As on June 30, 1988)

	No. of Unions[a]	*No. of Members*[a] *(1,000)*
Japan's Private Sector Trade Union Confederation (Rengo)[b]	8,806	5,323
General Council of Trade Unions of Japan (Sohyo)[c]	6,621	3,977
National Federation of Industrial Organizations (Shin-sanbetsu)[d]	76	56
Others (including non-federated)	19,762	4,167
Total	33,750	1,227

a. The members of Unions belonging to more than one national federation are double-counted. Therefore, the sum of total may not match the overall total.

b. Domei and Churitsu Roren were dissolved and Rengo was established in November 1987, Rengo will incorporate Sohyo in November 1989 and be renamed Shin Rebgo (Japanese Trade Union Confederation).

c. To be dissolved in November 1989 to join Shin Rengo.

d. Established in 1949.

Source : Ministry of Labour, Japan, Labour Union Basic Survey, 1989.

2. The development of service economy made the positions of service industries such as wholesale and retail, catering and other personal service business more important and overall union density had to drop. Unionization of small scale establishments is inefficient from the perspective of union organizers, so they can not be expected to contribute much to union density.
3. The middle class consciousness now spreading among worker is other reason for the loss of enthusiasm for the union movement.

Most unions try to improve their strength and put much effort to increase membership. Table 3.5 highlights the ratio of labor unions and efforts to organize. It indicates that they concentrate more on regular employee than temporary and part-time.

TABLE 3.3
Number of Enterprise-based Labour Unions and Members along with Type Organisation 1988

All Industries covered :	
Total	
Unions	72 792
Membership	12 157 134
Enterprise	
Unions	68 776
Membership	11 155 771
Occupation	
Unions	1 452
Membership	370 297
Industry	
Unions	1 135
Membership	468 490
Others	
Unions	1 429
Membership	162 576

Source : Year Book of Labour Statistics, 1988.

In larger enterprises with more than one plant or work place, there are independent unions or branches of the enterprising unions in each of the several work places. The allocation of bargaining issues and power between the enterprise and individual plants differs according to the history and structure of industrial relations in each enterprise. The degree and type of worker's participation in enterprise decision making also differs from enterprise to enterprise, as do the privileges and benefits which the unions receive from the management. It is only possible here to provide a general perspective on the many diverse industrial relations situations in Japanese enterprise.

The following bargaining pattern within the enterprise is followed in Japan:

TABLE 3.4
Ratio of Labour Unions, Showing Reasons for Increase and Decrease Union Members

	(%)	
Total	100.0	
Reasons to increase: (M.A.)		
Increased	27.3	(10.0)
New union members of newly employed workers	82.3	
To make retired persons under the age limit union members	0.1	
To make temporary or part-time workers union members	3.2	
Effort to organize	11.1	
Others	9.3	
Unknown	0.5	
Unchanged	27.5	
Reasons to decrease: (M.A.)		
Decreased	44.6	(100.0)
Decreased by curtailment of business and so on	18.7	
Moderation in employing workers	44.7	
Adopting part time workers instead of regular employees	16.8	
Increase of newly employed workers not to join unions	6.4	
Secession of retired persons under the age limit from union	34.3	
Increase of seceders exclucling the age limit from unions	16.8	
Others	19.1	
Unknown	0.1	
Unknown	0.5	

Source : Year Book of Labour Statistics, 1988.

TABLE 3.5
Ratio of Labour Unions, by Efforts to Organize

Sorts of Workers	*Regular employee*	*Temporary employee*	*Part time employee*
Total	100.0	100.0	100.0
With	99.8	62.6	63.9
To become union members	99.9	4.2	6.6
M.A.: Not to become	0.1	95.3	93.4
	(100.0)	(100.0)	(100.0)
To be semi-union member	...	2.2	1.8
To make efforts to organize	...	9.1	8.4
To make cooperation with	...	2.4	2.7
To be nothing particular	...	86.4	87.1
Without	...	37.2	35.9
Unknown	0.2	0.2	0.2

Source : Year Book of Labour Statistics, 1988.

1. The enterprise union bargains about general working conditions and other issues applicable to all the plants and work places in the enterprise and concludes agreements for the whole enterprise.
2. The plant branches of the union bargain with the plant managers about issues peculiar to the plant conclude agreements within the framework of the general agreement and negotiate over matters arising out of the application of the general agreement to the particular situation in the plant.
3. The division branches within the plant have almost the same scope within their own range, expect that on this level formal agreements are not generally concluded and informal understandings between the union representatives and the shop-floor supervisors are observed instead, as long as they do not contradict the principles established by the upper levels of institutionalized industrial relations in the enterprise.

The branches in each plant can be independent unions, in the sense that they have their own constitution and rules, their own finance and authority to make decisions and take actions independently of the parent enterprise union.

2. ORGANIZATION OF JAPANESE COMPANY UNION : AN EXAMPLE

The basic pattern of organization in the Japanese industry is enterprise level union. These unions are successful in negotiating the terms and conditions. The strength of a union depends upon its structure.

For example the Matsushita Electric Workers Union has a total union membership of 85,000 in her 66 local union chapters. It has three top organs: Annual National Convention, Central Committee and Central Executive Committee. The Central Executive Committee is supported five bureaus—Secretariat, General Affairs, Organization, Policy-making and politics (Appendix 3.1).

The Japanese unions are often considered as friendly or cooperative unions, but it seems they participate actively in management at all levels. We can identify union participation at top level, division level and workshop level. At tóp level it has Management-Labor Committee, Divisional Management Labor Conference and Central Labor Management Council and Central Labor-Management Authorities Committee. Likewise at Divisional level it has Department of Management-Labor Committee, Department of Group Management-Labor Conference, Department of Labor-Management Council and Labor-Management Authorities Committee. At workshop level it has Workshop Steering Committee. The objectives of Central Labor-Management Council are: to direct and facilitate democratic corporate operation, to improve working conditions of union members. The Divisional Labor-Management Council, conducts its business in accordance with prescribed procedures for Central Management-Labor Council, those matters not resolved by Divisional Labor-Management Council, shall be transferred to the Central Labor-Management Council to be settled. The objectives of Management-Labor Committee are: Conducting preliminary hearings by the management on opinions held by the union concerning important management policies. It handles suggestions from the union on business management. The Divisional Management-Labor Committee, procedure are conducted in accordance with prescribed procedure for the Management-Labor Committee. The Divisional Management-Labor Conference has two types: 1. Management-Labor Conference is attended by Functional Directors (of engineering, overseas and sales division) 2. Management-Labor Conference is held when necessary in each division group. Its objectives are to improve communication and exchange views concerning management problems, related to the responsibilities of each division. The workshops steering committee plays an important role. The committee is designed to provide the management and employees with opportunities to discuss daily problems rising in the workplace, such as production and sales plans, general business plans, lay out, production equipment and the working environment.

3. CHARACTERISTICS OF ENTERPRISE UNION

According to Shirai, enterprise unions have the following characteristics:

1. Membership is limited to the regular employees except supervisor personnel of the particular enterprise (other workers not regularly employed in the same plant or firm, temporarily or on part-time are not eligible for membership).
2. In general, both blue and white collar workers are organized in a single union.
3. Union officers are elected from among the regular employees of the enterprise and during their tenure in office, they usually retain their employee status but are paid by the union.
4. About 72% of the enterprise unions are affiliated with some type of federation outside the enterprise, but since most of these federations are loosely organized national industrial unions, sovereignty is retained almost exclusively at the local enterprise union level.[7]

The Trade Union Law (Article 5(2)) of Japan, emphasizes the notion of union democracy and therefore, it provides that the constitution of trade union shall include the following:

1. Members of trade union shall have right to participate in all affairs of that union and the right to receive equal treatment,
2. No one shall be disqualified for union membership because of race religion, sex and social status or family origin,
3. The officials of local union shall be elected by secret ballot directly by the member,
4. A general meeting shall be held at least once a year,
5. A financial report shall be made available to the members at least once a year,
6. No strike action shall be started without a secret ballot among the union members, and

7. The constitution of a union may be revised only by majority vote by direct secret ballot of the members.

4. FUNCTIONS OF ENTERPRISE UNION

The enterprise union will employ few full-time officers if they are big and can afford to pay, otherwise part time officers are appointed to do the job outside working hours or with unpaid leave of absence for union activities. Generally speaking the Japanese unions, being enterprise unions, are in close contact with rank-and-file on the shop-floor and are fairly capable of settling problems on behalf of their members. The union organizations at plant level, if they are majority unions, are responsible for accepting overtime agreements, voicing the employee's opinion of any proposed new work rules and representing the employees on several committees, including those on safety and hygiene in the plant. And even if they are not majority unions, the employers will have to listen to them if they want to avoid conflict.

The trade unions in Japan have three organs: General Meeting, Executive Committee and Central Committee. The general meeting members have the highest authority: it can draft and amend the constitution and rules, decide on the rights and obligations of members and authorize lower organs to carry out special function. Strike actions and power to conclude collective agreements are with general meetings. Executive Committee or the Central Committees take care of day-to-day matters and lead the union between general meetings. Central Committees which are usually larger than executive committees, are composed of members representing the rank-and file on a broader basis and are more inclined to co-ordinate the different interests and opinions within the membership than to perform decision-making and leadership functions. Also, when the union organizes a strike or some other action, they may establish special committees, often called 'expanded' or 'struggle' committees, to mobilize the rank-and-file and to control them for leadership.

The role and function of enterprise union are most important within the hierarchy of union organization since most of the bargain is done at enterprise level. The enterprise union enjoy complete autonomy including finance except few restrictions of union federations in their decision making process and their carrying cut of activities. The National Federations deal with political and institutional problems, which are beyond the scope any bargaining within a single enterprise and engage in activities such as education and propaganda. Thus their functions complement those of enterprise union. About 80% of industrial federations and confederations are now advisory bodies. Their functions are restricted to exchanging information and mutual assistance and their decisions are not binding on their affiliated member unions. However, even these 20% genuine federations are characterized as loose organization. Such a lack of authority of the main body over the member union is caused due to the strong independence of the affiliated enterprise union. In private sector enterprise unions, most unionized workers are concentrated in larger enterprise. Nearly 60% of organized workers are employed in enterprise with more than 1000 employees. About 70% of the workers belong to unions which have more than 1000 members. Due to large number of votes and strong financial position, the enterprise unions of large firms can influence more on the industrial federations. The larger unions are not always willing to follow the same policy about wages and working conditions as their colleagues in the federations, since each enterprise union will conclude her agreement with employer. The main task of industrial federation is political activity and collection and distribution of information among affiliated members. These information slogans and propaganda always aim to spread federations' ideology, however in most cases not effective or practical.

Trade unions in Japan have achieved respectable positions as an important social organization. Japanese trade unions have enormous potential to promote their goals. Most unions consider their important goal is to promote economic interest. Table 3.6 indicates the ratio of labor unions by points considered important for union activity. For example 73.4% considers their important goal is to get higher wages and other monetary benefits. Though only 16.0% considers activities such as educational and cultural important. Table 3.7 shows 91.2% of unions conducts educational and cultural activities. The

Table 3.6
Ratio of Labour Unions, by Points Considered Important for Union Activitism

	M.A. (%)
All industries covered:	
Total	100.0
Activity of acquirement of wage and lump-sum	73.4
Retirement allowance and annuity	46.3
Working hours and holidays	69.3
Security of employment	26.4
Reassignment and changing of occupation	9.4
Promotion	11.7
Age limit system	23.6
Welfare enterprise	27.1
Measures of technological innovations	5.5
Extension of organization	16.1
Activity of consumers insurance cooperatives, worker's cooperative credit bank and cooperation	7.0
Educational, learned and cultural activities of unions	16.0
Participation in management	13.1
Life time life planning of members	13.8
Activities of society and area	4.4
Demanding policy including tax reduction	5.0
Nursing and attending leave	3.1
Assistance to developing country and international cooperation	0.1
Unknown	2.2

Source : Year book of Labour Statistics, 1988.

Table 3.8 highlights the ratio of labor unions, whether they have mutual aid activities. One cannot ignore that the success of trade union today depends upon how many and what kind of activities it will develop and implement.

5. SPRING OFFENSIVE OR SHUNTO

Industrial federations[8] play a role of directing and coordinating the strategies and policies of individual enterprise

TABLE 3.7
Ratio of Labour Unions, by whether they Conduct Educational and Cultural Activities

All industries covered	(%)	
Total	100.0	
M.A.		
Enforeernent of educational activity	91.2	(100.0)
Edcuation concerning knowledge in union	83.3	
Education for fresh members	62.8	
Education for backbone members	55.2	
Study for managing staff	65.1	
General education concerning society and econany	34.0	
Improvement of special ability about management	24.8	
Education before age limit	13.1	
General culture (language study, literature, art, etc.)	10.7	
Cultural activity (recreation etc.)	90.7	
Not enforce	8.3	
Unknown	0.6	

Sources : Year Book of Labour statistics, 1988.

TABLE 3.8
Ratio of Labour Unions, by whether they have Mutual Aid Activities

All industries covered	(%)	
Total	100.0	
M.A.		
Doing the mutual aid	90.0	(100.0)
Fire mutual aid	62.4	
Life mutual aid	58.3	
Present of money for happiness and condolence	93.8	
Worker's accident compensation	44.6	
Present of money for personal injury and illness	82.7	
Present of money for calamity	74.9	
General loans	53.2	
Housing loans	39.1	
Annuity	38.4	
Others	4.4	
Not doing	8.9	
Unknown	1.1	

Sources : Year Book of Labour statistics, 1988.

unions. In Japan wages are negotiated between labor and management in spring (April). This unique kind of wage negotiation is called as "shunto" or "spring offensive". The spring offensive negotiations only decide the amount or percentage of the wage increase is calculated or on which the increase is added has already been decided by enterprise bargaining. Spring Offensive has become an established practice since 1956. The aim of these practices is to strengthen unions bargaining power, reduce disparities of wages and get wage increase. Generally wage negotiation starts with the Iron and Steel, Ship-building, Electrical machinery and Automobile industries affiliated with IMF-JC and major private industries follow. The results of these large negotiations are reflected in the wage determination of national enterprise and wage increases for workers in small and medium enterprises and even for unorganized workers. The results of Spring Offensive also affect the recommendations of National Personnel Authority, which is responsible for the determination of wages of public servants. Recently, the strategies and policies of trade unions in Spring Offensive, are putting a high priority on securing real wage, demand to the government for social and economic policies and institutional reforms on issues such as: price stabilization, employment security and social security, to improve standard of living of workers.

The federations carefully watch the negotiations of their member unions. If management becomes reluctant to their demands, unions formulate tactics such as refusal of overtime work, workshop rallies; one-or-two hours walk outs, strikes of limited time. These tactics are used to exert pressure and strengthen the union's bargaining powers. Using such tactics, major unions usually push up their wages by the end of April. Wage gains due to Spring Offensive are impressive. During 1965-73 the average rate of wage increase in major enterprises was 14.8% and in other total 9000 enterprise including small and medium it was 16.5.[9] In 1989 basic wage prior to increase was Yen 246,549, wage increase Yen 12,747 which is about 5.17% due to Spring Offensive.

National wages double in five years but real wages double in ten years. Japanese employees are enjoying a steady wage growth on the whole. The factors responsible for such increase as per Yakabe are:

1. Annual increase resulting from collective bargaining.
2. Increased term-end payments (bonuses) usually four months pay, following a business boom. The bonuses are paid twice or thrice a year.
3. Regular wage adjustments regardless of work content, job changes or skill level.

The most important of the three factors is the collective bargaining or "Spring Labor Offensive" or "Spring Struggle". The main driving force of the wage increase resulting from Spring Offensive is: unemployment rate, rise in price and enterprises ability to pay. Recently the rates of increase in nominal wage have decreased because of deterioration of situation of employment and unemployment, slow economic growth rate and decline in enterprises profits. However, due to the stability of consumer price level, the real wages have been growing steadily on the whole.[10]

Enterprise Unions are considered to be weak by labor specialists, in their bargaining power due to the small size. The unions are "captive" unions because of their nature of cooperation with the management and interest covers only members and company. In the opinion of Japanese scholars however, they are not weak but rather strong even to influence management policies on many occasions with their knowledge. Most enterprise unions are affiliated to Industrial federations and National centers, which will negotiate or make proposals whenever enterprise unions are not able to do. Industrial federations and National centers help, also to obtain an overall wage increase through Spring Offensive. Thus they complement the strength of enterprise union. Enterprise unions are also often criticized being too dependent and cooperative with management than industrial unions. Their bargaining power is inevitably limited to the financial position of their enterprise. Admitting the shortcoming of enterprise unionism, some of the National centers of the trade unions (such as Sahyo) invented a unique industrial bargaining system called "Shunto". According to Hanami, this effort could not improve the situation.

Why enterprise unionism still exists in Japan? One of the main reasons is that it is still the most suitable type of union organization to protect the interest of Japanese worker in prevailing life time employment system. Most of Japanese employees come under life time employment system in which employee is expected to stay in a particular firm till he retires. While western labor unions are job-based, industry-wise national organization, Japanese unions are enterprise unions. This system reinforces the worker's feeling that his fortunes are tied to those of his company, motivating him to work, to increase efficiency which has far-reaching effects. Wages and working conditions of other firms are of no concern to him, therefore, he prefers to be associated and protected by the enterprise union, which can bargain exclusively with his employer and get his better working conditions in his enterprise. Japanese trade unions' demands always depend on prevailing economic situations with their deep understanding of the national economic reality. Enterprise unions also play an important role in improving the internal market (within company) which would benefit their members.

The Japanese industrial relations are normally amiable, because employees under enterprise union are cooperating with the plans of the enterprise and also being enterprise-conscious. Therefore, for many foreign scholars Japanese Industrial Relations is paradise. They think employees here are friendly, cooperative, conscious, and obedient to their enterprise. Often conflicts or employees' grievances and dissatisfactions, are settled amicably in an informal way without resorting to formal procedure. On very few occasions conflicts might turn into confrontation and it will be hard to reach a settlement. While unions are not strong enough to confront management at the same time they are not weak enough to be completely controlled by management.

Enterprise unions in Japan are more interested in improving the working conditions in individual enterprises. In fact, most of the enterprise unions have limited their membership to regular employees only, thus denying temporary employees the chance of participating in the gain of union activities. In spite of the radical political speeches of the union leaders arguing for the welfare of members outside their organization, their activities are limited only to the welfare of permanent employees. Japanese trade unions are in dilemma, to solve the problem of an unequal distribution of wealth and welfare, while still enjoying the fruits of the activities of the enterprises. The unions are equally responsible, together with the enterprise to society in general. The only reasonable way for the unions to help the society is to participate in management and industrial policy-making, instead of bargaining with the enterprises in the traditional way which protects the well-being of workers only as employees.[11]

6. TRADE UNIONS AND GOVERNMENT

Apart from protecting and promoting their members' interest in improving substantially living conditions of workers, the Japanese unions always gave importance to social, economical and political functions. They influence the national and local policies by sending their delegates to more than 100 government committees.[12] Trade union delegates meet the Prime Minister with regard to politics and reforms at the time of annual reduction, tax reforms, reduction of working hours, pension plans and the stabilization of prices and employment. In Japan pressure groups are not very strong yet the trade unions are able to influence government, politics and society to some extent. According to Hanami, the large unions in Japan have not been able to mobilize their influence very effectively, because they have been closely committed either to the socialist or the democratic socialist, both of whom have been always been minority parties and have never had the chance of implementing their own policies. If the decline of the Liberal Democratic Party continues, the influence of the unions in the political field might grow, provided unions adopt a more practical and realistic approach and establish and implement some concrete policies in the future.

About the relationship between unions and political parties, Rengo leaves its members to decide themselves which party they support. Sohyo supports the Japan Socialist party in principle. Looking at individual federations under Rengo, those formerly affiliated with Domei, support Democratic Socialist

Party and who's formerly affiliated with Churitsuoren support reformist political parties, mainly the Japan Socialist Party. Generally speaking federations joining both Rengo and Sohyo support the Japan Socialist Party.

7. UNIFICATION OF TRADE UNIONS

During 1960's four separate national centers were formed—Sohyo, Domei, Churitsuroren and Shinsanbetsue (Table 3.2 and Figure 3.1). Each national center engages in activities with government and national problems, those can not be dealt with at the enterprise level. Most enterprise unions in Japan join industrial federations and through these federations they participate in national centers. As on June 1988, the major Japanese labor federations are:

1. Japan Private Sector Trade Union Confederation (Rengo).
2. General Council of Trade Unions of Japan (Sohyo).
3. National Federation of Industrial Organization (Shin-sanbetsu).
4. Others (including non-federated.

Table 3.2 shows Japan's major Labor Federations with their members of unions and number of member.

Japan's labor movement has advanced based on blue-collar workers. But with the growth of service sector industry, the proportion of tertiary industry workers, part time workers and white-collar worker has grown and there is an increasing trend among workers toward non-membership in unions.

As wage demand becomes unimportant issue and institutional and political demands gathered momentum, union leaders felt the necessity of united labor pronto. The labor union unification aims to strengthen the bargaining power of trade union *vis-a-vis* the management and influence government for policy and institutional reforms.[13]

In 1982 the Japanese private sector Trade Union Council (Zenminrokyo) was set-up beyond the frame work of the four national centers, comprising 41 industrial federation and 4.3 million union members. The creation of this new organization had a great influence on the whole trade union movement. Zenminrokyo had been active in wage struggle, and had made demands for political and institutional reforms. On November 20, 1987, Zenminrokyo developed the Japanese Private Sector Trade Union Confederation (Rengo). It holds 55 federations and 5.4 million union members. The dissolution of Domei and Chritsuroren accompanied the inauguration of Rengo. Both established new organizations such as Yuaikaigi and Churen respectively in order to keep going the activities which Rengo did not inherit and also to deal with remaining problems. Shinsanbetsu minimized its functions and Sohyo decided to support Rengo and accomplish an overall unification including public sector by the year 1990.[14]

Rengo was inaugurated on November 21, 1989 and it embraced the former Rengo a nationwide labor organization of private sector unions, Sohyo, public sector unions from the now defunct Domei, and some additional private sector unions and became the largest unified nationwide organization in the history of the Japanese labor movement. Rengo claims total membership around 8 million (about 65% of all organized labor). Rengo has 78 affiliates (including 4 friendly organizations) out of which 62 are private sector affiliates and 16 are public sector affiliates. Since 1987 Japan's labor movement succeeded in the grand unification as scheduled. The unifications could be realized because the majority of public sector unions which had played a major role in the disbanded Sohyo, Jichiro (All Japan Prefecture and Municipal worker's Unions) and Mikkyoso (Japan Teachers' Union) were determined to join privte sector unions in their unification efforts even at the risk of their own divisions. Today's trade union structure of Japan includes one national center (Rengo) and 8 industrial federation and of all trade unions, 94.9% are enterprise unions.[15] New Rengo has joined International Confederation of Free Trade Unions and will rank as the third largest after the AFL-CIO of the United States and TUC of UK in terms of number of members.[16]

This unification has brought bitter divisions in the Japanese trade union. The formation of Rengo, created the Japan confederation of trade unions—Zenroren, a second nationwide organization. Zenroren claims membership of 1.4 million. National Trade Union Council—Zenrokyo a third nationwide organization with 500,000 members was formed as a part of the mainstream left-wing faction of the old Sohyo. There are neutral unions which do not belong to any of the above organization. Such neutral unions claim 800,000 to 900,000 members.

Rengo's first task therefore, would be whether she will succeed in maintaining and expanding its organizational strength through competition with these groups or gain cooperation with them. The second task is whether it will be able to dissolve Liaison organizations such as YuaiKaigi or Sohyo-center and Sohyo. Even though nationwide organizations disbanded after grand unification, they continued their functions with this Liaison organization, because new Rengo can not take political activities. This is due to the fact that new Rengo does not support any political party and she can not afford to employ many full time staff members due to her weak financial strength. The third task is whether she will be able to continue to uphold or strengthen the dynamism of a movement for institution and policy change to solve broad social problem as have been exercised by former Rengo and its predecessor Zenminrokyo which have boldly clarified their policies over administrative reform and economic restructuring. Rengo feels extremely difficult to administer its organization as a whole, since it has embraced public sector unions, which are different from private sector unions in terms of the mode of organizational administration, occupational interest and ideologies. The fourth task would be whether or not she will be able to successfully consolidate and integrate industry-wide organizations and strengthen them functionally. The fifth task would be whether she will consolidate local organizations. The most important task thus, for Rengo is how it will relate itself to political parties regarding activities to improve government policies. New Rengo officially has taken a neutral stance toward political parties. However, due to sudden changes in the political climate, new Rengo is taking bold steps towards politics lately.

8. TRADE UNIONS AND EMPLOYER'S ASSOCIATIONS

The Japanese enterprise can be characterized as "business community maintained by labor and management" rather than a "capitalistic enterprise, in which the sovereign power of stockholder is predominant. It has features similar to or even identical to, the employee-owned or managed enterprise, now being tested in various ways in western countries, where employees or ex-employee executives are the mainstay of management.[17] The upward mobility is the norm of Japanese employees, bolstering morale while also cementing ties between workers and managers. The management plays the role of a referee between employee and stockholders rather than acting as servant of financiers.

There is a strong spirit of cooperation between unions and managements in Japan, which is evident in frequency of disputes, the approach to internalization and technological innovation. This is one reason why efficiency and competitiveness in Japanese enterprise has not been damaged and thus enjoy a number of advantages. For better mutual communication and consultations, the Japanese industrial relations have an interesting and typical "Labor-Management Consultation System". This system exists in more than 80% organized enterprises and is even active in non-unionized enterprises.

Labor-Management in Japan is typically stable. Why? In brief one can indicate the following factors:

1. Absence of class consciousness. No discrimination between white and blue collar workers. Once they are recruited they get internal promotion and wage increases. There is not much difference in wages, which are normally determined on the basis of education, age, length of service, ability and rank.
2. Due to life time employment practice and seniority wage system, workers are sensitive about the performance of their enterprise, therefore, they cooperate. On the other hand, managements consider labor as important partner and try to keep their moral high.

3. The philosophy of trade unions, take into consideration national and company interest, while determining their interests.

The employees associations are mainly concerned about defending the interests of the employers, and they always aim for the development of healthy and stable industrial relations, promoting collective bargaining and bringing a unified employer's views on the issues of industrial relations to the government in a concerted manner. The role and functions of enterprise union are most important in Japan since the bargaining is done at enterprise level. The enterprise level bargaining has restricted the role of employer's associations in Japan. Even labor law is responsible for bringing Employer's Association to the secondary position because workers enjoy the right to organize while employers have no such right.

At the national level, the Nikkeiren-Japanese Employers Association deals with industrial relations, with 47 local associations, 52 industrial associations of employers, and has nearly 30,000 under its coverage. The functions of employers association is limited to the exchange of information, consulting, providing advice and leading public opinion against trade unions' in the field of wages, prices and other policies connected with industrial relations. With regard to collective bargaining employer's association establish a general policy especially on wage issues in an attempt to cope with the spring offensive. Such policy often only serves as a guideline and is not binding on the affiliates.

The Japanese Labor Law gives excessive protection to labor, while an employer does not have any right to organize, but only the freedom of association. The Japanese Employer's Association mainly organizes the rather larger enterprises, the Shokokaigisho (Chambers of Commerce) and its local branches provide information and advisory service for smaller enterprises which cover all kinds of business problems and include industrial relations. The Japanese Employer's Association's role minor in comparison with Keidanren (Japanese Industrialists Association) the role of which is to function as a pressure group representing the interest of business in general. It can also be explained by the lack of importance attached to industrial relations by Japanese management in the face of all the other problems they have to cope with.

9. FUTURE OF ENTERPRISE TRADE UNION

The future of any trade union depends upon enlightened labor force, an honest leader and well defined constitution and objectives. According to George Meany, the trade unions must possess some basic essentials, if they are to be more effective and useful. The essentials are:

1. A good union must be to protect its members and win a reasonable measures of economic justice for them.
2. A good union must be run by the members and for the members. There must be leaders—strong leaders, able and willing to stand firm for what they believe is right, and to fight for it against what might appear at times to be a popular position. But they must always be subject to support or reject the general membership of the union
3. A good union must be an honest union. This goes beyond finance, just being 'money honest' is not enough. The integrity of good union is all inclusive. It extends to its relationship with employers, to what it says to its won members, the formulation of its policies and the evaluation of its won performances.
4. A union must look beyond its won horizons. It must recognize and fulfil its proper role in the life of the nation and community in which it lives.

If one has to evaluate the success of enterprise union in Japan on the above essentials, he can safely say with very little exception that it has achieved her goals and met the expectations of its members. However, the majority of the Japanese people believe that western societies are advanced, modern, democratic, efficient and reasonable compared to Japan and they criticize their own practice and institutions as backward, feudalistic, inefficient, and irrational and undemocratic.[18]

Like any type of labor organization, enterprise union has weak and strong points. For example Shrai, summarizes the following undeniable faults:

1. They disperse union resources for the total lab or movement because of their highly decentralized structure,
2. They impede the possible development of a united labor movement,
3. They lack the will to make an effort to protect the interest of retired workers who had long been union members,
4. They are unwilling to organize unorganized workers, including unemployed workers,
5. They suffer from administrative and financial inefficiencies,
6. They are susceptible to employer interference and pressure, and
7. They are relatively weak in their bargaining power against employers, including the government.

According to Hanámi, it has been often pointed out that splits in union organizations and the ideological obstacles put in the way of a united front have impeded the bargaining power of the unions to a considerable extent. Most union leaders in Japan are aware of these weaknesses of enterprise union; hence they are sincerely working towards unification. The picture is not yet clear, one has to wait to see how they will introduce the industrial unions, where enterprise union has dominated over 40 years. In Japanese labor movement especially with development of Spring Offensive, industrial unions and national centers are able to influence enterprise unions. It is necessary for Japanese trade union to widen their operational policies, participate in management and aim at almost complete employee management of enterprise. The focus of collective bargaining seems to be moving upward from enterprise union to industrial unions.

Despite of upward movement, union power in Japan is largely decentralized and the administrative autonomy of enterprise union remains almost unaffected. Industrial unions hardly can take any step that would force a decision on enterprise union. Enterprise union enjoys many virtues. The virtues are:

1. The rapid increase in union organization within a relatively short time.
2. The enlargement of the scope and subject matter of collective bargaining.
3. The success in the organizing of white-collar workers.
4. The sound and stable union finances.
5. Good communication between leaders and the rank-and-file particularly on the shop floor.
6. Easy access to management in handling day-to-day problems.
7. A single united union within each enterprise as a rule.
8. The flexible adjustment to structural changes in industries and the establishment of a very appropriate structure for dealing with problems emerging within a plant or enterprise.[19]

One can express great appreciation for the functional efficiency of enterprise unions in dealing with in—plant problems. Shirai, even insists that an enterprise union is the most relevant and instrumental form of union organization in the advanced stage of capitalism, where the internal labor market becomes the predominant form of labor market.[20]

Japanese enterprise union has turned out to be more efficient in meeting problems of modern industrial relations—development and utilization of manpower resources, their distribution and reallocation, technological change and job security of workers, collective bargaining and inflation, workers' participation and plant-wise negotiation and decision-making within enterprise.

In several industrialized countries, the focus of collective bargaining seems to be moving down from the national or industrial level to the enterprise, which has already been established in Japan. In West there is also an increasing effort to organize white-collar, managerial and supervisory workers on the Japanese model; however, they have structural problems. Because Japanese unions are structurally different, they have been relatively successful in organizing white-collar workers in the same unions with blue-collar workers. The enterprise union has worked well and met workers' expectations. Shirai concludes that within the socio-economic and cultural context of Japanese industrial society, the enterprise union seems to be the most acceptable ad effective form of union organization and it is unlikely, at least in the foreseeable future, that radical changes will be supported by the majority of rank-and-file Japanese unions. Enterprise union has some intrinsic weakness, therefore, more coordination among unions certainly needed to meet new problems and challenges under new circumstances and structural changes. Slowly there will be shift of power from enterprise union to industrial unions and federations, which mean unification efforts, will be successful. Labor federations must put more sincere efforts to minimize the adverse effects of competition among rival companies, in individualization and fragmentation of industrial relations and to improve working conditions not only for union members but also for unorganized workers. In modern society these days, what is required from labor unions is not a smug labor-oriented attitude, but a movement to benefit a wider range of social strata.

10. ENTERPRISE UNION : SURVEY INTERPRETATION

Apart from life time employment, enterprise-based labor union also has attracted increasing attention from labor specialists, as an important contributor to the remarkable economic growth. A Japanese worker under life time employment stays with one enterprise and he strongly believes that enterprise-based labor union can protect his interest. As mentioned earlier in this chapter, enterprise-based labor union do have many limitations, but on the whole Japanese worker still have faith. According to a survey report those firms which said that "it is better to have labor union" accounted for 78.6% of the total and a large 96.3% accept the existence of labor unions. Needless to say, labor unions referred here are enterprise unions.

According to the results of this survey, the attitude of workers has not undergone considerable change and they still prefer enterprise-based labor union. Tables 3.9, 3.10 and 3.11,

TABLE 3.9
Employee's Preferences on 'Enterprise Union' (YES)

Preference Ranking	*Reasons*	*Workers Responded (%)*
First	Able to solve labour problems at enterprise level	60.0
Second	Maintains harmonious relations between employer and employee	61.4
Third	Responsible for the prosperity of enterprise	57.0

TABLE 3.10
University (J.B.)* Preferences on 'Enterprise Union' (YES)

Preference Ranking	*Reasons*	*Workers Responded (%)*
First	Able to solve labour problems at enterprise level	58.3
Second	Maintains harmonious relations between employer and employee	59.7
Third	Responsible for the prosperity of enterprise	80.5

J.B. = Job seekers

TABLE 3.11
High School (J.B.)* Preferences on 'Enterprise Union' (YES)

Preference Ranking	*Reasons*	*Workers Responded (%)*
First	Able to solve labour problems at enterprise level	55.1
Second	Maintains harmonious relations between	54.0
Third	Responsible for the prosperity of enterprise	57.1

J.B. = Job seekers

highlights the preferences rankings of employees and job seekers. There is no difference in the preferences of employees and job seekers (even among university and high school graduates) except little variation in percentage. They all prefer enterprise-based labor union. The employee prefers this because:

1. It is able to solve labor problems at enterprise level (60.0%).
2. Maintain harmonious relations between employer and employee (61.4%).
3. Responsible for the prosperity of enterprise (57.0%).

According to the Social and Economic Congress of Japan's survey result, many respondents said that unions and managements are currently tackling various vital issues such as wages, working hours amicable. In other survey, it is discovered that the employees (57.7%) of large firms think that their union leaders have technical knowledge for discussing with management and items discussed cover all issues pertaining to investment plan, administration and personnel management. To a large extent enterprise unions also shares interests with management to a considerable extent. There are many areas where both labor and managements are "sailing in the same boat". The respondents in this survey strongly believe that enterprise union can solve their problems and also maintain harmonious relations with their employer, which means they believe in "cooperative labor-management". Unions in Japan share with management an understanding for technological change and thus contribute for the prosperity of enterprise. Looking more closely at the outcome of the survey, the employees consider the enterprise-based labor unions as friendly or cooperative, who participate actively in the management at all levels. This is the reason why enterprise-based labor unions still exist in Japan.

The survey also traced the negative attitude towards enterprise unions. Labor specialists have pointed out many weaknesses; however, they are more or less general in nature. They do not relate much to the worker directly. In this survey, though a small percentage shows that Japanese employees and even job seekers are aware of the limitations. Tables 3.12, 3.13 and 3.14, identify the reflection. The reasons for not favoring according to the order of preference of employee:

TABLE 3.12
Employee's Preferences on 'Enterprise Union' (NO)

Preference Ranking	*Reasons*	*Workers Responded (%)*
First	Weak and fails to bargain effectively	41.6
Second	Pro-employer Union	33.3
Third	Fails to achieve better working condition	41.6
Fourth	Fails to bring harmonious relations between employer and employee	58.3

TABLE 3.13
University (J.B.) Preferences on 'Enterprise Union' (NO)

Preference Ranking	*Reasons*	*Workers Responded (%)*
First	Pro-employer Union	29.1
Second	Weak and fails to bargain effectively	45.8
Third	Fails to achieve better working condition	41.6
Fourth	Fails to bring harmonious relations between employer and employee	45.8

* J.B. = Job Seekers.

TABLE 3.14
High School (J.B.) Preferences on 'Enterprise Union' (NO)

Preference Ranking	*Reasons*	*Workers Responded (%)*
First	Pro-employer Union	29.1
Second	Weak and fails to bargain effectively	45.8
Third	Fails to achieve better working condition	41.6
Fourth	Fails to bring harmonious relations between employer and employee	45.8

* J.B. = Job Seekers.

1. Enterprise-based labor union is weak and fails to bargain effectively (41.6%).
2. It is pro-employer union (33.3%).
3. It fails to achieve better working conditions (41.6%).
4. It fails to bring harmonious relations between employer and employee (58.3%).

These preferences are in harmony with those criticisms of labor experts. In case of job seekers we see the difference between university and high school is negligible. They differ with second and third preferences.

This survey covered variety of issues. Other interesting findings pertaining to enterprise union are based on age, work experience and level of income are:

1. The largest (52.2%) age-wise, who favored enterprise union belong to an age group 25 to 34 years.
2. The further classification of response indicate that the largest percentage (36.8%) however, belong to age group 25 to 29 (remaining 18.4% are from age group 30 to 34 years).
3. Out of those 89.5%) who favored enterprise union about 43.1% is from a group 1 to 6 years of experience.
4. As the years of experience increase the percentage in favor of enterprise union decreases.
5. Out of those 89.5% who favor of enterprise union, 31.3% of employees belong to the income group earning 200,000 to 300,000 Yen.
6. Another 30.3% responses came from income-group 100,000 to 200,000 Yen.
7. In other words the 61.6% of employees who favored enterprise union belong to 100,000 to 200,000 Yen income group.
8. As income increase the response in favor of enterprise union decrease.

As long as life time employment continues and enterprise-based labor union protects the interest of Japanese employees, it will remain as the most suitable type of labor union organization in Japan. On the basis of survey, we can conclude that Japanese employees neglect or overlook that the enterprise union is inefficient, backward, irrational and undemocratic. While enterprise unions are not so strong to confront with management, at the same time they are also not weak enough to completely control by the managements. Though some times the bargaining power of many enterprise unions have been hindered due to the splits in union organization and ideological difference but the administrative autonomy and functional efficiency remain unaffected. Most enterprise unions are affiliated to industrial federations and national centers from where they receive their strength.

NOTES AND REFERENCES

1. "Machine is the cause and the labor movement is the result". "Trade union appears as a group interpretation as the social situation in which workers find them and as a remedial program in the form of aims, policies and methods. "Trade unionism arises from the job consciousness and scarcity of job opportunities. "Trade union owns their origin to class-struggle between the capitalist employers and their workers. To get more and more profits, the employers exploit the workers, who because of their common interest to get more wages, unite in trade unions and then resist the employers". "Labor movement is always a reaction and protection against capitalism".
   Broadly speaking, the origin-and growth of trade unionism is the result of increased complexities of economic structure of man's life and the industrial revolution made it all the more essential, that is the stress and strain of industrial revolution (as quoted by Mamoria's Dynamics of Industrial Relations in India, Himalaya Publishing House, Bombay, 1986, p. 83).
2. Kuwahara, Yasuo, Industrial Relations System in Japan—A New Interpretation, Japanese Industrial Relations, Series No. 16, The Japan Institute of Labor, Tokyo, p. 9.
3. Nakamura Tadashi, Labor in Japan, (Questions and Answers), Japan Institute of Labor, Tokyo, 1990, p. 82.
4. Blanpain, R. (Rd.), International Encyclopedia for Labor Law and Industrial Relations, Vol. 7 (Japan section is written by Hanami T.A.) Kluwar Law and Taxation Publishers, The Netherlands, 1985, p. 41.
5. Kuwahara, Yasuo, *op. cit*., p. 9.
6. Nakamura, Tadashi, *op. cit*., p. 56.
7. Solomon, B. Levine (1958) rightly characterized the enterprise union as follows: In appearance the enterprise union resembles the local of an industrial union, organ "intermediate", organization like the Ford or General Motors departments of the United Automobile workers in the US. However, the similarity ends about there. The essential distinction between the enterprise union and the local industrial union is that the former is a unit in and of itself, it is not merely and administrative

component of a national union nor is it simply and "inside" independent company-wide union (as cited in Taishiro Shirai (Ed), Contemporary Industrial Relation as in Japan, p. 119).

8. Refer Hanami's Labor Relations in Japan, 1979. He has elaborately discussed enterprise unionism and the National setting—industrial federation and confederations—Shunto.
9. Katsumi Yakabe, Labor Relations in Japan—Fundamental Characteristics, International Society for Education Information Inc., Japan, p. 3.
10. Nakamura Tadashi, *op. cit.*, p. 74.
    Refer "Shunto Wage Offensive"—Historical overview and perspective, Japanese Industrial Relations, Series No. 15, The Japan Institute of Labor, and Tokyo.
11. Blanpain, R. (Ed.), *op. cit.*, p. 45.
12. Trade Union participant in the following councils.
13. Refer "Grand Unification of Japan's Labor Movement", *Japan Labor Bulletin*. The Japan Institute of Labor, February, 1990, pp. 4-8
14. Refer Nakamura's Labor in Japan, (pp. 66-69), for History of Post-war labor organization and his book Labor-Management Relations in Japan, for Trade Unions Structure of Japan and Rengo and Labor Front Unification.
15. Refer Macho Nitta's article—Grand Unification of Japan's Labor Movement, *Japan Labor Bulletin*, Japan Institute of Labor, February 1990, for detail analysis of Grand Unification—Formation of New Rengo.
16. *Ibid.*, pp. 4-8.
17. Refer Kuwahara Yasuo's Japanese Industrial Relations, series No. 16, "A Hypothesis on the structure of Industrial Relations in Japan", pp. 9-13.
18. Taishiro Shirai (Rd), *op. cit.*, p. XXXIII.
19. *Ibid.*, p. 141.
20. *Ibid.*, p. 143.

APPENDIX 1
Organisation of Matsushita Electric Workers' Union

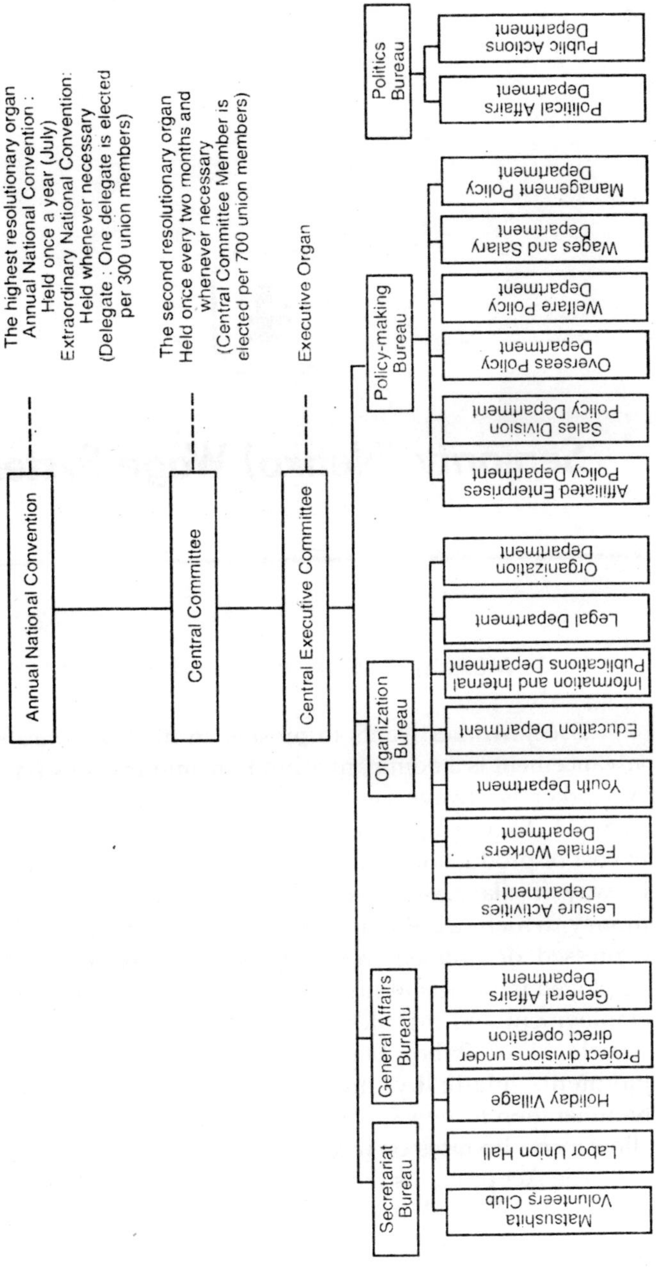

4

Seniority (Nenko) Wage System

1. MEANING AND PAYMENT OF WAGES

Every worker wants to prosper in his life; hence material advancement is a dominant aspiration among industrial worker. A worker is always vigilant about the wage he gets, for his survival. To an employer wage constitutes an important factor of cost of production. "Wage" means all remuneration (whether by way of salary, allowance or otherwise) expressed in terms of money which would, in term of contract of employment, expressed or implied, were fulfilled be payable to a person employed in respect of his employment or of work done in such employment and includes house rent allowance.[1] According to Article 11 of Labor Standard Act, wages include all the payments made by the employer to the employee as remuneration for work, whether they are called wages, salaries, allowances, bonuses or whatever.

The Act prohibits the employer to pay wages other than in cash, it is allowed if otherwise provided by law, order or agreement. Generally, such goods and benefits are regarded as a part of wages:

1. When they are provided in the place of wages in cash, usually accompanied by the deduction of the equivalent amount from the wages, and
2. When their provision is agreed in the contract as an addition to wages in cash.

However, they are not regarded as a part of wages if the employee pays a price or if they are part of welfare facilities. Often enterprises pay cash payments for employees marriages, for the funeral of a member of his family or for an accident or causality, these are not regarded as a part of wages as long as the precise detailed conditions of the payments are not laid down in the work rules or agreements. Housing provided by the employer is regarded as a part of wages only when the employer pays a housing allowance of equal value to those not living in company accommodation.[2]

One of the characteristics of Japanese wage system is the distinction between the portion earned of one's work and the portion paid by virtue of just being an employee. The wages paid for just being an employee includes payments to replace notice of dismissal, the payment of wages during the annual vacation, during time-off caused by an accident at work, family allowance, commuting allowance, etc.

For example, the following wage structure of Toyota highlights different part of wages:

Wages:

Regular Wage
- Basic wage
- Productivity allowance
- Grade allowance
- Age allowance
- Job title allowance
- Family

Special allowance
- Service area allowance
- Meal allowance

Premium Payments
- Special operation payment
- Overtime payment

- Night work payment
- Shift work payment
- Staggered work payment

Article 12 of the Labor Standard Act, defines the "average wage". According to this definition, the 'average wage' means the quotient obtained by dividing the total amount of wages for a period of three months (or the period of employment if this is less than 3 months) preceding the day on which the calculation of the average wage becomes necessary by the number of all days during the period, provided that the amount of the average wage shall not be less than the amount computed by one of the following methods:

1. In case the wage is computed by the labor days or labor hours, or defined by piece-rate or other contract price, 60% of quotient obtained by dividing the total sum of wages by the number of the labor days during that period.
2. In case a part of the wages is defined by month, week or any other fixed period, aggregate of the quotient is obtained by dividing the total sum of those parts by the number of all days during the period and the sum computed by the foregoing method.

If there is a fixed day for closing the wage account, the period of the preceding paragraph shall be calculated from the last fixed day.

If the periods mention in the preceding two paragraphs included any of the following periods, the days and wages in those periods shall be excluded from the days and total amount of wages in the preceding two paragraphs:

1. Period of rest for the medical treatment caused by injury or illness while on duty.
2. Period of rest before and after child birth according to the provision of Article 65.
3. Period of rest caused reason for which the employer is responsible.
4. Probation period.

The total amount of wages on which the 'average wage' is calculated does not include extraordinary wages, wages which are paid periodically with more than three month period and wages which are paid by anything other than money, that is not within certain scope. Concerning the inclusion of payments other than in money, the Labor Ministry provides detailed standards. The amount of 'average wage' for the daily worker is also defined by the labor ministry.

Chapter 3 of Labor Standard Act includes provision regarding regulations concerning the wage payments. Wage must be paid in cash and in full directly to the workers. Wages must be paid at least once a month at a definite date (Article 24), however, this shall not apply to extraordinary wages, bonus, etc. Deduction from the wages may be permitted if otherwise provided by law, order or a written agreement with the majority union or if there is no majority union, with the representative of the majority of employees. However, even if such agreement exists, deductions to offset the employer's claim against an employee are only permissible within the limit of one-fourth of the total amount of wages in a payment period. Exceptions to the above mentioned standards which are in common use are, the deduction of tax social security fees, union dues and fees under the check-off system, the repayment of debt to the employer and the payment of fees and payment for benefits and goods provided by the employer under an agreement to this effect. The employer may not make a contract fixing in advance either the sum payable for breach of contract or the amount of indemnity for damage caused by the employee's negligence, and neither may be deduct the money advanced or make any other claim of the condition to work.

Concerning payment in cash, payment by cheque and payment into the employee's bank account have recently become controversial issues. Payment into the employee's account is admitted on condition that the payment is made into an account designated by the employee and that the total amount of wages can be withdrawn on pay-day. Payment by cheque tends to be denied, at least legally, which perhaps reflects the unpopularity of the use of the cheque in Japan. The deduction of amount of over payment of wages is regarded as lawful even without agreement since it is only a matter of settlement or adjustment.

When the worker requires to appropriate money for emergency use such as child birth, disease, accident and other cases which will be prescribed by ordinance of the labor ministry in detail, the employer shall pay the accrued wages before the day of payment (Art. 25). For the rest day caused by reason for which the employer is responsible, the worker's average wage be paid (Art. 26). When the worker is employed by piece rate or other contract, the employer must assure the worker if fixed sum of wage proportionate the working hour (Art. 27). When the employer extends the working hours or employs the workers on rest days or employs the worker during 10 pm and 5 am, he shall pay increased rate wages by at least 25% of the normal wages, family allowance, commutation allowance and other wages prescribed by ordinance are excluded from the normal wage upon which increased rate wages should be computed (Art. 37). The employer shall grant six-day vacation with pay consecutively or separately to the workers who have been employed continuously for a year and were present eighty percent or more of the whole working days (Art. 39).

The Security of Wage Payment Act, 1975 protects the payment of wages and other monetary interest of employee in the case of their employer's insolvency. The delayed payment of wages can be punished by a fine. But when there are cases of insolvency, the civil law gives priority to wage claims for the last three months against other claims. However, in practice there are quite often other claims on the enterprise, especially large ones secured by bonds and mortgages and as a result the priority given to wages does not really mean much.[3] The Security of Wage Payment Act, 1975, introduced two principle measures:

1. The first measure is the creation of a program by which government undertakes to pay the employees wages left unpaid by an insolvent enterprise. The amount which workers are entitled is the lesser of 80% of the unpaid wages and retirement and ending on the day before the worker applied for payment.

2. The second measure is the establishment of a duty of an enterprise to adopt measures to protect employee's saving. The preservative measures required by this Act can be met through a contract with a bank or other financial institution under which such institution guarantee that it will repay the amount deposited by each worker.
3. The third measure is each enterprise shall endeavour to take preservative measures with respect to a certain amount of retirement allowances.

The Article 25 of constitution, which together with Article 27 paragraph 2, is the basis of Japanese minimum wage. The main purpose of minimum wage is to protect low-paid workers and their standard of living, to raise the quality of the labor force and secure fair competition among enterprises.

The employer must guarantee a fixed wage proportionate to the working hours of those workers who are paid piece-rates or by results. This minimum fixed wage is interpreted as guaranteeing a certain amount of the income to the employee, but the minimum amount is not specified in the law. The Labor Ministry says that the size of the fixed wage should be defined so as the guarantee an amount which is not drastically lower than normal income.

The minimum standard of wage has been prescribed by Minimum Wages Law. Minimum wages are determined by the Labor Ministry or Chief of the Prefecture Labor Standard Bureau, on the request of all the employers and unions covered by a collective agreement which applied to the majority of workers of the same kind and their employers in a certain district. Minimum wages must be based on research and study of Minimum Wage Council, a tripartite body composed of representative of public interests, labor and management. As yet minimum wages have been decided for the traditionally low wage applied to all industries at a national level.

Minimum wages are to be determined based on worker's cost of living, wages of similar categories of workers and normal capacity of firms to pay wages. The minimum wages are set by each Prefecture authority on the basis of regional minimum wage, applicable to all workers in the prefecture regardless of industry or occupation. Minimum wages are also set known as industry-wise minimum wages applicable to workers in specified industries. In short, minimum wage applicable to all workers does not exist.

The Central Minimum Wage Council, since 1978 has classified all 47 prefectures into 4 categories and proposed guideline for regional minimum wage to the Local Minimum Wages Council in order to ensure the consistency of regional minimum wages on a nation-wide basis. Normally the Local Minimum Wage Council determines the regional minimum wages on the basis of guidelines. Since 1989 industry minimum wages are determined by the method which is set when the Minimum Wages Council will admit, the necessity to decide higher wages than regional minimum wages, with the proposal of labor and management concerned, which belongs to a variety of council method. This means that minimum wages shall be decided under the initial leadership of labor and management concernd,[4] there is no much difference in the condition of minimum daily wage by region and industry (Table 4.1).

TABLE 4.1
The Condition of Minimum Daily Wage (Feb., 1988)

1. Minimum wage by Region—daily	
- The highest	- 3,884 ¥
- The lowest	- 3,328 ¥
- Average	- 3,661 ¥
2. Minimum wage by industry	
- Central	
- Coal Mining	- 5,772 ¥
- Metal Mining	- 5,772 ¥
- Regional	
- The highest: Paint Manufacturing, Osaka	- 4,754 ¥
- The lowest: Food beverage and feed Manufacturing, Kagoshima	- 3,460 ¥
- Average	- 4,042 ¥

Sources : Labour in Japan, Nakamura Tadashi, Ministry of Labour, Tokyo, 1988.

Japanese minimum wage system considered as realistic has been criticized:

1. For its departure from what the minimum wages system ought to be—nationally unified minimum wages or at least nation-wide industrial minimum wages.
2. The contemporary systems coverage of 3.3 million workers is an exaggeration, for only an insignificant number of employees are really affected favorably by the minimum wage.

The Labor Standard Act under Article 4 prohibits the employer not to discriminate women against men concerning wage by reason of the worker being a woman. It is not however, a violation of the Act if wage differentials are on the basis of efficiency or technical skills. When a violation is proved, the employer is subject to criminal penalties and must pay to the female employees the difference between the amount of wages already paid and the amount of wages paid to male employees doing the same work.

Equal pay for equal work as promulgated by the Labor Standard Act, is concerned both for men and women. The wage difference still prevails on the basis of education, length of service, age, size of enterprise, region and industry. Since most wages are determined by negotiation at enterprise level, the principle of "equal pay for equal work" is hardly acceptable except in ideology. The idea of equal pay for equal work has been advocated by younger workers who are becoming more and more aware of the value of their flexibility and efficiency at a time of rapid technological development. Wage differentials certainly narrowed in recent years because:

1. The shortage of younger worker is expected to continue in future as there is an increasing tendency of higher education amount younger generation.
2. Recruiting of young and competent workers is becoming difficult.
3. The Japanese society is facing the problem of older workers whose ability is destined to loose its value

given technological development and whose number is growing because of increased life expectancy.

4. The cost of these older workers. Resulting from the seniority wage system is now imposing a heavier burden of Japanese enterprise.[5]

Though wage differentials in Japan have narrowed in recent years, the average annual wage in private sector between male and female worker, on the basis of size of the firm differs. According to the national Tax Administration in Japan, total monthly wage and total annual wage of male worker is more than female worker in all size of firms. Male worker's average number of years employed is 12.6, whereas female worker's average is only 8.6 (Table 4.2). Chart 4.2 shows national wage, real wage, and labor productivity and consumer index. Wage differentials are very much visible on the basis of educational background and age. Chart 4.3 highlights the wage differentials between University, High School and Junior High School graduates based on age.

TABLE 4.2

Average Annual Earnings per Regular Employee (1989)[1]

Sex	*Total Annual earning*	*Contractual earning[2]*	*Bonuses and special premium*
Male	5 158 932	3 796 584	1 362 348
Female	2 597 112	1 969 104	628 008

1. Wages and salaries before deduction of income taxes and social security contributions payable by workers.
2. Scheuled earnings plus family allowances, overtime payments, cost.

Sources : Ministry of Labour.

2. WAGE AND LABOR PRODUCTIVITY

The annual wages or salaries of regular employees working at all establishments with 30 workers or more averaged 5.2 million yen for men and 2.6 million yen for women in 1988 (Chart 4.1). Of the total remuneration, about 75% is paid as regular monthly pay and a large part of the reminder is paid in the form of bonuses. As for monthly contractual earnings for

CHART 4.1
Monthly Contractual Earnings by Scale of Employment (1988)

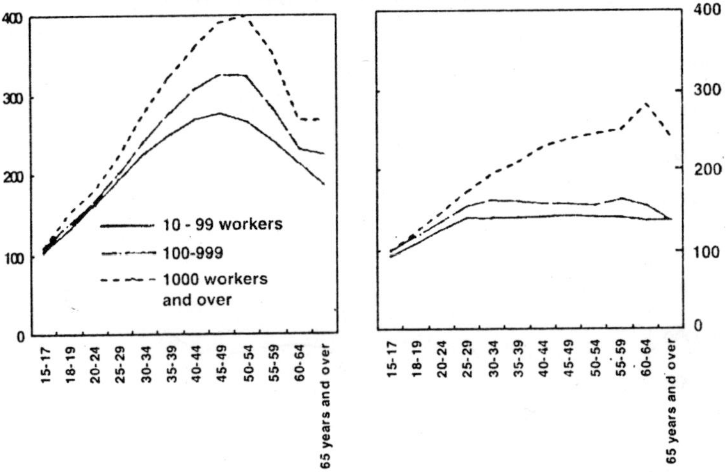

Source : Statistical Hand Book of Japan, 1990.

CHART 4.2
Manufacturing Industries (1985=100)

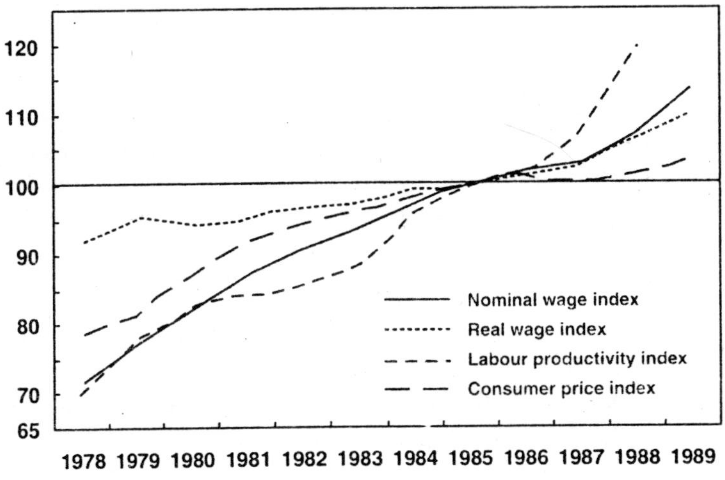

Source : Statistical Hand Book of Japan, 1990.

CHART 4.3

Wage Differentials by Educational Background and Age group (Scheduled Cash Earnings of Employees Working at Enterprise with 1000 Employees and more)

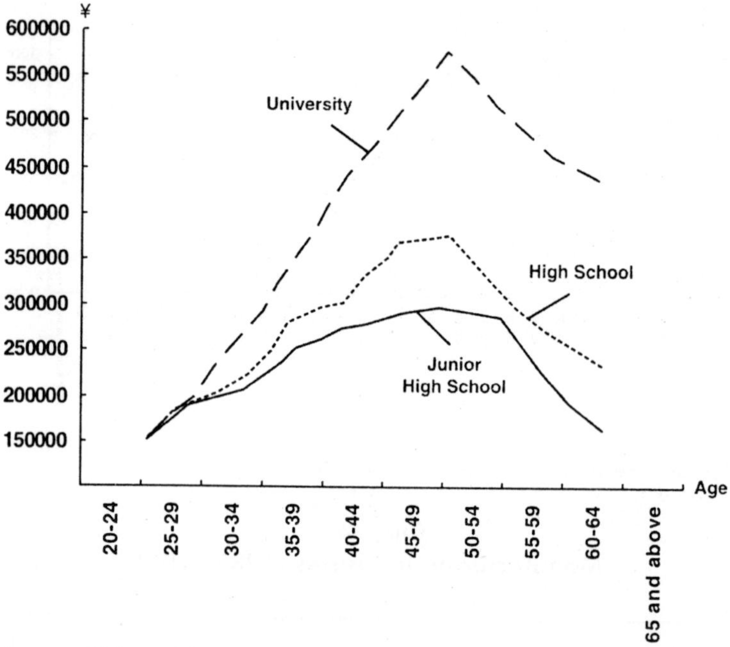

Source : Ministry of Labour Basic Survey on Wage Structure, 1988.

males, the average shows gradual increase as age increases from age at entry to the labor force to the 45-49 age group, wages for 45-49 age group are twice as high as those for workers of the 20-24 age group, while average earnings for females also show increases as age increases from age at initial employment to the 50 years age bracket, though there is no large disparity between age groups.

According to figures released by the Labor Ministry in December 1988, the average wage increase was 5.3%; representing a monthly increase averaging Yen 12,085 (equivalent figures for 1988 were 4.4% and Yen 9,731). Chart 4.4 indicates average rate of wage increase by size of enterprise. These figures represent the greatest level of increase since 1982.

CHART 4.4

Average Rate of Wage Increase by Enterprise Size (1988)

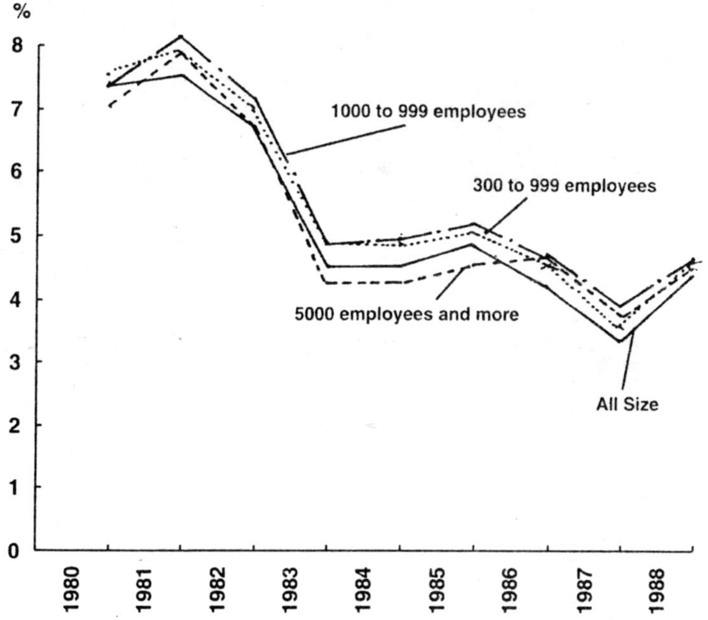

Source : Year Book of Labour Statistics (Japan) 1988.

While Japan's rate of wage increase was high from the late 1960's to the early 1970's, the rate has fallen since the late 1970's. Recent years, however, have seen moves to redress the imbalance. Table 4.3 shows average initial monthly salary, classified by type of work, gender and scale of the company according to the number of employees.

Due to the shortage in labor, many corporations are beginning to increasingly rely on part-time labor. According to a survey by the Labor Ministry, 75.2% of all corporations revised their part-time wage rates upwards in 1989 (compared to 70.4% in 1988) and the average rate of increase for those companies revising their wage rates was 6.0% (compared to 3.6% in 1988). In comparison, the rate of increase for all part-time labor was 4.3% in 1989 (compared to 2.8% 1988).

The main factors that determine increase in wages and salaries are—consumer's price index and labor productivity.

TABLE 4.3
Wage-Average Salaries
Average Age of Workers (June 1989) and their Average Monthly Salaries, Classified by Position (Surveyed between May and June 1989)

Position	Number Surveyed	Total No. of employees	Average age	Average monthly salary (¥) (A) Actual pay (A)	(B) Overtime included in (A) (B)	Fixed Salary (A)–(B)	Position entitlement (included in A–B)
(1)	(2)	(3)	(4)	(5)	(6)	(7)	(8)
Branch Office Manager	1 581	7 319	50.2	679 661	2 067	677 594	90 159
Office Department Manager	6 936	28 330	50.5	605 568	365	605 203	57 469
Office Section Manager	19 010	123 316	45.9	499 897	3 788	496 109	47 331
Ordinary Clerk	120 391 2	142 960	29.8	239 343	27 841	211 502	0
Plant Manager	787	2 660	50.8	566 818	464	566 354	50 772
Technical Dept. Manager	4 715	16 190	49.5	572 943	415	572 528	48 205
Technical Section Manager	11 918	70 149	45.1	470 893	2 252	468 641	39 155
Ordinary Technical Staff	54 470	814 371	31.6	292 023	54 265	237 758	0

Sources : Bureau of Compensation, National Personnel Authority.

Apart from these two main factors, most Japanese companies consider the following factors while determine the amount of wage increase: business results, regular wage, security of wage, consumer price and industrial relation stabilization (Table 4.5). While Table 4.4 highlights the ratio of enterprises and points considered most important when determining amount of wage

TABLE 4.4

Ratio of Enterprise—Points Considered Important when Determining Wages for Mid-career

	M.A. (%)
Total for all industries:	
Enterprises hiring	100.0
No. of years of previous position	34.0
Age	59.9
Specialized knowledge	23.3
Wage with previous employer	35.0
Balance with wages of persons currently in that occupatoon	71.4
Desired salary stated	21.0
Enterprises not replying	2.8

Sources : Year Book of Labour Statistics, 1988.

TABLE 4.5

Ratio of Enterprises—Points Considered most Important when Determining amount of Wage Increase, 1988

	M.A. (%)
All industries covered:	
Total	100.0
Business results	65.1
Regular wages	26.0
Security of labour	4.3
Consumer price	0.8
Industrial relation stabilities	2.8
Others	1.0

Sources : Year Book of Labour Statistics, 1988.

for mid-career employees, i.e. number of years of previous position, age, specialized knowledge, wage with previous employer, balance with wages of persons currently in that occupation and desired salary stated. In Japan in recent years, labor productivity has shown a constant improvement in manufacturing sector, representing an average annual increase rate of 6.4% during 1983-88 periods. Increase in equipment investment, rationalization and labor-saving are the major causes of productivity gains. Apart from this quality of labor force, high adaptability new techniques as a result of high levels of educational background, stable labor-management relations, limited number of disputes, low absenteeism and efficient operation are other factors responsible for high labor productivity and wages.

The Japan Federation of Employer's Association, argue that wage should follow productivity increase, it means wage increase beyond productivity would lead not only to inflations but also to employment stability. However, trade unions consider this would restrain wage and dampen economic growth by victimizing domestic demand. Trade unions always think, a steady economic growth, the stabilization of consumer prices and employment stability are the necessary conditions for an improvement of worker's standard of living. In order to achieve these three objectives, the demand for a wage increase should take due consideration of the prevailing economic conditions of the movement. Trade unions are also of the option that small wage increase would not be attended with economic performance and it would hamper a stable growth of the Japanese economy.

3. CHARACTERISTICS OF WAGE SYSTEM

Employee's wage in any country is governed by various factors, some controlled by employer and some by external constraints. The wage structure is often built on the premise that each job has its own price. The wage that an employer is willing to pay depends on his philosophy, his capacity to pay, his competitive position and his ability to attract and retain a work force by factors other than wages alone. Japanese wage system however, differs and exhibits unique characteristics. The following characteristics are peculiar when compared to other countries:[6]

1. The wages are calculated on monthly basis. Often wages are paid even if an employee is forced to miss a great deal of work. In another style of wages system, the wage earner is penalized for each day he is absent. In Japanese wage system therefore, wages are relatively stable as managements guarantee the employee's livelihood.
2. There is little wage difference between ordinary wage earners and staff employees. Furthermore, no distinction is made between these types of employees by labor unions—all are members of the same union.
3. The third characteristic of the Japanese wage system is the distinction between the portion earned for one's work and the portion paid by virtue of just being an employee. While the wages paid for one's work (according to efficiency, achievement and ability) fits the general concept of wages, the latter refers to allowances (family allowances, commuting allowances, housing allowance, etc.) paid by the employer.
4. Wages are accepted as permanent and lasting for the employee's entire career, this includes not only a guarantee of at least a minimum annual rise, but also a lump sum paid as a severance allowance at the time of retirement or separation-irrespective of whether this comes after only two or three years or after 30 years of continuous service. As long as labor contracts exclude clauses which suggest "no work, no pay", salaries will continue to be paid at least partially, even if the employee is absent from his job due to illness.
5. Japanese wage system, including retirement allowances, is highly dependent on age and length of service rather than on skill or job evaluation. Although lately more emphasis is made for job evaluation and economists suggest that the correlations between the amount of wages, the length of service and age is not different from the western countries. The difference still exists both in statistical fact and more especially in

attitudes and ideas. The differences in wages by age and length of service are greater in Japan than in the major European countries. Starting wages are decided according to the employee's level of education rather than his ability and thus basic wages are increased annually according to his length of service. Only after several years of service wage differences can be seen, caused due to promotion based on the individual merit. This does not deny however, the basic pattern of an annual wage increment automatically connected with the length of service.

6. The wage includes various types of allowances such as family, commuting, housing and regional allowances, allowances for foremen, supervisors and other positions. For special jobs, special work, technical work, high attendance rates and subsidized living expenses.

   Bonus are every important part of wages which are paid twice a year at the end of the year and in summer, which is equivalent to about 5 months wages in total for a year on average and often amounting to more than 6 months wages. This system is drawing attention from the other industrialized countries as a typical type of 'share system' or 'built-in-wage-profit system'. Retirement allowances paid in lump sum and often accompanied by pensions are also regarded as a part of wages and a very important part too, which may mean more than 25 months wages for those retiring after 30 years of service. The total amount of pension to be paid apart from the lump sum payment is equal to the amount of lump sum payment.

7. Since wage system is based on length of service and education, the wage differentials caused by the factors such as age and length of service have been rather conspicuous. Wages are determined through bargaining mainly at enterprise level, thus the differentials caused by differences in the size of enterprises and regional differences have been important.

8. Wage differences between regular and temporary workers or between workers of different status and sex have also been characteristics of Japanese wage structure.[7]
   The wage for a standard female worker of a senior high school in her 20's, who has remained employed by the same enterprise since her graduation, is about 90% of a wage for a similar male. The ratio declines as the women gets old, in her 50's the ratio is about 70%.
   - The wage differentials between men and women reflect not only worker's characteristics including age, length of service, educational background and position in household, but also employment factors such as industrial sector, size of enterprise, job and position classification where women are employed.[8] Chart 4.5 shows wage differentials by educational background and age group. In all the three categories wages increase until the age group of 50-54, where they reach highest level and wages deteriorate from this point.

CHART 4.5
Starting Salary for New Graduates and Educational Level (1988)

(in Thousands)

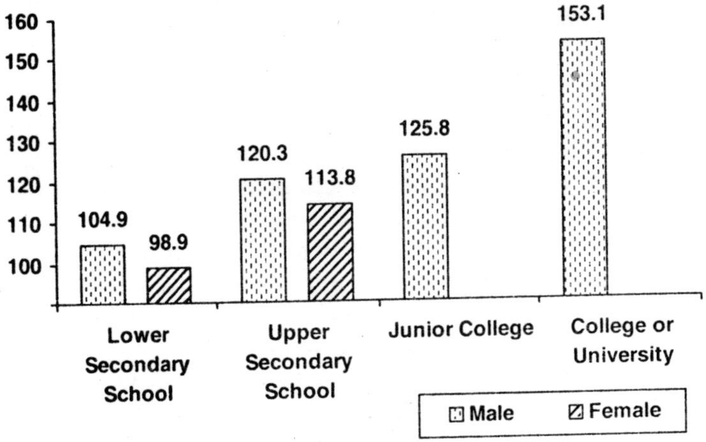

Source : Year Book of Labour Statistics, 1988.

9. Most Japanese enterprises maintain various facilities which can be termed "invisible remuneration" because they sustain well-being and living standards of the employees/employer provides welfare facilities such as medical and hospital care, meals, cultural, sports and recreation facilities, health and other insurance systems.

Although these characteristics do still exist, the differences have become narrower in every respect due to labor shortage.

The wage determination of a Japanese worker depends upon a variety of factors, some controlled by employer and some by employee. Wage system of Japan is unique and complex. Government laws or decisions of wage boards, local wages or courts decisions do not influence Japanese wage system. Figure 4.1 shows wage influencing variables and wage components in organized sector. Japanese wage consists of several components. Main components are regular monthly wage and Fringe benefits. Regular wage includes standard wage—wage paid for regular work and extra wage—mean allowance such as overtime work allowance and shift work premiums. Japanese worker gets very attractive fringe benefits, which includes bonus paid twice a year, retirement benefits and welfare benefits.

Basic wage is stable/fixed wage paid over a period of time, may be monthly or weekly. This wage is the normal rate for given output or job. Japanese basic wage is again peculiar, it is determined on the basis of age, job classification and job evaluation, Japanese worker gets very liberal allowances such as assignment allowance including position allowance, allowances paid for heavy duty staff, allowances paid for special duty staff and allowance for dependents, i.e. spouse and children.

Japanese companies follow very efficiently job classified wage system. Wage based on job classification has led to variations in wage packets. However, the objectives of job-classified wage system of Japan are fair and ideal—to adapt and accommodate the concept of equal pay for equal work to the Japanese traditional system and to set logical and clearly defined criteria in order to establish individual wages. The structure of job-classified wage system has established two job

FIG. 4.1
Wage Influencing Variables and Wage Components in Organised Sector

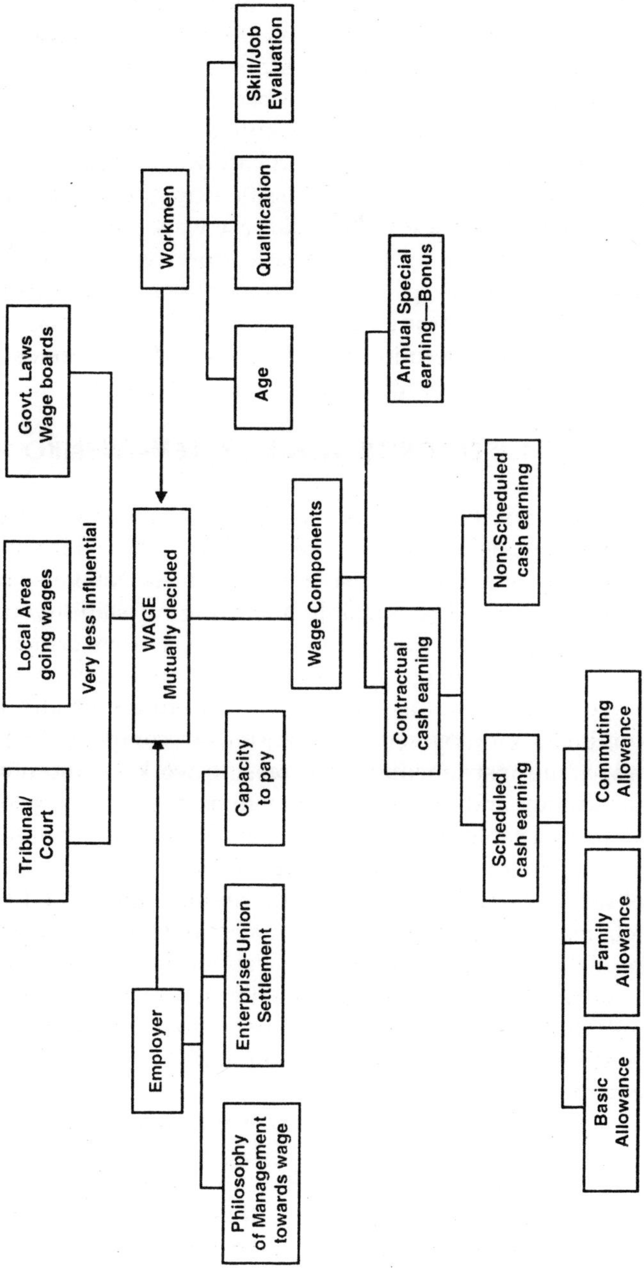

groups—first group includes skilled workers, office and engineering staff, special duty staff and second group includes managerial as supervisory staff, specialists and experts. Different rating standards have been assigned to job groups.

When workers are not classified by job groups, they are classified on education level and base wage paid on the basis of age. Generally, workers are classified by group and their basic wage comprises base wage 30%, base wage by job classification (30%) and wage by job classification evaluation (40%). At Matsushita base wage by job classification is determined by job group (7) and grades (8). The wage by job classification evaluation is determined on the basis of job groups (7) and evaluations (minimum, standard or maximum).

4. SENIORITY WAGE SYSTEM—NENKO

The stability of labor-management relations of Japan has drawn considerable international attention. Apart from life time employment and enterprise union, Japanese Nenko or seniority wage system is responsible for bringing stability in labor-management relations. However, it has been criticized that seniority-based wages are designed to hold down the general wage level as well as to force workers to be dependent upon continued employment in a particular company. The Nenko wages are instrumental in increasing worker's incentives and satisfaction and decreasing alienation by providing continuous and predictable rewards. According to Inagami, consciousness of belonging rests first on perception of structure of distribution of social resources (income, authority and status) and the rules relating to distribution of resources and opportunities which produces this structure. This relates not only to how the structure and rules of the distribution system contribute to individual member's need satisfaction but also how they contribute to the organizational ability to adapt to the environment.

What is the seniority based wage system?

1. The seniority-based wage system is the system whereby wages are determined at the time of recruitment by the enterprise, based on personal

attributes such as educational background, age, experience, etc. will continue to increase with a annual automatic increment given for each year of service. As the skills of employees improve in the directions required by the enterprise, their wage levels increase according to the firm-specific careers.

2. Based wage system can also be defined as a method of determining wages, salaries and other rewards from employment-based primarily on a worker's length of service, but partly on his age and education. Under this system worker is assured of sufficient earning to cover over his life cycle thus he is always willing to commit himself to his enterprise as family for long period and also has an interest to improve and learn his skills. In Japan's highly structured labor market, with its Nenko system, worker's basic interests, particularly in their employment, income security and opportunities to advance, depend on the prosperity of the enterprise.

Japanese workers still wish that their salary increase and promotion to be based on seniority. Chart 4.6 highlights the international comparison of factors to determine wage increase and promotion.

CHART 4.6

How would you Like Promotions and Salary Increases to be Decided?

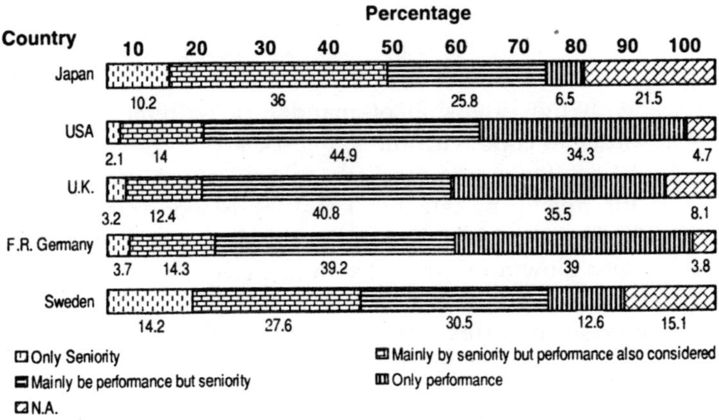

Source : The Japanese Youth, The Prime Minister's Office, Tokyo, 1978.

The seniority wages implies a set of features:

1. A positive slope in age-wage profiles,
2. Wage rates determined separately from jobs being performed, and
3. No significant differentials in basic wages according to workshop or occupation.

Although these features may appear unusual, they fit very well with the flexible operation of Japanese internal labor market.[9]

The seniority-based wage curves are found positive irrespective of industry, size of enterprises, level of educational background of the workers and sex, though the rate of increase according to seniority may be different. At each level of educational background, wages tend to increase consistently with age until worker reach the first half of the 50's and the peak gets higher in proportion to the educational attainment. Wages reach the peak when workers attain the first half of the 50's in each industry, and the peak is higher in tertiary industries than in manufacturing industries. The increase in the wage rate is bigger as the size of the enterprise becomes larger, wages reach the peak for workers aged 50 to 54 in larger enterprises, while in small enterprises, and they are highest at the age 45 to 49. The seniority wage system is also applied to female workers, but the rate of wage increase is smaller and the wage peak comes earlier than for male worker. In Japan in the recent years the seniority wage curve has decline due to:

1. With the extension of mandatory retirement age in order to cope with the aging society.
2. Wages for young workers, particularly starting wages for new graduate workers, increased dramatically during the high economic growth ear, though it has been slowing down after the oil crisis.[10]

Age-wise profiles, reflecting the degree of skill, differentiate three types of workers in small firms:

1. There are the white-collar workers whose wages

increase roughly according to age and whose age-wage profile is similar to that of blue-collar workers in large firms, suggesting that this subgroup has the internal promotion type of career pattern.

2. There are the blue-collar workers whose wages rise very little after they are about 35 years old, although their wage increases before that.
3. Third group is composed of laborers, whose wages are stable until middle age irrespective of size of firm after which they decline somewthat.[11]

Under life time employment system dismissal is very difficult and an employee gets wage increase automatically. Why then do Japanese workers work so hard or are so industrious? In Japan too payments based on results do exist and that certain segment of the paycheck is linked with the worker's efficiency. But these are not main factors which motivate Japanese worker to work hard. The key clues for Japanese hard work and efficiency are promotion system and employee's strong loyalty to and identification with their enterprise. Whenever the chance of promotion arises, difference in wage becomes clear since only some can reach higher positions. As the years pass the difference in wage becomes more pronounced. Workers compete fiercely for promotions and to improve their ranks and status, which result in substantial difference in total wages and in retirement benefits. Since Japanese worker often stays in the same enterprise till retirement, their fate and well-being depend almost entirely on the prosperity of the enterprise. Both parties' relations are bound as one by fate in conditions which produce a tie between man and man often as firm and close as that between husband and wife.[12]

The wage and promotion practices and the merit system will continue to be strengthened. Workers on their part have already laid the foundations for accepting the merit system, but depending upon how the resulting differentials are expanded. There may be resistance from workers. Chart 4.6 indicates that 52% prefer merit system and only 14% do not prefer merit system for determining wage increase and promotion. If resistance arises, it will result in the deterioration of morale of the workers, worsening human relations at the work place and increasing number of relatively good workers who change their place of employment voluntarily. Further the critical point regarding the expanded pay and promotion differentials will be whether or not stability for a greater portion of workers is sought so that they can work with a sense of security.[13] The Chart 4.7 highlights the wage increase by length of service and shows how wage differs between the best, average and worst workers.

CHART 4.7

Trends of Wage Increase by Length of Service

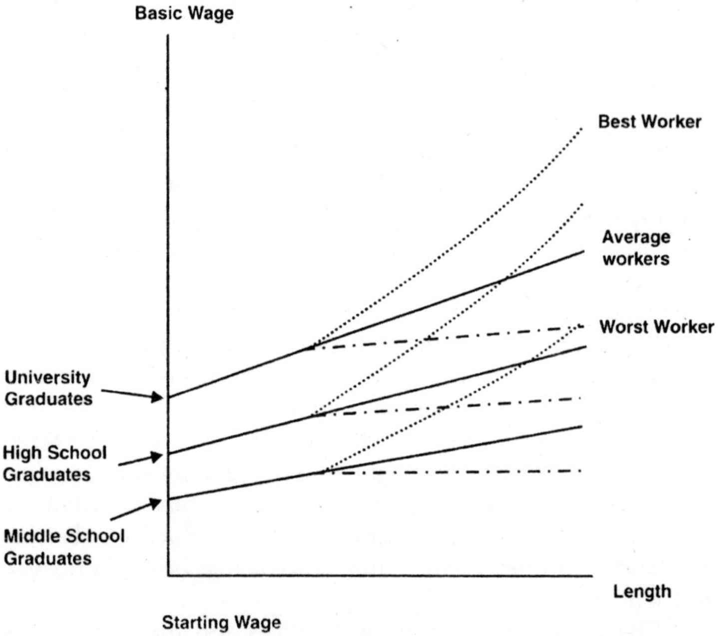

Source : International Encyclopedia for Labour Law and Industrial Relations, Vol. 7, Edited by Blanpain, R., 1985.

The Nenko system has gained high level of acceptance among regular workers for distribution of resources and opportunities and even avoids potential conflict between members. Regular workers do not object for a change in Nenko system (ability-oriented) with its egalitarian approach, if such changes are not drastic. However, it is difficult to escape from the traditional Nenko wage and promotion system in Japan, no matter with many revisions, which does not recognize the life-cycle needs of long-serving regular employees. This system with equal rights and opportunities for all, has not led divisions among regular workers. The system includes a tactic understanding that the distribution of resources and opportunities be made according to age and length of service within each group determined by sex and education. If potential for division exists, it is natural to expect it between regular and non-regular employees, between male and female worker and between workers with different educational backgrounds, but even here very little friction has been apparent. For example, the friction between regular and non-regular employees are house-wives working part time, who do not wish to become regular employees and whose central interest is outside the work-place. As for tension between male and female workers, since the orientation pattern have not changed significantly from "traditional" to "career" orientation, again the problem has not become very strong. The rules to certain amount of change, promoted by major changes in the technology and market environment in the past decade, which have forced management strategies and aging workforce which have created few problems in the contribution of human resources to management strategies.[14]

5. WAGE DETERMINATION—SHUNTO

The bonus and wage determination mechanism in the Spring Labor Offensive or Shunto, have attracted much attention from observers in the West. Wage determination in Japan is more flexible than those of West, which are based on collective bargaining.

The government of Japan does not interfere in wage negotiations; in fact she respects the autonomy of labor-management. In Japan wages are determined at a reasonable level by unconstrained negotiation between labor and management every spring. This negotiation is called "shunto" or "Spring Offensive" (see Chapter 3).

6. BASIS OF SENIORITY WAGE: SURVEY INTERPRETATION

The characteristics of Japanese wage system are very distinctive from other countries. One of the interesting features is that Japanese wage system including retirement allowance, is highly dependent on age and length of service rather than skill or job evaluation which is changing rapidly. As mentioned earlier, the wage determination of Japanese worker depends upon variety of factors, apart from age in the recent years. The factors determining the difference in wage profiles have been one of the most popular themes in labor economics and industrial relations research in Japan. This survey discovered that employees and even job seekers are well aware of the prevailing wage system ad departed from traditional system of wage, i.e. seniority-based wage. It seems due to environmental changes on wage system, the traditional factors supporting seniority wage are declining, giving room for other factors such as ability or job evaluation. Takeshi Inagami, in his survey report says that the following factors are likely to necessitate changes in the current wage system:

1. The ongoing aging of employees
2. Extension of the mandatory retirement age
3. Change in technologies and skills and the necessity of sustaining and improving the morale of workers.

However, economists believe that the basic pattern of wage is still connected with age and length of service.

Those firms which have placed importance on seniority-based wage are about 61.2% for reasons such as:

1. To provide stable lives for their employees
2. To reward the employee's past contribution to his company
3. To appropriate for the natural environment and customs in Japan
4. With long years of service the employees will have high ability
5. The labor unions have strongly demanded the system.

The results of this survey predict that wage determination based on ability or merit will be modified and strengthened very significantly in years to come.[15] The Prime Minister's Office Report (1978) also found that only 10.2% would like promotions and salary should be decided on seniority, 36.0% mainly by seniority but performance also considered, 25.8% mainly by performance but seniority also considered and 6.5% by performance. To be more precise even in this survey, seniority wage is in the hearts of Japanese people and so hard to disappear. In Tables 4.6, 4.7 and 4.8, we should pay attention to the second to fifth preferences, in which the reflection of their feeing can be found on seniority. Although it is not doubtful to believe, merit or ability or individual achievement are gaining popularity in Japanese enterprises, however, seniority wage system will not disappear.

TABLE 4.6

Employee's Preferences on the 'Basis of Wage'-I Preference

Preference Ranking	*Basis of Wage*	*Workers Responded (%)*
First	Ability (Individual achievement)	39.5
Second	Ability plus Seniority (Length of Service)	36.0
Third	Ability plus Education level	26.7
Fourth	Ability plus Seniority plus education level	41.8
Fifth	Seniority plus Education level	54.6
Sixth	Seniority	37.2
Seventh	Education level	65.5

Another survey also agrees with the results of this survey, that the younger generation like "meritocracy" more than the older. About 52% employees preferred a change to meritocracy, 14% not preferable, and 20% can't tell which and 6% any answer.

The Tables show a drastic shift from "seniority" to "ability" and surprisingly the "educational level" received least response. Looking at the outcome of this survey, employees do not object

TABLE 4.7
University (J.B.)* Preferences on 'Basis of Wage'-I Preference

Preference Ranking	*Basis of Wage*	*Workers Responded (%)*
First	Ability (Individual achievement)	42.7
Second	Ability plus Seniority (Length of Service)	33.3
Third	Ability plus Seniority plus education level	27.0
Fourth	Ability plus Education level	37.7
Fifth	Seniority	27.9
Sixth	Seniority plus Education level	52.0
Seventh	Education level	64.5

*J.B. = Job Seekers.

TABLE 4.8
High School (J.B.)* Preferences on 'Basis of Wage'-I Preference

Preference Ranking	*Basis of Wage*	*Workers Responded (%)*
First	Ability (Individual achievement)	53.6
Second	Ability plus Seniority (Length of Service)	40.5
Third	Seniority	39.1
Fourth	Ability plus Seniority plus education level	47.8
Fifth	Ability plus Education level	37.6
Sixth	Seniority plus Education level	46.3
Seventh	Education level	79.7

*J.B. = Job Seekers.

for a change in the seniority wage system and adopt for ability-oriented practice. The response to the question, "what should be the basis of wage determination?" is very interesting. According to the responses, the orders of preference rankings are as follows:

1. Ability or individual achievement (39.5%).
2. Ability plus seniority or length of service (36.0%).
3. Ability plus educational level (26.7%).
4. Ability plus seniority plus education level (41.8%).
5. Seniority plus education level (54.6%).
6. Seniority (37.2%).
7. Education level (65.0%).

It is very clear therefore, that ability factor has been considered most important and the emphasis on seniority is deteriorating. From first to fourth preference ability criteria is common and unfortunately Japanese workers gave least importance to education and seniority has very low profile.

In case of job seekers, there is slight variation in the response of university high school students. The ability criteria is common from first to fourth preference and seniority from second to fifth but preferred along with ability. It seems university job seekers prefer more the criteria of ability than high school. However, the response for education is very low, which is very interesting. The survey result therefore, indicates the belief in the ideal concept of "equal pay for equal work" contrary to the Japanese tradition wage system. The ability criteria is first among employees and job seekers, which is expected to be strengthened, education preferred last, will have very low profile and seniority which is preferred between these two will deteriorate. On the basis of these findings, employees and job seekers wish that their wage should be determined more on the basis of ability or merit than on seniority, though it is difficult to escape from the traditional seniority age system.

Notes and References

1. According to The Payment of Wages Act, 1936 (India), "wage" means all remuneration (whether by way of salary, allowance or otherwise) expressed in terms of money or capable of being so expressed which would, if the terms of employment, expressed or implied, were fulfilled, be payable to a person employed in respect of his employment or of work done in such employment and includes: (a) any remuneration payable under any award or settlement between parties or order of a court; (b) any remuneration to which a person employed is entitled in respect of overtime work or holidays or/and leave period; (c) any additional remuneration payable under the term of employment

(whether called a 'bonus' or by any other name); (d) any sum which by reason of termination of employment of the person employed is entitled under any scheme framed under any law.
Wage however, does not include the following:

(a) any bonus which does not form part of remuneration payable under the terms of employment, or which is not payable under any award or settlement between the parties or order of a court;
(b) the value of any house accommodation, or of supply of light, water, medical attendance or any other amenity or of any since excluded from the commutation of wages by a general or special order of the state government;
(c) any contribution paid by the employer to any pension or provident fund and the interest which may have accrued thereon;
(d) any traveling allowance or the value of any traveling concession;
(e) any sum paid to the employed person defray special expenses entailed on him by the nature of his employment; and
(f) gratuity payable on termination of employment.

2. Refer Blanpain R. (Ed.), International Encyclopedia for Labor Law and Industrial Relations, Vol. 7, for detailed discussion on pay systems, the notion of wages, regulations concerning the payment of wages, the guarantee of the payment of wages on the employer's insolvency, the minimum wage, wage levels, equal pay, remuneration during time-off, etc.
3. Blanpain, R. (Ed), *op. cit.*, p. 79.
4. Refer Kagawa Kozo, Introduction of Japanese Labor Law, for more discussion of The Security of Wage Payment Act, 1975, Minimum wage and equal pay.
5. Blanpain, R. (Ed.) *op. cit.*, pp. 73-83.
6. Refer Katsumi, Yakabe, Labor Relations in Japan, Fundamental characteristics, International Society for Education Information Inc., 1974, Chapter II for more discussion of the wage system where he has explained characteristics and determination of wage.
7. Wage characteristics from 5 to 8 have been highlighted by Hanami, Vol. 7. International Encyclopedia for Labor Law and Industrial Relations, p. 75.
8. Refer Nakamura Tadashi, Labor in Japan (question and answers). The Japan Institute of Labor, p. 134, for an interesting discussion on "what is the seniority-based wage system?" and for a table dealing with wage differential by industry and age group. Difference of wages on the basis of age and industry group—for example, manufacturing, wholesale and retail trade, eating and drinking places and service are evident.
9. Refer Taishiro Shirai (Ed), Contemporary Industrial Relations in Japan, Chapter 3. Kazuo Koike, describes and interprets for the western audience the operation of the "Internal Labor Markets" of large Japanese firms and offers his white-colorization" hypothesis. Blue-collar workers in the large firm in Japan, he argues, resembles white-collar workers in Western European countries and the US, in many respect, but

particularly in the wages and fringe benefits they enjoy their labor mobility and commitment, their prospects for promotion and their occupation and career patterns.

10. Nakamura Tadashi, *op. cit.*, p. 134.
11. Kazuo Koike also re-examines the nature of employment and the working conditions of workers in small firms and female workers in general largely by comparing descriptive official statistics of Japan and some of the western countries, but partly by using results of his own questionnaire survey.
12. Hanami, T.A., Labor Relations in Japan Today, Kodansha International Ltd., Tokyo, 1972, p. 28.
13. Refer article by Inagami Takeshi—"Changing Japanese Style Employment Practices. Here he has reviewed the seniority-based wage system. He Highlighted in Japanese Industrial Relations, Vol. II, the Japan Institute of Labor, Tokyo.
14. The traditional pattern here means starting work immediately after graduating from school, leaving at marriage or child birth and starting mainly part-time work when the children reach a certain age changing management strategies refers to the diversification of management and operations, crossing industrial boundaries, introduction of micro-electronics, multi-nationalization, setting subsidiaries, group cooperation, organizational restructuring including matrix structures, etc.
15. Job evaluation factors used by Firms to determine basic wage:

	%
Pay according to comprehensive assessment (Including 26.7% with no fixed wage scale)	50.8
Pay according to function skill	10.0
Pay according to type of work only	15.7
Pay according to experience and ability	12.0
Pay according to age, education and seniority only	11.5
Total	100.0
(Percentage refer to number of companies).	

(As quoted by Katsumi Yakabe, Labor Relations in Japan p. 30).

5

Labor Disputes

1. LABOR DISPUTES : GENERAL VIEW

A dispute is a difference, or a controversy. Various terms such as 'Industrial dispute', 'Labor dispute' or Trade dispute' are used in different countries to identify the differences between the employer and workers. The Labor Relations Adjustment Law, under Article 6 defines 'Labor dispute' as "a disagreement over claims arising between the parties concerned with labor relations regarding labor relations and resulting in either the occurrence of an act of dispute occurring."[1] The policy Planning and Research Department of Ministry of Labor, defines labor dispute as "any dispute over worker's status between labor and management for the settlement of which a third party intervenes through conciliation, mediation or arbitration or where act of disputes have occurred". Article 7 of the Labor Relations Adjustment Law, defines 'act of dispute' as "strike, go-slows, lockouts and other acts and counter-acts hampering the normal course of work in an enterprise and performed by the parties concerned with labor relations with object of attaining their respective claims". These definitions are given to specify the necessary conditions for the initiation of the disputes settlement procedures provided by Labor Relations Adjustment Law, they are also relied on for the interpretations of the law which deals with the legal effect of act of dispute. Through the constitutional guarantee of the right to act collectively and the rather broad definition of an act of dispute in Labor Relations Adjustment Law, there is a remarkable tendency in Japanese industrial relations to admit the legality of a variety of actions taken by the unions which hamper the normal course of business. Also because the constitutional guarantee of the right to act collectively[2] only applies to worker, the employer's right to lock out suffers badly from being very extensively restricted—especially when compared with the extensive legal recognition granted to acts of dispute by the unions.[3]

Although a multitude of causes, blended together, result in industrial conflicts, it is not always easy in specific instances to ascertain the particular cause or causes involved. Surface manifestations of unrest and dissatisfaction which appear to be responsible for work stoppage may cover deep-seated and more basic cause which cannot be observed at first sight. Moreover, the relative importance of the causes, when more than one is present, is often very difficult to gauge.[4] The experts in industrial relations believe that causes of industrial conflict between labor and management usually remain the same wherever capitalistic economy prevails. "The development of capitalist enterprise which means the control of the tools of production by a small entrepreneur class has brought to the fore the cuts problem of friction between management and labor throughout the world".[5] Lester observes: "when people sell their services and spend their working lives on the premises of purchaser of these services, a varying amount of dissatisfaction, discontent and industrial unrest are likely to occur. According to ILO declaration labor is not a commodity to be sold and purchased. The labor remains a human being first and last". Gandhi also said, "A worker is not merely a means of production, he is essentially a personality having a sense of responsibility towards his family, industry and nation. He therefore, desires economic enlistment as a dutiful husband, a good neighbor and an intelligent citizen". Employees are especially interested in higher wages, healthy working conditions, opportunity to progress and satisfying work, some voice in industrial affairs, and protection against loss of wage, over-work and arbitrary treatment. When such things are denied to them, they are forced to exert their rights and stop working to make the employers understand their grievances and redress them.[6] The causes of industrial conflicts are rooted in historical, political, socio-economic factors and the attitude of workers and their employers.[7] An element of conflict of interest always exists between the employee who wishes to sell his labor dearly and the employer, who wishes to buy it cheaply. The employer wants to earn the largest possible profit in competitive markets, while the unions want to secure and improve the terms and conditions of employment of their members as efficiently as possible.

In Japan, though the industrial relations have been peaceful in major industries in the past, a number of labor disputes have occurred. Chart 5.1 highlights the number of the labor disputes, the workers involved and the working days lost during 1984-88. The total number of disputes during the period has declined from 4,826 (1985) to 1,897 (1988) and number of employees affected also declined from 3,249,173 (1985) to 1,239,687 (1988). It is interesting to note that the number of labor disputes accompanied by dispute tactics is much higher (39.4%) than the number of labor disputes not accompanied by dispute tactics e.g. in 1988. Though the percentage of labor disputes accompanied by dispute tactics is higher only 36.9% of these tactics were involved with work stoppage. Table 5.1 indicates that in 1988, 594 work stoppages were resolved out, this 57.8% were resolved within one day only 3.8% took more than one month.

It is found that more than seven out of ten disputes concerned wage increase, bonus and allowances and out of that 60-70% was over the general wage increase. Of 53,926 cases adjusted by the central and local Labor Relations Commissions, wage increases were at issue in 30.7%, bonuses in 19.1%, retirement allowance and pensions 4.1%, discharge 4.0%, dismissal allowances 3.6%, dismissal 2.6% and hours of work and vacations 3.6%.[8] Table 5.2 shows the number of enterprises with labor disputes and principal demands in 1988. This includes only private enterprises. There were a total 1,927

CHART 5.1
Number of Disputes, Accompanied/ Not Accompanied by Dispute Tactics

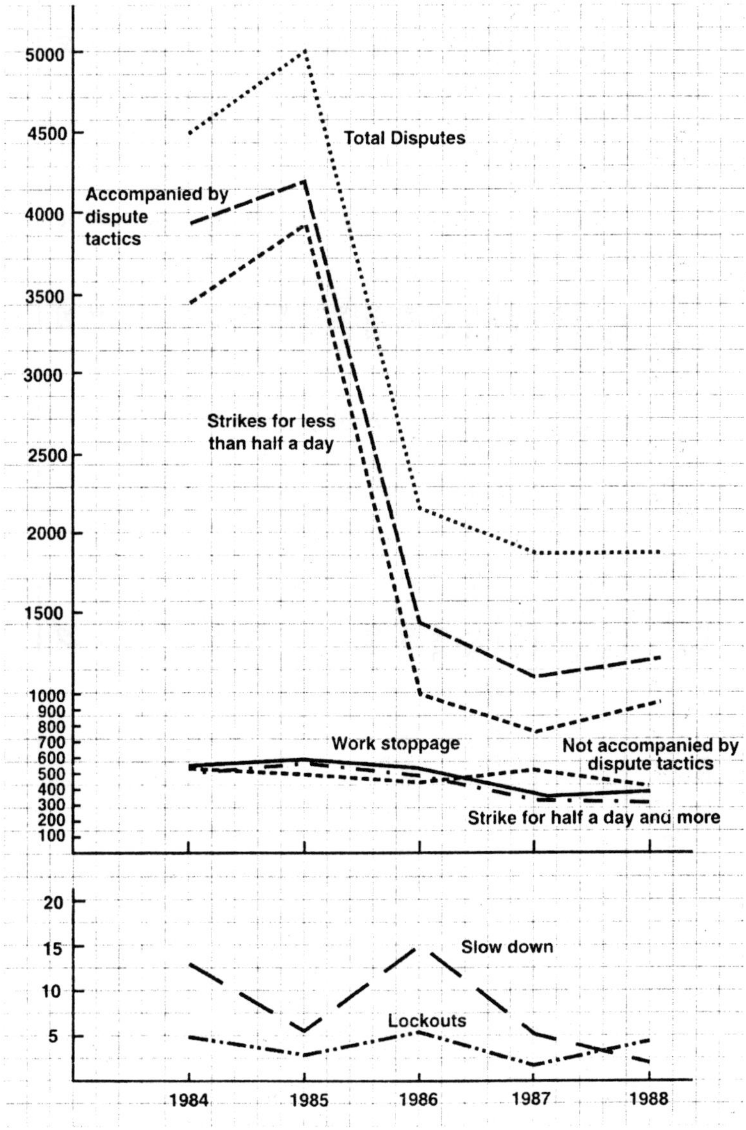

Source : Year book of Labor Statistics, 1958.

TABLE 5.1

The Number of Enterprises with Labor Disputes, by Size and Principal Demands (Including only Private Enterprises) (1988)

Size of enterprise	*Total*	*More than 5000 employees*	*1000 to 4999*	*300 to 499*	*100 to 299*	*30 to 99*	*Less than 29*	*Not Classified*
(1)	*(2)*	*(3)*	*(4)*	*(5)*	*(6)*	*(7)*	*(8)*	*(9)*
All Enterprises	1 927	155	12.4	357	563	2	194	33
Total issues	2 638	191	161	505	767	3	269	52
Conclusion or overall revision of agreement	49	17	—	8	8	—	4	1
Wage increase	10 90	63	72	224	359	2	69	19
Temporary allowance	542	16	30	118	167	—	57	9
Establishment or increase of retirement allowance	29	1	—	6	6	—	8	—
Revision of working. hours	87	—	2	13	25	—	7	5
Vacations and holidays	100	3	4	11	23	—	18	2
Opposition to discharge or issues to reinstatement of discharged	91	2	8	8	12	—	34	2
Opposition to suspension closing or reduction of business operation	11	—	1	2	1	—	2	—
Others	1 55	11	7	25	45	—	20	7

Sources : Year Book of Labour Statistics, 1958.

Table 5.2
The Number of Labor Disputes, by Industry and Principal Demands (1988)

Industry	Total Disputes	Total Issues	Conclusion or overall revision of agreement	Wage incr-ease	Temporary allowance	Establishment or increase of retirement allowance system	Revision of working hours	Vacation and holidays	Oposition to discharge or issues to reinstate-ment of discharged	Opposition to suspension closing or reduction of business operation	Others
(1)	(2)	(3)	(4)	(5)	(6)	(7)	(8)	(9)	(10)	(11)	(12)
Total	1 879	2 629	45	1 036	359	24	74	255	93	12	171
Agriculture Forestry	1	1	—	1	—	—	—	—	—	—	—
Fisheries	1	1	—	—	—	—	—	—	—	—	—
Mining	8	9	—	1	1	—	—	2	2	—	3
Construction	10	13	1	5	2	1	—	—	2	—	1
Manufacturing	560	723	6	305	161	13	54	10	28	6	19
Electricity, gas, Gear supply and water	27	35	1	13	4	—	—	5	—	—	5
Transport and communication	346	447	20	154	81	4	9	7	20	1	27
Whole sale and retail trade, eating and drinking place	55	72	2	21	14	2	—	3	7	—	2
Finance and insurance real estate	22	27	1	12	6	—	—	—	—	—	—
Service	474	638	11	246	90	4	9	30	34	2	48
Government	374	602	3	278	—	—	2	200	—	1	65
Not described	1	1	—	—	—	—	—	—	—	—	1

Source : Year Book of Labour Statistics, 1988.

enterprises that had disputes (in all enterprises) involving 2,638 issues. Only 49 cases reached conclusions or revision of agreement out of 1,927. The largest (563) enterprise employing 1299 employee involved 897 issues. As Koshiro, also the policy planning and research department of the Ministry of Labor pointed out the largest number (1,090) of demands were pertaining to wage increase and 542 of temporary allowances. The other principal demands were for vacation and holiday (100), opposition to discharge for issues to reinstatement of discharged (91), revision of working hours (87), establishment or increase of retirement allowance (29), opposition to suspension closing or reduction of business operation (11) and other demand (155). The number of disputes and principal demands based on industry is highlighted in Table 5.2. Manufacturing industry dominates as per the number of disputes (560) and demands (723), out of 1,879 disputes and 2,629 demands. Other industries according to the size of disputes are—services (474), government (374) and transportation (346). Here again leading demands are: wage increase (1,038), temporary allowances (359), vacation and holidays (255), opposition to discharge or issues to reinstatement of discharge (93), revision of working hours (74), opposition to suspension closing or reduction of business operation (12) and other demands (171).

Hanami, while emphasizing cultural elements in the nature of industrial conflict, admits that the Japanese workers do not enjoy equality with their employers, that the employers are "feudalistic" and that the workers are servile. American workers do not bow politely to their employers when they meet on the street as their Japanese counterparts always. However, he feels at the work place, there is less class distinction between manager and workers in Japan than in western societies.[9]

The industrial disputes are fundamentally group conflicts. In every industrial relations, disputes tend to become institutionalized by the emergence of unions and their involvement in dispute settlement, especially through collective bargaining process. Labor dispute being group conflicts are usually associated with so-called mirror image phenomenon, according to which "reality is not the same for observers belonging to different groups".[10] The present industrialization has created a big gulf between labor and management. The workers have now come to realize that most of their demands can be achieved if they resort to concerted and collective action, while on the other hand employers are aware of the fact that they can resist those demands. In most cases, the disputes in Japan (e.g. 1960's) ended in the defeat and split of labor union, typically as a result of the emergence of rival unions. This disorderly labor-management relation often left deep scars on relations between the two parties for a long period even after the resolution of the dispute. Labor-management learns a bitter lesson from their experience: not to engage in self-defeating and futile confrontation.

"The members of competing groups build up and maintain differential images of reality, images so formed that 'our' group is virtuous and free from sin . . . 'their' group is bad, aggressive, treacherous and not quite human . . . if we can perceive the opponent as less than human, superego controls do not operate and no guilt is felt". The above quotation makes it clear that industrial violence occurs elsewhere besides in Japan. The author quoted above distinguishes the hostility between labor and management from ordinary economic conflict and lists industrial conflict alongside civil and international conflict by pointing out the similarities in picket-line violence to the violence of a lynch mob are of Nazi SS men".[11]

Labor disputes have become day-today affair and normal rather than exception. Early settlement is essential for industrial progress, thus most countries have developed autonomous institution[12] such as works committees or councils, grievance committees and voluntary arbitration to process grievances and for settlement.

2. TYPES OF INDUSTRIAL DISPUTES

The most common categories of industrial dispute are: Interest dispute, Grievance disputes, unfair labor practices and Recognition disputes. The interest disputes are called 'Conflict of interests' or 'Economic disputes'. In certain countries these are called 'collective labor disputes'. Grievance disputes are also known as 'conflicts of rights' or 'legal disputes'. These involve individual workers only or a group of workers in the same group and correspond largely to what in certain countries are called 'individual disputes'. The most common 'unfair labor practices' in industrial relations parlance are attempts by management of an undertaking to discriminate against workers for being trade union members or for trade union activity. These unfair labor practices are also known in various countries as 'trade union victimization'. This type of disputes arises when the management of an undertaking or an employer's organization refuses to recognize a trade union for purposes of collective bargaining. Other classification of industrial disputes can: individual disputes *v.* collective disputes, disputes of vested rights *v.* dispute of interest, economic disputes *v.* political disputes and organized disputes *v.* unorganized disputes.

Hanami observes that these distinctions are theoretically recognized in Japan too, but are not very meaningful in the actual industrial relations situation. There is no clear-cut distinction between individual and collective conflicts since both of them are handled by the ordinary law courts, whenever they are brought to court. The distinction between conflicts of rights and conflicts of interest has never been very clear because the law courts often give rulings on questions of appropriateness. The reasons for this confusing situation are rather complicated. The most important factor is the Japanese neglect of the binding character of a contract. Parties rely on personal relation or mutual trust. Most problems are settled on the basis of personnel understanding. Clear cut decisions based on certain universal standards are not at all popular in Japanese society. Another factor responsible for such confusion is underdevelopment of some distinct dispute settlement procedure designed to deal with certain categories of disputes in the industrial relations system. There are procedures such as bargaining, consultation and grievance procedure only on the official documents but in actual industrial relations informal procedures of a more personal nature prevail. If such informal method fails to work the parties tend to move on the find confrontation, appealing to the courts or resorting to drastic action such as strikes or other acts of dispute.[13]

Theoretically disputes of interest between unions and employees are taken care of by the dispute settlement procedures: Conciliation, Mediation and Arbitration, while disputes of vested rights between employers and individual workers or the unions are the responsibility of the courts. Unfortunately these distinctions often fade away in practice (refer Chapter 6).

3. ACTS OF DISPUTES

The industrial disputes will have far reaching adverse impact on employee, consumer, community and nation suffers in more than one way. Act of disputes means "action taken by either or both parties to attain an objective which disrupts normal business operation (strikes of a half-day or more, lockouts, strikes of a half-day or less, slow downs and production takeover". Any act of disputes will result in huge wastage of man-days and production, loss of wage to the employee, profits to the employer. As Callin has put, "the strikes and lockouts are a great menace of public safety. They infringe upon property rights and become malicious in their effects, if not in their purpose and they are regarded as a war or at any rate of blockade".[14] Pigou has observed, "When labor and equipment on the whole or any part of an industry are rendered idle by strike or lock-out, national dividend must suffer in a way that injures economic welfare. It may happen in two ways: On one hand, by impoverishing the people actually involved in the stoppage, it lessens the demand for the goods the other industries make, on the other hand if the industry in which the stoppage has occurred is one that furnishes a commodity or service largely used in the conduct of other industries, it lessens the supply of them of raw material or equipment of their work. This results in a loss of output, ultimately reducing the national income.[15]

The theorists differ with regard to the purpose of acts of dispute. The most orthodox theories and majority of legal decisions confine indemnity to those actions taken for the purpose of getting better working conditions by means of bargaining with the employer. The claims of proper act of dispute must be supported by economic purpose and any act done for political purposes are not be given indemnity. These orthodox theorists and legal experts regard act of dispute as a means of negotiating and recognize its legality only in so far as it is used to increase the bargaining strength of the union. The other theorists, opposing this view, regard the right to act collectively as being independent of the right to bargain and insist that the constitution has legalized every action of the union, regardless of its purpose, if the action itself is proper.[16] If the acts of disputes to be protected, unions need not be registered or qualified under Trade Union Law, however, act should be carried out by a *bona-fide* union. The qualified recognized unions are those which promote worker's interest against the employer, not workers, political parties and are not company dominated.

The unions in Japan have discovered a variety of acts of disputes with which they try to embarrass the management. Strike is one among many types of industrial actions which are normally used, it is not even the most typical or the most representative of all acts of disputes used in Japanese industrial relations[17]. Through the constitutional guarantee of the right to act collectively and the rather broad definition of an act of dispute in the Labor Relations Adjustment Law, there is a remarkable tendency in Japanese industrial relations to admit the legality of a variety of actions taken by the unions which hamper the normal course of business. Also, because the constitutional guarantee the right to act collectively only applies to workers, the employer's right to lock-out suffers badly from being very extensively restricted—especially when compared with the extensive legal recognition granted to acts of dispute by the unions.[18]

The acts of dispute are no less than war. As in modern wars, the casualties and sufferings do not remain confined to fighting soldiers on the front, so in case of strikes, the adverse effects do not confine to employee and employer but like war acts dispute affect the entire community. Trade Union Law (Art. 1, section 2) declares that in no event shall act of violence be construed as appropriate acts for trade union. Needless to say, not only violence but also threats, coercion, defamation and injury, not to mention homicide and similar criminal acts, are not permitted even as acts of dispute. The same article on the other hand lays down a criminal indemnity. This superficial contradiction is solved by interpreting it to mean that there is criminal indemnity for those criminal acts which would possibly amount to threats, coercion or trespass in ordinary civil life but which are usually accepted by trade unionists as ordinary acts in the course of industrial relations when they are demanding to negotiate, trying to persuade strike-breakers and so on. In any case the law allows criminal and civil indemnity for acts of dispute, a phrase which is regarded as including a variety of acts and not just strike or go slows. Thus, what is a proper act of dispute should be considered separately for each category of acts, which is generally used in Japanese industrial relations.[19]

The term 'conflict' is always viewed as unhealthy and dysfunctional. But if we look at the effect of conflict objectively,

FIG. 5.1
Manifestation of Conflict in Japan

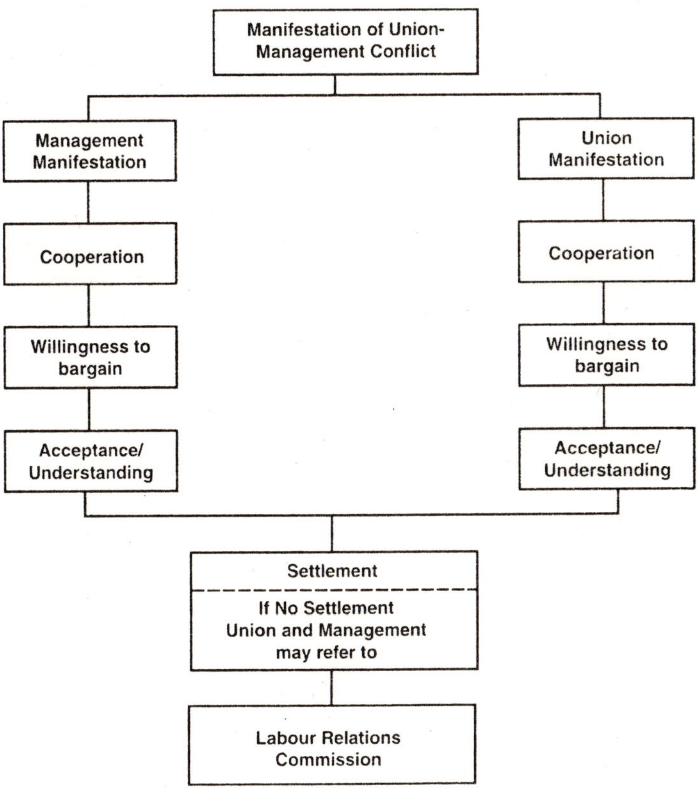

we see that sometimes conflict is beneficial as it brings about social change as a consequence.[20] Industrial conflicts often help to maintain stability of the group by forcing groups to air their grievances and resolve their problems thus preventing unhealthy upheavals and ill-feelings within and between groups. Figure 5.1 highlights the manifestation of conflict in Japan. If conflict is not settled cooperatively and willingly parties may go to the Labor Relations Commission.

The parties to a collective agreement have an obligation which is inherent in its very nature to refrain from engaging in acts of dispute—including strikes and lockouts, aimed at challenging the contents of the agreement during its term of effectiveness. According to the majority view this obligation, can not be denied even with the agreement of both parties since it is inherent in the collective agreement. However, it is relative in the sense that acts of dispute are prohibited only during the effective terms of the agreement and even then only acts of dispute which challenge the contents of the agreement. Otherwise, acts of dispute are permitted both after the termination of the agreement and during the effective term of the agreement if the act of dispute is over an issue not mentioned in the agreement.

The parties in dispute whether organized or unorganized, manifest their conflict in various forms, some over while others do not. The ultimate manifestation of industrial conflict is a strike on the part of workers and a lockout on the part of manager. Conflict is not confined to strikes and lockouts but there are other expressions of conflict which have significant effects on the working of an enterprise.[21]

(a) Strikes

For Doten, "strike is merely symptoms of more fundamental mal-adjustments, injustices and economic disturbances". Petterson views strike as "a temporary cessation of work by a group of employees in order to express grievances or to enforce a demand concerning changes in work conditions.[22] Strike (of a half day or more) means "temporary work stoppage by a worker's organization to obtain an objective". Strike of a half day or less is defined as "temporary work stoppage by a worker's organization to obtain an objective, with an aggregate duration of less than one-half of one working day". The Indian Industrial Dispute Act, 1947 (section 2 (q)), defines a strike as a "cessation of work by a body of persons employed in any industry, acting in combination or a concerted refusal under a common understanding, of a number of persons who are or have been employed to continue to work or to accept concerted action. These definitions a strike postulate three main ingredients, namely: 1. Plurality of workmen, 2. Cessation of work or refusal to do work, 3. Combined or concerted action.[23]

Kumar has observed "the definition and use of the word 'strike' has been going constant transformation around the basic concept of stoppage of work or quitting of work by employees in their economic struggle. It can take various shapes such as pen-down strike, tool-down strike, sit-down strike, sympathetic strike, token strike, hunger-strike, lightning strike, relay strike, wild cats mass leave, gherao,[24] etc. Classified from objective standards, strikes are 'economic strikes' launched for economic demands by the workmen or 'political strikes', organized by registering protest against the policies of the government or demonstrating power behind some opinions and policies or 'individual strikes', carried only by individuals from attendant circumstances. Whatever the form or method be, it is strike.[25] Strike may also be classified as 'primary' and 'secondary' strikes. Primary strikes are generally pointed against the employer with whom the disputes exist. Secondary strikes are the strikes in which the pressure is applied not against the primary employer with whom the primary workers have a dispute but against some third person who has good trade relations with him which are severed and as a result the primary employer is at a loss.

Trade unions in Japan use variety of acts of dispute with which they embarrass the management. Strike is just one of the many industrial actions which are normally used in Japanese industrial relations.

One of the interesting characteristics of Japanese industrial relations is the short duration of strikes. Actually one or two hours strikes are very common and majority of strikes continue for one or two days, hence any strike which lasts for a week will be regarded as a very long strike. In Japan 'partial strikes' are legal which means some of the union members go on strike while the other continues working. In case of the sympathetic strike which supports another enterprise, the Japanese courts consider them improper simply because the employer of members of the labor union, which is engaging in a sympathetic strike, has no competence to settle the dispute at another enterprise. Organized conflicts and unorganized conflicts are distinguished in legal theory and wild-cat strikes and unauthorized strikes are regarded as illegal. Political strikes are, with few exceptions regarded by the courts as illegal but some theorists advocate their legality.[26] In Japan the strike is not the final weapon in collective bargaining. Often there is a strike before any bargaining has even taken place and so quite naturally the unions may stop the strike and the members go back to work without the dispute having actually been settled. During any dispute there may be a series of strikes and this can be explained by the fact that strikes in Japan are designed to attract the employer's attention. In fact strike is regarded as a demonstration of feeling rather than as a weapon with which to press the management after negotiations have reached deadlock. Trade unions do not distinguish very clearly between bargaining and strike action, seeing both as ways of demonstrating their will to fight. The act of dispute therefore, need not be something which causes serious economic damage, like a long-standing strike, minor irritating embarrassment will do instead. This is the reason why Japan is there are so many different acts of disputes.[27]

A strike can be regarded as proper act of dispute:

1. If it is launched for economic demands,
2. If the demands of the workmen should be reasonable and legitimate,
3. When existing facilities are summarily withdrawn,
4. If there is any unfair labor practice on the part of management, and
5. When there is no response from the management in spite of referring a demand and issuing reminders. Strikes are justified in Japan if their purpose causes no problems. A compromise interpretation on criminal

> indemnity has been reached in Japan, i.e. some of the less serious criminal acts which are certainly punishable if they are committed in ordinary circumstances by ordinary citizens may be justified if they are done in the process of collective bargaining or during the act of dispute. Such concept of the legality of acts of dispute in Japan might sound much too tolerant and rather absurd to western readers. Many experts and judges have agreed that acts of dispute should include something more positive than the more passive refusal to work. Trade unions are heavily protected, judges and theorists support because they think employers are tyrannical.[28] However, Article 8 of Trade Union Law provides that 'no employer shall claim indemnity from a trade union or its employees the damage caused by strikes or other acts of dispute which are proper. As an employer he is responsible for the acts of his employees. Few consider that the act of dispute should be regarded as an act of God, since it is legally guaranteed and the employer can not help it and majority claim that the act of dispute cold have been avoided if the employer had tried hard enough and anyway he must bear even more responsibility for his employee's acts if they are legal.[29]

The value of strike has been recognized as a legitimate weapon for the workmen for ventilating his grievances in every democratic country. Unlike Japan 'right to act collectively' or 'strike' is not guaranteed in country like India (constitution), because it is controlled by statutes like Industrial Dispute Act, The Indian constitution does not consider the right to strike as a fundamental right. The general right to resort to strike has been recognized by defining the circumstances under which a strike is to be regarded as illegal. The right to strike is a relative right and it should be used only as a last resort in India.

Trade unions in Japan have invented variety of acts of dispute to embarrass the management. Apart from strike they use techniques such as: Going-slow, working to-rule, taking holidays, pasting posters, wearing ribbons, picketing and sit-downs.

In 1988 for example number of labor disputes reported were 1,879 of which in 532 disputes did not accompany dispute tactics while in 1,347 disputes accompanied disputes tactics. Out of 1,347 disputes in 498 disputes involved work stoppage resulting strike and lockouts. The disputes resulting strikes for a half a day or more are 496 and resulting lockouts only 5. The large number of strikes in Japan involves very short duration. Therefore, in 1988 the number of strikes for less than half a day is high, i.e. 1,031 and only on two occasion's parties used slow-down tactics (Chart 5.1).

The overwhelming number of disputes 560 out of 1,879 has been reported from manufacturing industry in 1988. The other industries where more number of disputes reported are: service sector, government and transport and communication (Table 5.2). Chart 5.1 deals with number of disputes, workers involved and working days lost by size of enterprise. This includes only private enterprise. In 1,412 enterprises labor disputes were accompanied by dispute tactics. As per the size of the enterprise the largest (451) are those who employed 100-299 employees. It is very clear therefore, that the number of enterprises, those involving dispute tactics is less than as the number of the employee. For example, the enterprises employing more than 5000 employee involving dispute tactics are only 100 and in only 41 occasions work stoppages due to strike and lockouts have been reported while in smaller enterprise it is more.

(b) Go-slow and Work to Rule

Go-slow and work-to-rule are very common in Japan, partly because of the nature of industrial action as a demonstration and partly because of the comparatively poor financial position of the unions. There are alternatives to strike in the sense that many times the workers resort to go-slow when the union does not want to resort to full-fledged strike but still wants to take some alternative action which may be less risky, less expensive but equally effective. Go-slow is a tactic of workers, where they intentionally reduce the speed of work to adopt dilatory tactics to reduce the production or efficiency while pretending to be engaged in the company. Slowdown also means reduction in work efficiency by a worker's organization to obtain an objective while continuing to work. On few occasions employees use another technique known as 'production takeover', which means a business establishment is occupied by workers against the will of the employer and production and operation are conducted according to the worker's policies. Go-slow is misconduct and viewed seriously by labor commissions and tribunals in India. It is not however, a strike for it is not a cessation of work, but rather a deliberate concerted reduction in the pace of work. Go-slow by workmen has been held to be an insidious method of undermining the stability of a concern and is reprehensible in character. It has been castigated as worse than strike for the simple reason that it means not only loss of production but added loses on account of the running of all machines and equipment without putting these to proper and adequate use. Therefore, go-slow has been considered as serious type of misconduct and the workers who resort to go-slow can even be dismissed in countries like India.[30]

In Japan go-slow technique is frequently used in public sector, where the law prohibits acts of dispute. The unions claim that they are not engaging in an act of dispute by taking such an obscure type of action. However, go-slow and work-to-rule are regarded as acts of dispute in so far as they actually disturb the everyday running of the business, even if they do not disturb in a strict legal way. They are not regarded as illegal as such, since the workers are merely refusing to provide the whole of it—so according to this logic they are causing less harm. But even these acts of dispute can cause problems. Particularly in respect to the wages of those who are partially refusing to work. Such acts of dispute should be regarded as improper and illegal if they are in any way malicious.[31] Some believe that work-to-rule is not a strike; it is not a cessation of work, but a very strict 'adherence to regulations not normally observed'.

(c) Picketing and Sit down

'Picketing'[32] is an act of posting pickets and implies marching or patrolling of the workmen in front of the premises of the employer, carrying and displaying signs, banners and placards for the purpose of preventing others from entering the place and drawing attention of the public to know that there is a dispute between the employer and employee. In other words, it is 'watching and dissuading those who go to work during a strike'.[33] Picketing is frequently used by trade unions in Japan. 'Sit-down' is only another form of picketing, since picketing in Japanese industrial relations means more or less shuttling down the flow of traffic through gates. Sit-down strike[34] is an act when a group of employees or others interested in obtaining certain objective in particular firm take possession of property of such business, establishment themselves within the plant, stop its production and refuse access to the occupiers or the others desiring to work. It is the strike in the traditional sense to which is added an element of trespass of the strikers upon the property of the employers.[35]

In Japan often union members resort to such techniques, where they form lines in front of the gates standing arm-in-arm. The predominant theories and some of the court decisions admit the properness of picketing or sit-down on the companies' premises as long as the union members do not engage in violence. The justification for such illegality is found in the constitutional guarantee of the right to act collectively, which means more than the simple freedom to refuse to work and freedom of speech which together are the sole legal grounds for picketing in the Anglo-American countries.[36]

Picketing and sit-sown or stay-in strikes are more effective because the employer is deprived of the use of the plant and machinery, besides, a great burden is placed on the management when the striking workers remain inside the firm, to arrange for the production on its property.

(d) Taking Holidays

This type of act of dispute was originally started and has often been resorted by public sector where act of dispute is prohibited. Here unions order all or most of their members to take their annual holiday on the same day, which will have the same effect as that of a strike. Unions claim that they are only taking legally recognized holiday and not committing any of disputes. When strikes are financially heavy, unions in private sector also have resorted to this kind of act of dispute. This is an interesting and peculiar kind of act of dispute during which union members continue to claim wages. Such wage claims have been denied by Japanese courts and held that such a kind of act of dispute disturbs the normal course of business to assert the union demands against management. However, a difficult problem arises when we consider the legal effect of a worker taking a holiday and then participating in some union activity at a work place other than his won. In this case some court decisions including a Supreme Court decision and some of the theories say that the act of taking holiday does not disturb the normal course of business in the worker's own place and that such an act should be regarded simply as engaging in union activity while on holiday, like attending a union meeting. From this point of view there is no reason why the worker's wage claim should not succeed.[37]

(e) Pasting Posters and Wearing Ribbons

In Japanese industrial relations today, pasting posters and wearing ribbons is mainly sued with an intention of disturbing the normal course of business or embarrassing the management, rather than just for purposes of communication. Originally such act of disputes were sources of information to the union members, non-union workers, customers and the general public about the position of the union and the situation which gave rise to the dispute. These techniques are often used where unions paste hundreds of posters, rather shabbily and poorly-made in a disorderly fashion on the elegant company buildings. The wearing of arm-bands, head-bands or ribbons disturbs the normal course of business when the appearance of the employees is important, especially in the service industries. These acts are not necessarily improper because acts to hamper the normal course of business are allowed as acts of dispute, and so only the most extreme acts, which are felt to be unfair or abusive, will be deemed to be improper and illegal.[38]

(f) Control of Means of Production

This kind of act of dispute is called 'seisankari' which means production control. It was often used after World War II but it is not used today. The effect of this act is similar to that of a picket or a sit-down, here the unions sometimes take away certain things which belong to the company—production means and keeps with them until the dispute is settled. The most frequent example of this kind of act is the action taken by the unions in the taxi industry, whereby they take the keys, the car licenses or the tiers and hide them somewhere. Another possibility is for the unions to keep the money collected by its members from the company's customers for the company and deposit it in the bank in the union's name until the end of the dispute. The reasoning behind such decisions which support the legality is that the unions do not intend to take the goods or the money for ever, but only for the time being and thus it does not amount to, for example, the criminal embezzlement.[39]

Judicial decisions affirm the right of the employer to make disciplinary dismissals against union officers who ordered and led improper act of dispute. In judging disciplinary dismissal the courts consider whether improper acts were so vicious that union officers ought to be expelled from the company and so forth.

4. LOCK-OUTS

"Lock-outs means the action of an employer in temporarily closing down or shutting down his undertaking or refusing to provide his employees with work with intention of forcing them either to accept demands made by him or to withdraw demands made by them on him. Lock-out can also be said as stoppage of business activity by an employer as a means of dispute accompanied by employer's announcement to that effect. According to Indian Industrial Dispute Act, "Lock-out means the closing of a place of business of employment or the suspension of work, or the refusal by an employer to continue to employ any number of persons employed by him".

The Constitution of Japan guarantees the right to act collectively only to workers, while the employer's right to lock-out is recognized or not is a confusing question, because there is no provision which admits the employer's right to lock-out in the constitution and the union law. There is a difference of opinion. Many theorists admit the right of employers to lock-out for balance or fairness between employer and worker, but few do not agree on the basis of civil principle. They maintain that the employer can refuse to pay wages when the workers are not providing work in accordance with the contract. The legal effects of a lock-out are not just limited to wage claims but also involve the possibility of the expulsion of workers from the company's premises. The question is whether the employer can actually turn out workers who are sitting-in on the premises, and the answer is in the affirmative but it is rather unnecessary to regard it as having the effect of a lock-out since in any case the employer has the legal right, based on this right to property, to expel anyone who enters and stays on the company premises against his will. The majority of theorists do not recognize the employer's property rights and therefore, have to explain the legal effect on the basis of his right to lock-out. Any way, there is no doubt that the employer may expel workers only after he has gone through the procedures the courts, having gained an injunction from the court he may then enforce it.[40] The Supreme Court holds the view that an employer who conducts a lawful (proper) lock-out should be exempt from liability for "delaying in accepting performance" by the employees so long as parity is maintained between employer and employee. The courts take the position that locking out the workers as an offensive tactics is not lawful, and that a lock-out must be passive and defensive. The employer for example can lock the workers out only when the labor union is engaging in some acts of dispute and there must be a prospect of acts of dispute which would cause severe damages exceeding limits which the employer can endure. If the lock-out is lawful, the employer is exempted from an obligation to pay wages and even can expel the workers from the company's premises.

5. DISPUTES IN SMALL ENTERPRISES

Conflicts in small enterprises are mainly due to employers' aim for higher profits, authoritarian administration of the enterprise, closer supervision of workers, maintenance of strict discipline and complete obedience of the rules of the enterprise.

The employers in the smaller enterprise are the ones who seem to have the most negative views of unions and the most anti-union policies. The management of such enterprises, mostly take conservative view in their industrial relations because they firmly believe that they can not afford to do anything else, considering the environmental constraints under which they must operate—excessively competitive market, heavy dependency on a parent company, client companies or financial institutions, the relatively low productivity of their employees, their low profits and the high ratio of their labor costs to total costs. Often they may even reckless at times in their efforts to weaken or destroy unions. The large number of unfair labor practice cases brought before the labor Relations Commission has their sources in these smaller companies.[43]

Table 5.1 shows that the number of disputes in smaller enterprise are comparatively less than large and medium size enterprise. For example, in 1988 number of enterprises with labor dispute were two, in enterprise where 30-99 workers are employed and 194 where less than 29 workers are employed. Small enterprises accompanied by dispute tactics are very negligible.

6. DISPUTES IN PUBLIC SECTOR

It is necessary to understand the problems and characteristics of labor-management relations in the public sector, to understand industrial relations in Japan. Labor-management conflicts since World War II has been a common feature in Japan. Public sector is divided into different categories. Article 36 of Labor Relations Adjustment Law, prohibits "any act which hampers or causes a stoppage in the maintenance or normal operation of safety procedures in factories, mines and other places of employment". Article 37 of the same law requires the parties concerned in a case involving public welfare work to give notice of any act of dispute to the Labor Relations Commission and Ministry of Labor or the Prefecture Governor at least 10 days before the day on which the act of dispute is scheduled to begin. In public sector any act which hampers the normal course of operations in a public corporation, a government enterprise or the public service of the government, is completely prohibited. Article 17 of Public Corporation and National Enterprise Labor Relations Law (PCNELR) states, "employees and unions shall not engage in a strike, slowdown or any other acts of dispute hampering normal course of operation of a public corporation and national enterprise, nor shall any employee or union members and union officers conspire to effect, instigate or incite such prohibition". "The public corporation and national enterprise shall not engage in a lock-out". Article 18 imposes dismissal as a possible penalty for violations. Similar provisions are also found Articles 11 and 12 of the Local Pubic Enterprise Labor Relations (LPELR) law. However, such a prohibition of acts of dispute in the public sector has been severely criticized. Hanami feels the legislations prohibiting all acts of disputes in public sector has been one of the major causes of trouble in Japanese industrial relations.

Going-slow and working-to-rule are frequently used in public sector where the law prohibits the acts of dispute. The Supreme Court in 1969 stated that employees in public corporations and national enterprises are "workers" as defined in Article 28 of the constitution of Japan and therefore, in principle, they deserve to be protected by the provisions concerning the basic rights of worker. The Supreme Court further said that "it is not permitted to deny the basic right of workers in the public service on the grounds that they are servants of the whole community and not of any group thereof, as stipulated in Article 15 of the constitution.[41]

The civil servant's approved rights are limited according to the existing laws, though constitution under Article 28 guarantees the rights of wage earners and salaried employees to organize unions, the right to bargain collectively and the right to act collectively (it refers to strikes and other union activities). Table 5.3 highlights the legal rights of public sector employees and how they are limited under existing law. The Article 108-2 of National Civil Service Law, gives civil service employees the right to organize what are called employee's associations. There are some exceptions; policemen, firemen, prison employees and members of the self-defense forces and the coast guard may not form employee's associations. According to Table 5.3, except policemen and Firemen and Prison employees all other public

TABLE 5.3
The Legal Rights of Public Sector Employees

	Organisation	*Collective Bargaining*	*Right to Organise*
Policemen, Fishermen, etc.	No	No	No
National Civil Servants	Yes	No	No
Public Corporation and National Enterprise	Yes	Yes	No
Public Employees in Local Government	Yes	No	No
Local Public Enterprise	Yes	Yes	No

Source : Koichiro Yamaguchi, "The Public Sector" : Contemporary Industrial Relations in Japan, Edited by Talshiro Shirai, University of Wisconsin Press, 1983, p. 304.

sector employees have right to organize. About the right to collective bargaining except Public corporations and national Enterprise and Local Public Enterprise and others do not enjoy. Right to strike is not granted to any of the public sector employee, they are strictly prohibited. The National and Civil Service Law, Article 108-7 says that civil servants shall not be subject to any discriminatory treatment by reason for their membership in a union, for attempting to join or organize a union, or for having performed proper acts of a union. Article 108-5 of the National Civil Service Law says registered employee's associations have the right to negotiate but they may not conclude agreement. However, this regulation has more form than substance.[42]

As per Article 98-2 of National Civil Service Law, civil employees shall not strike or resort to delaying tactics which reduce the efficiency of governmental operations and that any employee takes part in strike or other unlawful actions shall not contest the government about his discharge and he will be also subject to up to three year's imprisonment or a fine not to exceed 10,000 Yen. Participants in a strike in the civil service are likely to be subject, not only to criminal liability but also to civil liability and disciplinary sanctions.

7. LABOR DISPUTES—COUNTRY COMPARISON

The right of workers to organize, guaranteed by Article 28 of the constitution of Japan of 1946, is "eternal and inviolable". According to most Japanese Labor law scholars, this right is sacred and holy—a mythology that can be found in hardly any other civilized country. They are also proud of this constitution provision, since few countries other than socialist and development nations recognized as human rights in their constitutions the right to bargain and to act collectively.[44]

Normally employee's demands are made only within the limits of the capacities of a single company. Even if certain demands seem to be excess of the company's financial capacity, union cooperation in labor-saving efforts and raising productivity, plus an absence of actions detrimental to management goals, has resulted in balance. Long range analyses show that all wage hikes have been carried out only within the limits of Japan's overall economic growth. Non-Japanese observers, felt, Japanese unions rarely strike, and strikes that do occur usually are short duration. They also claim that the strikes by Japanese unions are not intended to damage employers, but just to show the worker's determination to struggle or to embarrass the management. Therefore, they are called "demonstrative strikes". The number of labor law cases in the courts or before the Labor Relations Commission in Japan is surprisingly small in comparison with the Western countries.

It is not correct to conclude that Japanese unions rarely strike. The number of industrial disputes in Japan is as great as it is in France. The total number of Japanese industrial disputes does not include strikes of less than four hour's duration, which occur quite often. As compared to US, Canada, England and Australia the strike duration is short in Japan. Short duration strikes are not only seen in Japan but elsewhere. If we estimate the average duration of strike in each country by dividing the number of working days lost by the number of workers involved, we find that strikes in France and Germany, Sweden and Italy are also in general shorter duration.[45] In 1986, number of disputes in Japan are comparatively less than other countries except US. Though the number of dispute in Japan is more than in US, her number of workers involved and working day lost is very less. Even though number of disputes of Japan is very close to that the Canada her number of workers involved and working days lost is comparatively very less. This is a unique nature of Japanese industrial relations.

Why Japanese enterprise unions are generally regarded as relatively weak in comparison with unions of west? Why in most Japanese Unions, strikes are short? Both leaders and the rank and file of Japanese unions have a very distinct mentality, which distinguishes strikes by Japanese enterprise union from those by other countries, Japanese unionists are reallv hesitant to cause any severe damage to the enterprise to which they belong. This is not because of their identification with or a sense of belonging to their enterprises. The enterprise becomes a community to which employee tends to commit himself for better wages, fringe benefits, skills, position and status. Thus the employer and the employee share a common desire to maintain the enterprise and keep it prospering. Strike minded and militant union leaders can not ignore or over ride this feeling of belongingness to the employee and the employer. If he ignores then a prolonged strike may take place that causes or threatens to cause severe damage to the enterprise, the consequence may be a breakup of the union. It is this reason that makes the union to be more cooperative with management. Japanese unions are often very law abiding and respect democratic role of union administration. Law-abiding attitude of unions is not completely admirable, since they regard the majority vote as only a legal requirement and disregard its real meaning as support strike action.

8. PREVENTION OF LABOR DISPUTES

It is recognized in every country that labor disputes are a great menace to the industry and the countries' economy. The strike and lock-outs always lead to grave industrial and social dislocation, therefore, it is necessary to preserve industrial peace. "Industrial peace is not merely a negative concept signifying the absence of industrial unrest, the reconciling of the hostile forces, in order to avoid ruinous strife, but it also signifies the active presence of harmonious and good industrial relations, generating amity and good-will between the partners in an industry—a condition which is both the cause and the effect of fruitful cooperation. The proper development of industrial peace demands a suitable background of happy industrial relations, marked by such essential requisites as laying down of fair standards by the state, the desire of the employers to bargain on equal terms with his employees, anxiety on the part of employers to promote the welfare of their employees and genuine sympathy of the general public.

The responsibility of maintaining peace, harmony and efficiency lies on the shoulders of the labor and management to achieve full production, peaceful industrial relations and stable economy. It is said that in industrial negotiations perfection of machinery counts far less than good faith and good will.

The basic causes of labor disputes can be prevented by effective management, union action and active government participation. Therefore, the keynote to industrial peace is the cooperation between the employers and the employees. Whenever the interest of the employee and the employer differs—it often strains industrial relations and creates industrial unrest. The most powerful weapon with the workmen in dealing with an employer, who is refusing to accede to their demands, is strike. The corresponding weapon in the armory of the employer as means to reprisal is lock-out or closing of the place of employment.

The consequences of strike and lock-out damage the economy of a country. Neither all strikes or lock-outs can be regarded as justified nor are all strikes or lock-outs unjustified. Laski has said, a strike is unjust in that it is an appeal to force in a matter of disputed right, it is human because of misery it causes to the workers, it is wasteful of resources of capital and labor, it is wicked, because it stirs up hate, it is anti-social in that it denies and disrupts the solidarity of community. Therefore, frequency of strikes lock-out should be minimized through persistent efforts by management, labor and government.

There are provisions to prohibit and restrict acts of disputes in Japanese labor law, when an act of dispute endangers human life and public welfare work. Article 36 of the Labor Relations Adjustment Law, prohibits 'any act which hampers or causes a stoppage in the maintenance or normal operation of safety procedures in factories, mines and other places of employment'. This means, the law prohibits any act which endangers human life in the work place but not those acts which merely destroy the property of the company. Negative acts which may eventually cause the destruction of the property are not necessarily illegal because in such cases the employer can and may take the steps required to avoid destruction as long as the unions do not obstruct him.

Whenever the work stoppage would pose a serious threat to the national economy or the life of the nation, the prime minister may decide on an emergency adjustment. After prime ministry's publication of a decision to make emergency adjustment the parties are forbidden to engage in any act of dispute for 50 days from the publication.

Though prohibitions of acts of disputes in public sector have been severely criticized, in Japan any act which hampers the normal course of operations in public corporation, a government enterprise or the public service of the government is completely prohibited. This prohibition of acts of dispute in the public sector is extremely strict and very broad in two senses. Firstly, all kinds of acts of disputes, including those which are small-scale and fairly harmless, are prohibited if they hamper the normal course of operations in public sector. Secondly, it covers the whole range of major public corporations and government enterprises and all categories of public employees.

Notes and References

1. According to the Indian Industrial Dispute Act, 1947, section 2(k), "Industrial disputes means any dispute or difference between employers and employers, or between employers and workmen or between workmen and workmen, which is connected with the employment or non-employment or terms of employment or with the condition of labor of any person".

   "A conflict (labor disputes) which may include a dispute between parties to a collective bargaining agreement over the terms (interests) or the interpretation of the term (rights) of their contract" (According to AAA—American Arbitration Association).

   The term "Labor dispute' include any controversy concerning terms of conditions of employment or concerning the association or representation of persons in negotiating, fixing, maintaining, changing or seeking to arrange terms or condition of employment, regardless of whether or not the disputants stand in the proximate relations of employer and employee" (The Norris-La Guardia Act of March 23, 1932).

2. Basic Trade Union Rights:

	Right to Organize	*Right to Negotiate*		*Right to Strike*	*Union member*
		Right to Bargain	*Right to Conclude Contracts*		
Employees in the Private Sector (including public Corporation)	YES	YES	YES	YES	9,382
National enterprise employees and local public enterprise Employees	YES	YES	YES	NO	735
Public employees in the Non-operational sector	YES	YES	NO	NO	2,226
Police officer (immigration control officer), maritime Police officer, prison officer, fire defense officer, self-defense force	NO	NO	NO	NO	....

Tadashi Nakamura, Labor in Japan, Japan Institute of Labor, Tokyo, 1988, p. 84.

3. Blanpain, R. (Ed), International Encyclopedia for Labor Law and Industrial Relations, Vol. 7 (Japan section is written by Hanami, T.A.) Kluwer Law and Taxation Publishers, The Netherlands, 1985, p. 132.
4. Dankett, Clyde E. Contemporary Unionism in the US, p. 389.
5. Mukerji, R.K., The Indian Working Class, Hind Kitabs, Bombay 1951, p. 372.
6. Lester, R.A. Economics of Labor, p. 3.
7. Momoria, C.B. and Momoria, S., Dynamic of Industrial Relations in India, Himalaya Publishing House, Bombay, 1986, p. 266.
8. Taishiro Shirai (Ed.), Contemporary Industrial Relations in Japan, University of Wisconsin Press Ltd., Wisconsin, 1983, p. 218 (Koshiro, in his article: Development of Collective Bargaining, discussed the content of labor disputes of issues an interesting table)
9. Dore describes the difference between British and Japanese Factories: "English Electric employees have a conception of the status system of the factory (and for that matter of their society) in terms of a few more or less homogeneous layers separated by marked gaps. The extent to which people are conscious of the gaps depends on the variety of differentiating criteria which coincide on the same time of division—income, method of

payment, toilets, canteens, holidays, pension rights, dress, accent, union membership, etc. in addition to functional authority positions. In the Hitachi system there are far fewer discontinuities—toilets, canteens etc., do not demarcate status groups. Pay scales are a single continuum".

10. Ross Stagner, The Psychology of human conflict, in the Nature of human conflict, Ed. Elton B. McNeil (Engle Wood Cliff, N.J. Prentice-Hall, Inc., 1985, p. 47.
11. Hanami Tadashi, Labor Relations in Japan Today. Kodansha International Ltd., Tokyo 1979, p. 121.
12. Prevention Measures in India: Labor Welfare Officer and Labor Welfare Work, Tripartite and Bipartite Bodies, Standing Orders and Grievance Procedure, Ethical Code and Industrial Relations, Wage Policy and Wage Regulation Machinery, Workmen Participation in Management and Collective Bargaining.
13. Blanpain, R. (Ed.), *op. cit.*, p. 153.
14. Catlin, W.B. The Labor Problem, p. 416, as quoted by Mamoria's.
15. *Ibid.*
16. Blanpain, R. (Ed.), *op. cit.*, p. 132.
17. Refer for Fig. 1, which shows the classification of strikes and lock-outs, Mamoria's, p. 274.
18. Blanpain, R. (Ed.), *op. cit.*, p. 131.
19. *Ibid.*, p. 132
20. Kornhauser, Dubin and Ross (Ed), Industrial Conflict, New York, McGraw-Hill, 1954, p. 14.
21. *Ibid.*, p. 132.
22. Refer for more definitions of strikes, Mamoria's, p. 272.
23. Mamoria's, *op. cit.*, p. 272.
24. Except those acts of disputes that have been dealt in this book other forms are not often used in Japan.
25. Buckingham and Caranatic Mills Co., Ltd. *v.* Their workers, 1952, LAC 491 (LAT): Swadeshi Industries Ltd. *v.* Their Workmen 1955, II LLG, 404 (LAT).
26. Blanpain, R. (Ed). *op. cit.*, p. 153.
27. *Ibid.* p. 133.
28. *Ibid.*, p. 141.
29. *Ibid.*, p. 139.
30. Mamoria's, *op. cit.*, p. 277.
31. Blanpain, R..(Ed.), *op. cit.*, p. 136.
32. "Bycott" aims at disrupting the normal functioning of the enterprise. It is an appeal for all voluntary withdrawal cooperation and so, it is persuasive in nature and negative in approach.
33. Mamoria's, *op. cit.*, p. 277.
34. The "Stay-in-strike" is one which develops when the demands of the workers are not met on the strike day and the workers remain determined on the "sit-down strike" and do not leave the plant.
35. Mamoria's, *op. cit.*, p. 275.
36. Blanpain, R. (Ed), *op. cit.*, p. 138.
37. *Ibid.*, p. 137.

38. *Ibid.*, p. 137.
39. *Ibid.*, p. 138.
40. *Ibid.*, p. 142.
41. Taishiro Shirai (Ed), *op. cit.*, p. 283 (Koshiro's article).
42. *Ibid.*, p. 307, (Yamaguchi's article: The Public Sector. He has dealt with disciplinary sanctions against union activities among civil service employees).
43. *Ibid.*, p. 379.
44. *Ibid.*, p. 162 (Hanami's article: The Function of the Law).
45. *Ibid.*, p. 177, see for a table that shows.

6

Dispute Settlement Machinery in Japanese Industrial Relations

Disputes are expected to occur in every country at various levels. Dispute of interests between management and labor or between management and union causes severe frictions and sometime lead to prolonged strikes and lockouts. The consequences of disputes will have a reaching effects on the workers, employers, the consumers and the community which disturb the economic, social and political life of a country. Peace, harmony and efficiency are essential for proper development of industrial relations. Some of the basic causes of conflicts can be prevented or at least reduced to a great extent by effective management and union action. Employee communication, grievance procedure and its speedy settlement, joint consultation at different levels of the plant, worker's education programs, healthy and stable unions and their due recognition as bargaining agents, sincere observance of the Code of Discipline, labor-management association, revision of wages in the context of price index level, helpful attitude of the supervisors towards worker's problems and improvement in working conditions and provision of welfare amenities, would all go a long way in preventing industrial disputes and pave the path for industrial peace.[1] From an enterprise perspective industrial peace is desirable because industrial unrest reflects adversely on its efficiency and capability, in fact its survival could be at stake. Workers and trade unions are not actually antagonistic to the idea of peace but they are not its devotees either. Prevention of industrial disputes is no doubt more desirable than their settlement. However, it would not be wise enough exclusively to rely on prevention and ignore the question of settlement. Many attempts have been made in all countries to reduce the conflicts and an antagonistic attitude between management and workers. Marxist remedy is most radical which demands worker ownership and management of enterprise. Other latest devices that are becoming popular are: worker's committees, labor management committees and participate management.

In this chapter I would like to deal with dispute settlement machinery of Japan, essentially inter-group conflict—management and workers or unions. To me Japanese dispute settlement machinery seems to be interesting because:

1. Acts of disputes are very brief and unions have invented variety of acts of Dispute.
2. There is absence of grievance arbitration.[2]
3. Courts in Japan sometimes act like arbitrators.
4. There is a development of voluntary resolution of disputes by means of Compromise.

I do not intend to examine the legal framework for dispute settlement but wish to deal with the methods of dispute resolution. In other words, I will explain "what is being done" and "how it is being done rather" than "what the best way of doing it".

In a traditional Japanese society a dispute is not expected and even if dissatisfaction is expressed, often parties try to make concessions to each other in an attempt to resolve and resume their former harmonious relations. The traditional way of dispute settlements very well expressed by the idiom:[3]

arasoi o mizu ni nagasu	- let the dispute flow to the water
kenda ryo-seibai	- both disputants are penalized equally
arasoi o maruku osameru	- to settle the dispute in a circle

This means lets forget the conflict and be friendly again by following traditional approach. Normally, industrial relations in Japan are peaceful. The workers having committed to the life time employment practice co-operate with their enterprise; and the enterprise unions being enterprise conscious are friendly and cooperative too. Practically most of the employee's grievances and dissatisfactions are taken care of by the management in an informal way, without resorting to formal procedure or applying any universal norms. Most disputes are settled by mutual understanding without ever being raised in any explicit form. Thus Japanese employers and managers are not used to overt confrontation and the logical settlement of conflicting interest. Therefore, it is inferred that there is a tendency in Japanese industrial relations, i.e. once a conflict has become explicit, settlement would be very hard to reach. In such cases the dispute tends to be prolonged and may turn into a fierce confrontation which often involves violence.[4]

The labor relations between management and union are not very different from the other countries. Whenever labor-management fails to reach an amicable settlement by themselves, like in any other country they agree to submit it to 'arasoi o azukeru—third party'. The effectiveness of this method of dispute settlement depends upon the third party's prestige and the degree of trust.

The distinction between individual *versus* collective disputes, disputes of vested rights *versus* disputes of interest economic disputes *versus* political disputes and organized conflicts *versus* unorganized conflicts are theoretically recognized in Japan as in other countries, but are not very meaningful in the actual industrial relations. The dispute settlement procedures—industrial relations commission, conciliation, mediation and arbitration. Disputes of vested 'rights' between employers and individual workers or the unions are the responsibility of courts. Unfortunately, this distinction often fades away practice.[5]

The purpose of Labor Relations Adjustment Law, in conjunction with Labor Union Law, is to promote a fair adjustment of labor relations and to prevent or settle labor disputes and thereby to contribute to the maintenance of industrial peace and to economic development (Article 1). The parties make special efforts to reach a mutual settlement and only in the event of their failure they approach to the Labor Relations Commission. When acts of dispute occur, the parties concerned should notify thereof without delay to the Labor Relations Commission or To (Tokyo), Do (Okido), Fu (Osaka), the prefecture governor or the Director of the Maritime Bureau (including the Director General of the District Maritime Administration Department). It is a government responsibility to assist the parties for fair and prompt settlement with appropriate machinery.

1. MUTUAL SETTLEMENT

The principle of autonomy is recognized in almost all industrialized countries so that parties themselves can settle their differences or conflicts mutually. We can mention various reasons in favor of autonomy principle:

1. Disputes are increasing day-by-day and the time needed for settlement is too long, therefore, it would be hard to depend on government agencies for their settlement.
2. Parties need to continue friendly relations and if they wish so, they should prefer to reach a settlement by themselves or through private agencies. Continuous harmonious relationship between labor-management is not just a wish but is of necessity in industrial relations.
3. Most of the disputes are of conflict of interest not related to rights and obligation; hence they are not suitable for government dispute settlement agencies or the law courts.

However, the principle of autonomy is suitable only for certain specific types of industrial relations, it can not be an absolute rule to fit any circumstance. Where principle of autonomy is preferred, labor dispute settlement by private institution has priority and government intervention is exceptional. Before utilizing prescribed statutory procedures, the law lays emphasis on the right—even the duty—of the parties to use voluntary, mutual procedure. Section 20 of the Labor Relations Adjustment Law, provides that "the parties concerned with labor relations shall make special endeavors mutually to promote proper and fair labor relations and fix by trade agreement matters relating to the establishment as well as management of regular agencies to adjust differences constantly and in the event that labor disputes occur to endeavor to settle them autonomously in all sincerity".

As I have mentioned earlier parties always try to find amicable settlement on the basis of personal understanding and are reluctant to go for a third party's help. The rate of voluntary or mutual settlement of labor disputes is high, which indicates that the parties are generally unwilling to seek third-party intervention in settling their disputes.[6] Why do parties hesitate to take third parties help?

1. In Japanese society clear-cut decisions based on certain universal standards are not at all popular.
2. The underdevelopment of some distinct dispute settlement procedure is designed to deal with certain categories of dispute in the industrial relations system. There are various procedures, such as bargaining, consultation and grievance procedure, which have been formally set-up by the unions and management, but these normal procedures introduced in accordance with the western model often exist only in the official documents such as collective agreements and in actual industrial relations, informal procedures of a more personal nature prevail.
3. Japan's labor dispute adjustment system is based strictly on the principle of voluntarism. Unions and employers, particularly the employers are always hesitant to submit their conflicts to a third party and they always try to resolve conflicts of interest by establishing substantive norms. The Labor Relations Commission's Adjustment service is invoked only with

the consent of parties except for public utility disputes and essential industries including those covered by the Public Corporation and National Enterprise Labor Relations Law.

4. Japanese courts and Labor Relations Commissions frequently lay the role of arbitrator and decisions often are more favorable to workers and unions than they might achieve by using the collective bargaining method. By and large unions, particularly minority unions in multi-union situations, seem to fare better under court and commission decisions. Therefore, Matsuda assumed that among the labor disputes that are recorded as being settled by collective bargaining, there are many that have in fact been resolved through court or unfair labor practice procedures, wither by decisions, orders or compromise. Further he found that every year more than 60% of the civil cases on labor and more than 80% of the unfair labor practice cases are settled by compromise or are withdrawn.
5. In Japan collective bargaining tends to conclude with unions and employers reacting an agreement to establish procedural rules, such as for joint consultation and other meet-and-confer clauses, rather than substantive norms. According to the Labor Ministry report the number of unions with joint consultation clauses in their collective agreements has been increasing at an annual rate of 10%. A large number of labor disputes except wage and hours are settled by various forms of consultation.

There are various dispute resolution methods to cope up with industrial dispute. Broadly, these can be categorized as statutory and non-statutory measures. Non-statutory measure encourages a resolution through negotiation. Compromise is primarily on a give-and-take basis not by applying any substantive rules. Dispute resolution based on mutual compromise is basically *ad hoc* and popular in Japan. By the very nature this speeds up the process and cuts short the long procedures and promotes long-term harmonious relations without damaging continuing relations. The third party intervention can be considerably minimized or done away with altogether. Whenever parties share common interests and goals, it is easier for mutual compromise.

Over the years mutual compromise institution has become powerful in Japanese industrial relations, regardless of whether it involves an interest rights or a vested right disputes. This may be because of various pressures, from outside and within the enterprise. In 1989 of 1721 total disputes, labor-management negotiation settled 719 disputes without third party help, 76 disputes with third party assistance and 131 by third person (Table 6.1). This indicates that a total of 41.8% disputes settled through negotiation. A compromise over rights has often been condemned as undesirable, if not illegal, particularly when it is the worker's constitutional right that is at stake, as in an unfair labor practice case, notwithstanding the rate of compromise in both courts and unfair labor practice procedures has been increasing. Even legal framework of Japan indirectly pressurizes voluntary resolution by means of compromise. Therefore, the greater the pressures on the parties, the easier it is for the parties

TABLE 6.1
Labor Disputes Settled by Method of Settlement, 1970-89

Year	*1970*	*1975*	*1980*	*1985*	*1987*	*1988*	*1989*
Total	4365	8326	4253	4692	1604	1716	1721
Direct negotiation between caiptal and labour	2992	4431	1958	1177	935	925	719 (41.8)
With third person	221	361	224	194	133	101	7S (10.5)
By a third person	475	483	318	217	194	180	131 (7.6)
L.R.C.	444	464	299	187	192	171	123 (93.9)
Conciliation	401	438	277	169	181	165	120 (97.5)
Mediation	28	1 1	5	4	1	4	1 (1.2)
Arbitration	15	15	17	14	10	2	2 (1.3)
Labour Policy Officer	9	5	12	2	1	1	1 (0.8)
Other	22	14	7	28	4	8	7 (5.3)
Other	898	3412	1971	3291	475	611	871 (50.6)

Note : Figures in parenthesis indicate percentage.
Source : Japan Statistical Year Book, 1990.

to compromise. Nearly 50% to 60% of all cases handled by District Courts are concluded by compromise or withdrawn (mostly outside court). It is also found that more than 75% of all unfair labor practice cases submitted to the Local Labor Relations Commission, are settled by compromise or by withdrawal. The reason for such compromise in both procedure seems to be the same, i.e. pressure or suggestion from a court or commission. A survey by the Central Labor Relations Commission (1952-55), revealed that one-forth of all compromises were reached with the advice of the Labor Relations Commission or of the members thereof representing labor or management. More than 15% of the conciliated settlement was made because the labor felt that it had attained its aim by making an employer sorry for what he had done or by forcing him to reflect on it. Also nearly a quarter of the employers and some 8% of the employees agreed on a compromise because they preferred a monetary settlement. Finally, 13% of the employees and unions responded that they had compromised for the purpose of maintaining restoring better industrial relations and 15% of the employers and employees answered that their relationship had actually improved as a consequence of a compromise.

Labor Relations Adjustment Law, Article 4 endeavors for autonomous settlement. "Nothing in this law shall be construed either to prevent the parties from determining for themselves their labor relations or from adjusting the differences of their claims concerning labor relations by direct negotiations or collective bargaining or to relieve the parties concerned with labor relations of their responsibility for making such endeavor". The constitution of Japan provides the right to bargain, therefore, the principle of the superiority of collective bargaining under the autonomy of the parties in industrial relations is firmly established. In Japan bargaining is done on the basis of 'good faith' with few exceptions. In 1982 some 9 million employees, which is nearly 90% of the organized labor force were covered by collective bargaining. More than 50% of the unions engage in joint consultation on nearly all matters, including management of work force and production. In addition to general consultation, there is extensive use of prior consultation on specific issues: 80%-90% of the unions take part, in one way or another, in decisions of personal changes, 83% participate in the administration of welfare facilities, 88% discuss safety and health matters and 90% consult on workforce adjustment.[7]

In Japan collective bargaining is to be used to decide about matters such as working conditions, while consultation is used to deal with problems which are not supposed to be for bargaining which is, after all, a form of confrontation. Those issues which are not suitable for bargaining are: dismissal, transfer and promotion, changes in production, sales or other management policies, the introduction of new methods, technology or facilities, the abolition of certain plant or work division and so on. Matters which are regarded as matters of managerial prerogative by the management side are certainly not suitable for collective bargaining, especially in Japan where bargaining tends to be more or less a matter of confrontation. The various aspects of bargaining can cause for serious conflict between unions and management. In such circumstances, it is expected that employees will respond with a wave of acts dispute, a series of unfair labor practice charges and litigations and a mass of employee complaints charging an employer with violation of the Labor Standard Law and the employer's reaction will be to take all kinds of unilateral actions.[8]

The government cannot be a silent spectator because labor-management disputes injure not only the parties in the dispute but also the society at large. Figure 6.1 explains conflict resolution system in Japan. The autonomy of union-management has long been emphasized in Japanese industrial relations and the government refrains from intervention.

However, government agencies (Labor Relations Commission and Courts) play an active role in labor dispute settlement, only when parties appeal. The government intervention is justified or even inevitable whenever parties are unable to settle a dispute by themselves. Generally, Japanese people are more reluctant to go to courts and therefore, prefer Labor Relations Commission. Why do unions and managements use Labor Relations Commission? According to Hanami:

1. The Japanese respect government authority.

FIG. 6.1

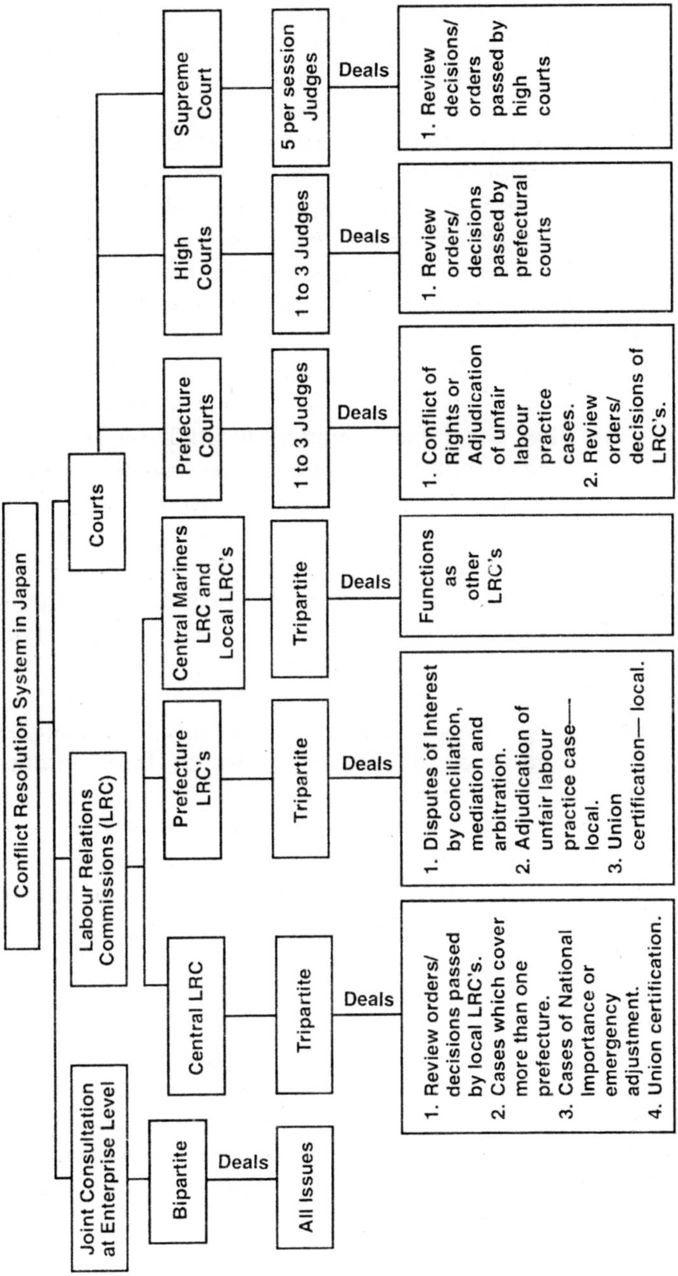
Conflict Resolution System in Japan
Joint Consultation at Enterprise Level
Bipartite
Deals
All Issues
Labour Relations Commissions (LRC)
Central LRC
Tripartite
Deals
1. Review orders/ decisions passed by local LRC's.
2. Cases which cover more than one prefecture.
3. Cases of National Importance or emergency adjustment.
4. Union certification.
Prefecture LRC's
Tripartite
Deals
1. Disputes of Interest by conciliation, mediation and arbitration.
2. Adjudication of unfair labour practice case—local.
3. Union certification— local.
Central Mariners LRC and Local LRC's
Tripartite
Deals
Functions as other LRC's
Courts
Prefecture Courts
1 to 3 Judges
Deals
1. Conflict of Rights or Adjudication of unfair labour practice cases.
2. Review orders/ decisions of LRC's.
High Courts
1 to 3 Judges
Deals
1. Review orders/ decisions passed by prefectural courts
Supreme Court
5 per session Judges
Deals
1. Review decisions/ orders passed by high courts

2. It would be difficult to find a person who could command enough power and prestige to be respected by both parties. In Japan private arbitration and conciliation have no role to play and are very rare.
3. There is accessibility and availability of Labor Relations Commission system which is tri-partite body.
4. Parties feel that access to Labor Relations Commission is easier than courts and it handles all important labor disputes. In this section let us examine the nature and functions of Labor Relations Commission and Courts.

2. LABOR RELATIONS COMMISSIONS

A Labor Relations Commission shall be set-up which consist of equal number of persons representing employers, workers and public interest. The Central and local Labor Relations Commissions, cover labor relations in private industry and local public enterprise, while the public Corporations and National Enterprise Labor Relations Commissions (PCENRLARC) cover labor relations in public corporation and government enterprise under Public Corporation and National Enterprise Labor Relations Law (PCNELRL), Seamen's Labor Relations are by the Seamen's Central Labor Relations Commission and the Seamen's Local Labor Relations Commissions. Matters relating to Labor Relations Commission other than those laid down in Labor Union Law, shall be prescribed by cabinet order. The Central Labor Relations Commission shall be under the jurisdiction of the Ministry of Labor (Article 19 of Labor Union Law).

The Central Labor Relations Commission is to be composed of a total of nine members equally representing the employers, workers and public interest. A Chairman, who will preside over the business of the Central Labor Relations Commission, is elected by all members from among the public members. The Ministry of Labor appoints the employer members and labor members according to the recommendations by the employers' association and labor unions respectively and the public members according to the agreement of the employer members and the labor unions. The term of office of the members is two years but they may be re-appointed. The Central Labor Relations Commission has an executive office to handle the administrative affairs of the commission (Article 19).

While Central Labor Relations Commission members are appointed by the Ministry of Labor those of Local Labor Relations Commission members are appointed by the governor of the relevant prefecture. The Local Labor Relations Commission has 5 to 13 members depending on the importance of industrial relations in the prefecture.

The Labor Relations Adjustment Law has been enacted in order to prevent and to facilitate the peaceful settlement of labor disputes. This law provides for three types of adjustments: Conciliation, mediation and arbitration, which is carried out by the Labor Relations Commission. The Central Labor Relations Commission reviews the orders and decisions taken by the local ones in the field of unfair labor practices and deals itself with cases which cover more than one prefecture or which are clearly of national importance. The Central Labor Relations Commission performs the following function:

1. The adjudication of unfair labor practice cases.
2. Dispute settlement by conciliation, mediation or arbitration.
3. Screening the qualifications of unions to participate in adjudication procedures or to be registered as legal persons.
4. Extending the effect of collective agreements.

The aim of Labor Relations Commission is to provide relief which is more informal, more flexible, simpler, quicker and cheaper than judicial remedies.

(a) Unfair Labor Practice cases—Adjudication

A complaint against the employer can be filed either by a union or an individual who claims to be suffering from an unfair labor practice (Table 6.2 and 6.3). The Article 7 of the Trade Union Law prohibits three categories of unfair labor practice by the employer:

TABLE 6.2
Number of Complaints (ULP) for Adjustment (First Instance) 1983-87

Classification	*No. of Cases*					*Percentage*				
	1983	*1984*	*1985*	*1986*	*1987*	*1983*	*1984*	*1985*	*1986*	*1987*
(1)	*(2)*	*(3)*	*(4)*	*(5)*	*(6)*	*(7)*	*(8)*	*(9)*	*(10)*	*(11)*
New cases	1333	572	560	546	578	100	100	100	100	100
Complaints by:										
Union	456	374	386	373	486	34	65	69	68	84
Individual	834	146	136	127	36	63	26	24	25	6
Union and Individual	43	52	38	36	56	3	9	7	7	10
Only Private Sector										
New cases	483	402	405	401	555	100	100	100	100	100
Complaints by:										
Union	414	352	353	352	476	86	88	87	88	86
Individual	32	10	20	17	29	6	2	5	4	5
Union and Individual	37	40	32	32	50	8	10	8	8	9

Source : CLRC, Chuo Rodo Jiho, Gogai, 1988.

TABLE 6.3
Number of Complaints (ULP) for Adjustment (Second Instance) 1983-87

Classification	*No. of Cases*					*Percentage*				
	1983	*1984*	*1985*	*1986*	*1987*	*1983*	*1984*	*1985*	*1986*	*1987*
(1)	*(2)*	*(3)*	*(4)*	*(5)*	*(6)*	*(7)*	*(8)*	*(9)*	*(10)*	*(11)*
New cases	66	70	61	85	67	100	100	100	100	100
Complaints by:										
Labour side:										
Union	14	15	7	14	19	21	22	11	16	28
Individual	1	3	3	3	—	2	4	5	4	—
Union and Individual	—	2	4	5	2	—	2	7	6	3
Management side :										
Management	51	50	47	63	45	77	71	77	74	67
Individual	—	—	—	—	—	—	—	—	—	2
Mangement and Individual	—	—	—	—	—	—	—	—	—	—

Source : CLRC, Chuo Rodo Jiho, Gogai, 1988.

1. Discrimination or unfavorable treatment,
2. Refusal to bargain, and
3. Domination or interference.

After receiving the complaint the Local Labor Relations Commission investigates the case and if necessary hold hearing sessions to examine witness or evidence. The remedies provided by Labor Relations Commission include:

1. For the employer to refrain and desist from discrimination, control interference,
2. To reinstate the employee in his former position, and
3. To bargain with good faith.

In 1987 out of a total number of 2238 unfair labor practice cases, 309 ended in compromise or withdrawal, while only 97 were settled by order or decision of the commission (Table 6.4).

Table 6.5 highlights the number of unfair labor practice cases by the type of industry and their size. The largest (42.7) percentage of cases have been reported by transport and communication and next by manufacturing (27.2) percentage. The number of unfair labor practices increases as the size of enterprise becomes larger. For example only 17.2 percentage cases are from an enterprise having less than 29 employees while 40.6 percentage cases are from an enterprise having more than 1000 employees.

In Japan the aggrieved becomes the charging party unlike in the USA National Labor Relations Board in unfair labor practice. At hearing sessions the parties usually are represented by lawyers and act as opponents. Therefore, Japanese system tends to be of a more legal nature. Although the labor and employer members participate in the process, but in practice the instigation is done by the public members and orders and decisions are made and reached by a meeting of the public member alone. It is quite interesting to note that during the entire proceedings the Labor Relations Commission, encourage settlement by conciliation. In fact figures show that, the majority of unfair labor practice cases brought before commission is settled either by withdrawal or by conciliation. Within a given period, if either of the parties are not satisfied with the order or

TABLE 6.4

Number of Unfair Labor Practices (ULO) Cases Completed by the Manner of Settlement in 1987 (First Instance)

Classification	*No. of Disputes*			*No. of Settlements*								
				Withdrawals and compromises			*Orders and Decisions*					
	Pending from last year	*New cases*	*Total*	*With-drawals*	*Compro-mises*	*Total*	*Remedial Orders*	*Dismissal*	*Total*	*Remitted*	*Total*	*Pending*
(1)	*(2)*	*(3)*	*(4)*	*(5)*	*(6)*	*(7)*	*(8)*	*(9)*	*(10)*	*(11)*	*(12)*	*(13)*
Total	1660	378	2238	54	255	309	86	11	97	—	406	1832
Only Private Sector												
Total	839	555	1394	50	247	297	84	11	95	—	392	1002

Source : CLRC, Chuō Rodo Jiho, Gogai, 1988.

TABLE 6.5
Number of HLP Cases by Type of Industry and Size (First Instance)

Classification of Industry	*Less than 49*	*50-99*	*100-499*	*500-999*	*More than 1000*	*Total*
(1)	*(2)*	*(3)*	*(4)*	*(5)*	*(6)*	*(7)*
1. Agriculture	—	—	—	—	—	—
2. Forestry	—	—	—	—	—	—
3. Fishing	—	—	—	—	—	—
4. Mining	—	—	—	—	—	—
5. Construction	—	1	—	—	3	4
6. Manufacturing	34	25	54	13	31	157
7. Electric, Gas and Water Supply	1	—	—	—	—	—
8. Transportation and Co-communication	20	24	30	8	165	247
9. Wholesale and Retail and Restaurant	16	6	14	3	9	48
10. Banking and Insurance	—	—	3	4	3	10
11. Real Estate	—	—	—	—	—	—
12. Service	28	17	31	5	6	87
13. Public Administration	—	—	—	6	17	23
14. Not Classified	—	—	—	—	—	—
Grand Total	99	73	132	39	225	578

Source : CLRC, Chuo Rodo Jiho, Gogai, 1988.

the decision of Local Labor Relations Commission, they may appeal to the Central Labor Relations Commission or may bring administrative suit or to the law courts for a review of the order. The Central Labor Relations Commission may sustain or cancel the order of the Local Labor Relations Commission may sustain or cancel the order the Local Labor Relations Commission after it has examined the case using substantially the same procedure as that described above for the Local Labor Relations Commission. If parties are dissatisfied with Central Labor Relations Commission results, they may seek judicial review. When parties select to bring a suit in the district court, the commission may find it necessary to seek an emergency court order to enforce its own order, in full or in part, from the court where the administrative suit is pending. A commission's order becomes final when:

1. It is sustained by a court,
2. No appeal is filed, and
3. The time period allowed for challenge has lapsed.

An employer who violates the court orders can be fined. The employer is not allowed to challenge the enforcement order but he may seek a suspension of execution of the original commission's order in advance and thus be able to prevent the court from issuing an emergency order. An employer can also file a complaint in a higher court, contesting any fine imposed upon him for violation. It is possible for him to appeal even up to the Supreme Court.

We can observe one peculiarity, in the way the Labor Relations Commission deals with unfair labor practice cases. These days at Labor Relations Commission the hearing procedure is becoming more and more like a court procedure but the remedial orders are more diverse and do not resemble to that of mediation or even arbitration. Since commission's procedures have become more like court procedures, the delay has become a serious problem. On an average in 1976, unfair labor practice cases before Central Labor Relations Commission, took 624 days from the date complaints were filed until orders or decisions were issued.[9] In 1976 the average number of days needed to complete an unfair labor practice case was 429 in

Local Relations Commission and 637 in Central Labor Relations Commission (Table 6.6 and 6.7). Such a long delay makes the function of the Labor Relations Commission almost meaningless in the sense of giving effective administrative remedies to the unions. The unions therefore, rely on the courts for provisional order. Why does Labor Relations Commission take such a long time for its decision? Hanami pointed out the multiple reasons for the delay and they are:

1. There is a long established practice to conduct hearing in a way that is very similar to court procedure, with lawyers participating and formal cross-examination of witnesses. In 1976 on an average, more than 10 hearing sessions were held and more than 6 witnesses were examined for each case. In an extreme case, 51 hearing sessions were held in which another 32 witnesses were examined. This situation is completely different from European labor courts where in general and on principle only one session is held for each case.
2. Intervals between each hearing are more and more prolonged.
3. It is difficult to set the dates for the public commissioners who are busy with their own work. For example, Tokyo Metropolitan Labor Relations Commission in 1976 had only 13 public members and more than 400 cases were pending.
4. The employers cause intentional delay.
5. Unions are not very eager to settle a case since they regard the appeal to the commission as another stage on which to challenge the management.
6. An adversary system is employed and lawyers for each part are involved at every level.
7. The complexity of the employer's unfair labor practice cases in recent years and the mixture of issues of rights and interests in labor disputes brought to the commission.

Although unfair labor practice cases have raised tough and complicated issues for the courts and commissions, they have not, as a whole caused serious disorder in the work places of the

TABLE 6.6
Number of Days taken for Adjustment (HLO Cases) (First Instance) 1987

Classification	*Number of Cases*			*Percentage*		
Days	*Total*	*By order of settlement*	*Withdrawal and compromise*	*Total*	*By order of settlement*	*Withdrawal and compromise*
(1)	*(2)*	*(3)*	*(4)*	*(5)*	*(6)*	*(7)*
Total	406	97	309	100	100	100
Less than 100 days	70	3	67	1.7	3	21
100-199	50	4	46	1.2	4	15
200-299	27	3	24	7	3	8
300-399	36	6	30	9	6	10
400-499	29	10	19	7	11	6
500-599	30	4	26	7	4	8
600-699	24	9	15	6	9	5
700-799	19	7	12	5	7	4
800-899	8	2	6	2	2	2
900-999	10	4	6	3	4	2
1000 and more	10.3	45	58	25	47	19

Source : CLRC, Chuo Rodo Jiho, Gogai, 1988.

TABLE 6.7
Average days needed for Adjustment First and Second Instance (HLP Cases) 1983-87

Classification	*1983*	*1984*	*1985*	*1986*	*1987*
First instance					
Total	404	771	76	867	732
By order to settlement	885	680	984	939	1176
Withdrawal and Compromise settlement	322	794	744	848	592
Second instance					
Total	1215	1134	1003	990	1024
By order to settlement	879	954	947	1296	1125
Withdrawal and Compromise settlement	1346	1187	1120	758	983

Source : CLRC, Chuo Rodo Jiho, Gogai, 1988.

firms involved. This indicates that instead of fighting the employee's discrimination by resorting to disruptive activities, the minority unions have sought review in the Labor Relations Boards and have gained redress to a considerable extent. The courts and commissions have established and developed many substantive and procedural rules which have made such disputes easier to adjudicate.

The lengthy procedures of Labor Relations Commission, serve both parties well. They are using litigation not to resolve a conflict but to demonstrate their devotion to a cause. For an employer, this sort of demonstration of an indomitable resolve to litigate a case, regardless of whether they expect to win or lose may well is for the purpose of discouraging other employees from making unfair labor practice complaints. As for the employees or the unions, when they are particularly sure that they will win, they pursue a case to higher courts not only to publicize an employer's unfairness, but also to get a governmental institution, such as a commission or the court to certify they are legitimate unions or that they have been pursuing legitimate cause.[10] Often an employer can contest the legality of Labor Relations Commission's order at three stages: District Court, High Court and Supreme Court. If the employer appeals first to the Central Labor Relations Commission and then to the court, he may have to go through five stages. Thus, it is possible for a case to take more than 10 years to reach a final settlement.

Though parties by and large approach the Labor Relations Commission only when they fail to reach an amicable settlement because it is government agency with authority, on few occasions they bring their cases without having made an effort to bargain in good faith. It means the reliance upon the "authority" of the Labor Relations Commission is just passing the buck. The parties say, "we are not responsible for the settlement since the commission said so and so". Therefore, the Labor Relations Commission dispute settlement procedure is a game, which has for its objective saving the "face" of all parties especially the "face" of the leaders *vis-a-vis* their constituents, which include union officers and members, personal managers and the directors, subsidiary companies and the parent company, as well as individual companies and the employer's organization.[11]

According to Hanami "after more than 30 years of enforcement of unfair labor practice system in Japanese industrial relations, we must admit that it has many limitations and deficiencies in promoting harmonious industrial relations, particularly in those enterprises which are facing awkward labor relations". The growing number of cases involving frequent complaints in a particular enterprise and prolonged procedure for resolving such cases is an evidence of such deficiencies in the system. Nevertheless, there is no doubt that it has introduced and established respect for the union's rights by the employer and the system is founded in firm growing in Japanese industrial relations.

The Labor Relations Adjustment Law, 1946 and Trade Union Law, 1949 regulate the procedure of dispute settlement in the Labor Relations Commission system. Dispute settlement method of Labor Relations Commission by conciliation, mediation and arbitration is similar to the western type machinery. Since Labor Relations Commission is a government agency, its procedures are more or less based on legal norms and specific standards or policies. Settlement of disputes is the second and most important function. In principle conciliation, mediation and arbitration can only be brought into use with the consent of both parties of the dispute, unless it is pubic welfare work or in the public sector.

(b) Conciliation

Conciliation is the most popular and frequently used method for settling disputes in Japan. According to ILO conciliation can be defined as "the practice by which the services of the neutral third party are used in a dispute as a means of helping the disputing parties to reduce the extent of their differences and to arrive at an amicable settlement or agreed solution". The objective of this method is to expedite settlement of disputes and to terminate work stoppages if they have already occurred. Conciliation is a method of settlement whereby a conciliator appointed by the commission works to confirm claims of both labor and management.[12]

The Labor Relations Commission appoints and keeps a panel of conciliators with the knowledge and experience to assist for the settlement of labor dispute. In the event of a dispute, the chairman of the competent Labor Relations Commission, upon the request of parties nominates conciliators from the panel. The conciliator endeavors to contact both parties, ascertain their respective points of view and assist them in arriving at a settlement. If he fails to bring settlement, he sends a report with salient facts of the case to the Labor Relations Commission. There is no specialized formal procedure for the conciliator to follow. During conciliation proceedings, parties can reach a mutual agreement (Articles 11, 23, 14 and 16 of Labor Relations Adjustment Law, 1946). Conciliation is the most favorite type of settlement procedure, because it is the most informal and the closest to the traditional Japanese method of settlement by amicable understanding.

Many times conciliation procedure serves as an auxiliary to the bargaining process. The conciliator is not like an adjudicator who is concerned with the substance of a settlement. However, today he not only acts as a helper but also plays an active role in the process of settlement. Conciliators are very conscious about public policy and they propose and persuade the parties on a particular way of settlement. Their persuasion is guided by industrial relations situations and not the legal norms.

The overall situation of labor dispute settlements in Japan is quite good. In 1989 1,721 total disputes were reported, out of which 1,057 disputes were settled. Labor and management through mutual negotiations could settle 719 (41.8%) disputes, which is really appreciable. The manner in which other disputes settled are: third party involvement—76 (10.5%), Labor Relations Commission—123 (93.9%), (Conciliation—120, Mediation—1 and Arbitration—2), Labor policy officer—1 (0.8%), other settlements 7 (5.3%) and 871 (50.6%) disputes remained pending for the next year (Table 6.1).

(c) Mediation

'Mediation' is the ancient art of peace-making. Mediation is a process by which a third party brings together the opposing groups not only to iron out the differences between them but also actively find an answer to the problems of specified proposals and alternative suggestions. Mediation can also be called as an attempt to settle disputes with the help of an outsider who assists the parties in their negotiations. It takes place on invitation or at least with the consent of both parties. The role of a mediator is very vital. He is often described as a 'confidential advisor' and 'industrial diplomate'.[13]

Mediation committee in Japan consists of tripartite representatives (equal number of labor, employer and public), who make a proposal to settle the dispute and recommend both labor and management either to accept it or not but under no circumstances can the parties be forced to accept the proposal. The chairman of the Labor Relations Commission will nominate the mediation committee. The chairman of the mediation committee is elected from among mediation committee representing the public interest.

As per Article 18 of the Labor Adjustment Law, Labor Relations Commission carries out mediation in any of the following cases:

1. Where a petition for mediation has been made to the

Labor Relations Commission by both parties concerned with dispute.

2. Where both or either one of the parties petitions mediation to the Labor Relations Commission is in accordance with the stipulations of a labor agreement.
3. Where in a case involving public welfare work a petition for mediation has been made by either party to the Labor Relations Commission.
4. Where in a case involving public welfare work or a case having great scope or involving war of a special nature and for those reasons seriously affecting the public welfare, a request for mediation has been made by the Minister of Labor (as regards the seamen, it is covered by the Seamen Law, the Minister of Transportation) or the To, Do, Pu or prefecture governor to the Labor Relations Commission.

Japanese mediation is typical in a sense that the committee not only drafts a proposal for settlement, it recommends, publishes and even may request the newspapers and radio for assistance in making them public. Often the proposal for settlement accepted by parties but later the disagreement arises over interpretation or implementation of the settlement. If such occasion arises, the parties may go for mediation committee for clarification of the interpretation or implementation and within 15 days they get clarification (Article 26, Sections 2 and 3). Special expedition and precedence in consideration is given to all mediation cases involving public welfare work.

In case of mediation the Labor Relations Commissions submit its proposal only after both the parties have reached an "understanding". It is interesting to note that parties rarely refuse to accept the Labor Relations Commission proposal, which would mean to destroy the "face" of the commissioners. Similarly, the commissions also do not submit proposal which might be rejected because they do not want to lose "face". Therefore, it seems, in actual practice, that the Labor Relations Commission system follows the tradition of amicable dispute settlement by an authority whom the parties respect and obey.[14] A commissioner should be wholly/completely familiar with the law and regulations concerning industrial relations and the settlement of industrial disputes. Hanami agrees with Ota that the success of a Japanese commissioner depends on whether both the parties have confidence in him or not, rather than his knowledge or his ability. Often the public commissioner claim parties confidence because the law requires the parties consent on his appointment like on the appointment of an arbitrator in USA. Public commissioners need to maintain their independence from government to remove union's suspicion.

(d) Arbitration

Arbitration can be distinguished from conciliation and mediation not only by the fact that its decision is binding on the parties but also by its different approach and spirit.[15] Arbitration can be said as a means of securing an award on a conflict issue by reference to a third party. According to Kurt Braun, "the objective of arbitration is not compromise . . . but adjudication, though parties are at liberty to compromise". In Japan, "arbitration is a method of settlement where by arbitration committee composed of public members offers an arbitration award, although worker and employer members may attend an arbitration award, although worker and employer members may attend the meetings of the committee and express their opinion. The arbitration award, having the same effect as collective agreements, binds both parties and brings the dispute to a final settlement".[16]

As per Article 30 of the Labor Relations Adjustment Law, the Labor Relations Commission can commence arbitration in any one of the following cases:

1. Where a petition for arbitration has been made to the labor Relations Commission by both parties concerned with dispute, and
2. Where a petition for arbitration has been made to the Labor Relations Commission by both or either one of the parties according to the labor agreement which stipulates, that the petition for arbitration by the Labor Relations Commission must be made.

The arbitration of a labor dispute by the Labor Relations

Commission is carried out by setting up the arbitration committee consisting three arbitration committeemen. The chairman of Labor Relations Commission will nominate arbitration committeemen from among the members or the special adjustment committeemen representing the public interest of the Labor Relations Commission, who have been selected with the agreement of the parties concerned. The chairman is being selected from among the public interest of the Labor Relations Commission (Article 31). With the approval of the arbitration committee the members representing the employer and the workers, may attend the meeting and state their opinions. The decision or a written award of the arbitration committee is made by a majority of the arbitration committeemen.

It is necessary to understand one more Japanese unique character of industrial relations: that is settling disputes by compromise rather than clear cut orders. Though the law provides three types of settlement machinery, i.e. conciliation, mediation and arbitration, the parties prefer the most informal kind of settlement, i.e. conciliation, mediation is rare and arbitration is very rare in Japan.

The tendency of parties to compromise is greater the Labor Relations Commission than in the courts. Why so it is? Let me mention Hanami's findings. According to him:

1. Courts are purely judicial institutions, while Labor Relations Commission's are administrative commissions,
2. Labor Relations Commissions have greater latitude and discretion in its judgments than do the courts,
3. Labor Relations Commission's commissioners are convinced that Labor Relations Commissions should settle all cases by compromise and only when they are unable to do should they issue orders, and
4. Unlike courts, which give clear-cut judgments, the Labor Relations Commission's functions are to normalize the relationship between labor and management.

The following tables highlight the functioning of Labor

Relations Commission. The Table 6.8 deals with the number of adjustments by Labor Relations Commission based on matters involved and size of the union. Out of total 1888 cases 417 (22.01%) pertaining to wages, 299 (15.8%) labor conditions except wages, 147 (7.7%) management and personal matters, 219 (11.5%) promotion of collective bargaining, 69 (5.0%) union recognition activities, conclusion and overall revision of agreements and the effect and interpretation of agreements and others 737 (39.0%), were settled by Labor Relations Commission in 1987. The largest (35.5%) number of cases came from small unions whose strength is less than 100.

Table 6.9 deals with the number of adjustments by Labor Relations Commission based on type of industry and union size. The largest number of cases belongs to manufacturing (36.5%), service (25.4%) and Transport and Communication (25.1%). And again 52.4% cases are from small unions with less than 100 employees.

The Labor Relations Commission normally takes much time for final adjustment. Table 6.10 explains the number of days taken for final adjustment at conciliation, mediation and arbitration machinery. It indicates that in 1987, out of the 502 cases dealt 117 (23.3%) took more than two months.

The Labor Relations Commission adjustment service can be invoked only by parties with their consent. Only in disputes of public utility and essential service industries, conciliation procedure can be invoked by Labor Relations Commission's own initiative. Table 6.11 highlights the number of adjustments by Labor Relations Commission with reasons and parties. For example in 1987 out of 787 majority 727 (92.3%) request came from union, 46 (5.8%) from management, 14 (1.7%) from both and no cases from Labor Relations Commission authority. Conciliation was used in 762 (96.8%), mediation in 21 (2.6%) and arbitration in 4 (0.5%).

In Japan courts and commissions play the role of an arbitrator. A small number of cases concerning the interpretation and application of collective agreement reach the courts. The parties including Labor Relations Commission can appeal to District Court, High Court and eventually Supreme Court challenging Labor Relations Commission's orders. Table 6.12 shows the number of administrative litigations dealt

TABLE 6.8

Number of Adjustments by L.R.C., Matters for Adjustment, Union Size, 1987

Matters Adjustment	*29 and less*	*30-99*	*100-299*	*300-499*	*500-999*	*1000-4999*	*5000 above*	*Total*
(1)	*(2)*	*(3)*	*(4)*	*(5)*	*(6)*	*(7)*	*(8)*	*(9)*
Union recognition and activities	17	8	2	2	2	10	4	45
Conclusion and overall revision of agreements	2	1	2	5	3	—	1	14
The effect and interpretation of agreement	3	6	—	1	—	—	—	10
Wages :								
Wage increase	37	41(1)	38(1)	9	6(1)	17	7(3)	155(6)
Temporary Payments	45	39	26	8	11	22(1)	2	153(1)
Allowances	7	3	4	2	2	6	2(1)	26(1)
Others	16	17	9	4	5	2	1	54
Retirement allowance and pension	10	7	4	1	—	5	—	27
Dismissal and-lay off payments	—	1	—	1	—	—	—	2
Sub-Total	115	108(1)	81(1)	25	24(1)	52(1)	12(4)	417(8)
Labour conditions except wages:								
Number of working hours	33	52	12	2	3(1)	34	—	136(1)

Holidays and vacation	31	51	14	3	3	19	1	122
Changes in working conditions	2	7	5	1	—	—	—	15
Retirement age	4	4	2	—	1	3	1	15
Other labour conditions	3	3	2	1	1	—	1	11
Sub-Total	73	117	35	7	8(1)	56	3	299(1)
Management and personal matters:								
Business closure and reduction	7	2	2	—	—	5	1	17
Merger and transfer of business	1	—	—	—	—	1	—	2
Reduction of staff	5	5	—	—	—	3	—	13
Transfer of labour to another firm	9	11	3	—	3	6	1	33
Dismissal	9	7	4	3	5	7	2	37
Other mangement related human relations issues	17	9	4	2	2	11	—	45
Sub-Total	48	34	13	5	10	33	4	147
Welfare	1	—	1	—	—	—	1	3
Promotion of collective bargaining	65	54	25	11	26	29	9	219
Advance negotiation	1	—	1	—	1	2	1	6
Others	11	8	6	—	—	3	—	28
Total	336	336(1)	166(1)	56	74(2)	185(1)	35(11)	1888(1)

Source : Central Labour Relations Commission (CLRC), 1988.

TABLE 6.9

Number of Adjustments by L.R.C., Industry and Union Size-wise, 1987

Classification of Industry	*Less than 49*	*30-99*	*100-299*	*300-499*	*500-999*	*1000-4999*	*More than 5000*	*Total*
(1)	*(2)*	*(3)*	*(4)*	*(5)*	*(6)*	*(7)*	*(8)*	*(9)*
Agriculture	—	—	—	—	—	—	—	—
Forestry	—	1	—	—	—	—	—	—
Fishing	—	—	—	—	—	—	—	—
Mining	—	—	1	—	—	—	—	—
Construction	—	3	—	—	1	4	—	8
Manufacturing	74	83(1)	40(1)	12	1491)	57	8	388(3)
Electric, Gas and Water Supply	1	2	3	—	—	-	—	6
Transportation and Communication	67	62	20	5	20	20	4(1)	198(1)
Wholesale and Retail and Restaurant	10	5	9	16	6	12	—	48
Banking and Insurance	1	7	—	1	1(1)	1(1)	—	11(2)
Real Estate	5	—	1	—	—	3	—	9
Service	56	47	. 36	12	11	26	12(2)	210(2)
Public Administration	2	4	2	—	5	2	—	15
Not Classified	1	—	—	—	—	—	—	2
Grand Total	218	213(1)	112(1)	36	58(2)	128(1)	25(3)	787(8)

Source : CLRC, Chuo Rodo Jiho, Gogai, 1988.

TABLE 6.10

Number of days taken for Final Adjustment and Method of Adjustment at L.R.C. (1987)

Days	*Conciliation*		*Mediation*		*Arbitration*	
	LRC Total	*CLRC*	*LRC Total*	*CLRC*	*LRC Total*	*CLRC*
1-2	14					
3-4	34					
5-6	22		1			
7-8	33					
8-10	·		1			
11-12	24	2				
13-14	14					
15-16	33					
17-18	17	1	1			
19-20	16	1			4	
21-22	15					
23-24	12		1			
25-26	11					
27-28	22	1				
29-30	12		2			
31-32	6					
33-34	8		1			
34-36	7					
37-38	6					
39-40	10					
41-42	10					
43-44	7	1	1			
45-46	3					
47-48	5					
49-50	5					
51-52	5					
53-54	1					
55-56	1					
57-58	3					
59-60	4					
61 and above	117		3			
Total	502	6	11		4	

Note : Number of final settlement excluding withdrawal.
Source : CLRC, Chuo Rodo Jiho, Gogai, 1988.

Table 6.11
Number of Adjustments by L.R.C., Reason-wise, 1983-87

Reasons foı Adjustments		1983	1984	1985	1986	1987
(1)		(2)	(3)	(4)	(5)	(6)
Total		975 (31)	736 (15)	689 (13)	673 (8)	787 (8)
Labour Union requests:		839 (26)	694 (14)	694 (12)	623 (6)	727 (7)
Management		83 (3)	30 (1)	41 (1)	42 (2)	46 (1)
Both		27 (2)	11	3	7	14
L.R.C. Authority		26	1	1	1	—
Conciliation :						
Sub-Total		38 (7)	25	17	17	21
Labour Requests						
Labour Adj. Law	18 2	9	1	3	1	1
	18 3	13 (7)	3	6	6	19
LPELR Law	14 2	3	16	5	1	1
	14 3	6	2	2	6	—
Management Requests						
Labour Adj. Law	18 2	3	—	—	—	—
	18 3	—	—	—	—	—
LPELR Law	14 2	—	1	—	1	—

Request Both						
Labour Adj. Law	18 1	1	1	—	1	—
	18 2	—	1	—	—	—
LPELR Law	14 1	—	—	—	—	—
	14 2	—	—	—	—	—
L.R.C. Authority						
Labour Adj. Law	18 4	3	—	—	—	—
Arbitration :						
Sub-Total		7	3	3	1	4
Labour Request						
Labour Adj. Law	30 2	2	—	—	—	—
LPELR Law	15 2	1	—	2	1	—
	15 4	4	2	—	—	—
Managements Requests						
Labour Adj. Law	30 1	—	—	—	—	—
	30 2	—	—	—	—	—
LPELR Law	15 1	—	—	—	—	—
	15 2	—	—	—	—	—
L.L.R.C. Authority						
LPELR Law	15 3	—	—	—	—	—

Source : CLRC, Chuo Rodo Jiho, Gogai, 1988.

TABLE 6.12
Number of Administrative Litigation dealt by Courts against L.R.C., 1983, 1985 and 1987

Classification	L.L.R.C.			C.L.R.C.		
	1983	1985	1987	1983	1985	1987
(1)	(2)	(3)	(4)	(5)	(6)	(7)
Appeal against order at District court (First instance)						
Cases pending in court or previous year cases	45	46	39	27	37	38
New Cases:						
By Labor	1	1	1	3	1	2
By Employer	17	8	11	11	8	16
Sub-Total	18	9	12	14	9	18
Grand Total	63	55	51	41	46	56
Conclusions:						
Withdrawals and compromises:	17	12	8	6	2	13
Decisions:						
Rejection, Dismissal	9	1	7	3	10	2
Partial Revision	1	2	2		2	
Fully Revision	2	2	1			
Total Conclusions	29	17	18	9	14	15
Appeal against order at High Court (Second instance)						
Cases pending at court or previous year cases	14	7	11	1	6	7
New Cases:						
Persons concerned	7	2	8	3	12	2
L.R.C. as litigant	2	3	1		2	
Sub-Total	9	5	9	3	14	2
Grand Total	23	12	20	4	20	9

(*Contd.*)

TABLE 6.12 (Contd.)

(1)	*(2)*	*(3)*	*(4)*	*(5)*	*(6)*	*(7)*
Conclusions						
Withdrawals	4	1	2		1	1
Judgements :						
Amicably						
Dismissal						
Rejection		2	1		6	3
Partially settled	3					
Revocaton						
Grant Total	7	3	3		7	4
Appeal against order at Supreme Court (Thrid instance)						
Cases pending at Court or previous year cases	13	16	7	12	12	9
New Cases :						
Persons concerned	1	1			4	2
L.R.C. as litigant	2	1		1		
Sub-Total	3	2		1	4	2
Grand Total	16	18	7	13	16	11
Conclusions						
Withdrawals, Compromises	1	2				1
Decisions :						
Rejection, Dismissal	2	1	3		2	2
Revocation of Original Decisions		2	1		3	1
Total number of conclusions	3	5	4		5	4
Total of pendings	102	85	78	58	82	76

Source : CLRC, Chuo Rodo, Jiho, Gogai, 1988.

by courts against Labor Relations Commission's orders in 1983, 85 and 87. For example, 1987 out of 76 cases 56 (77.3%) reported to District Court, 9 (11.8%) to High Court and 11 (14.4%) to Supreme Court. Among new cases more (6) cases have been reported by the employer while only (2) cases by labor. Here again we can see large number of cases settled by way of compromise or withdrawals.

3. EMERGENCY DISPUTE SETTLEMENT MACHINERY

On few occasions the government's active intervention is called for. To settle the disputes by forcing parties to follow a system that is sponsored by the government. Normally the government in many countries interferes when:

1. Parties fail to arrive at a settlement by voluntary method,
2. There is a national emergency which requires that wheels of production should not be obstructed by frequent work stoppage,
3. The country is passing through grave economic crisis,
4. There is a grave public dissatisfaction with the existing industrial relations,
5. Industries of strategic importance are involved, and
6. Public interests are threatened.[17]

In Japan the Prime Minister may, decide on an emergency adjustment only when he deems that, because of the case being related to a public welfare work or being of a large scale or being related to work of special nature, the suspension of operation thereof arising from an act of dispute seriously threatens national economic activities or daily life of the nationals, if there exists such a threat (Article 15.2).

What is public welfare work? The Labor Relations Adjustment Law, defines public welfare work as a work which is indispensable to the daily life of the public within the following industries: transportation, posts, telegraphs and telephones, water, electricity and gas supply, medical care and public hygiene.

1. He may designate certain work-stoppage of which will seriously affect the national economy or seriously endanger the daily life of the general public—as public welfare work for a specified period of less than one year, with the approval of the Diet, and
2. He has power to make a decision of emergency adjustment if he considers that the stoppage will threaten the national economy or the life of the nation, either because the dispute is related to public work or because of its size.

Whenever the Prime Minister decides on the Emergency Adjustment, he seeks the opinion of the Central Labor Relations Commission, publicize the decision with reasons and notify the Central Labor Relations Commission and parties concern. One of the most important duties of the Central Labor Relations Commission may perform her duty through conciliation, mediation or arbitration, investigation and publication of the case and making proposals for a settlement (Article 35.2). The act of dispute is prohibited for a period of 50 days of the publication of the Emergency Adjustment. It is interesting to note that up to now; only (coal mine strike case in 1952) has been put into Emergency Adjustment.[18]

4. DISPUTE SETTLEMENT IN PUBLIC SECTOR

Like many countries, Japan too has special adequate framework to deal with public sector to ensure industrial peace. The Public Corporation Labor Relations Law provides the Public Corporation and National Enterprise Labor Relations Commission to handle the matters pertaining to the public sector. This law aims at securing the un-interrupted operation of the public corporation and national enterprise, at maximum efficiency for the promotion and protection of the public welfare, by establishing the usages and procedure of collective bargaining in order to bring out an amicable and peaceful adjustment of grievances or troubles over working conditions of employees of the Public Corporation and National Enterprise (Article 1 of Public Corporation Labor Relations Law). This demands that all parties concerned should fully exert and put maximum efforts to minimize industrial strife and secure the amiable settlement.

The Public Corporation and National Enterprise Labor Relations Commission is formed by the Ministry of Labor, which consists of seven commissioners representing the public interest, five commissioners representing the Public Corporation and five commissioners representing the workers. The worker's representatives are appointed from among those recommended by the unions and employer's representatives from among those recommended by the Public Corporation and National Enterprise. The public members are appointed from among those candidates chosen by the Labor Minister after he has heard the opinions of both labor and the employer members. The chairman will be elected by the commissioners from among the public commissioners.

The functions of this commission are almost the same as those of Labor Relations Commission (conciliation, mediation and arbitration procedures). However, the commission may start mediation on its own initiative with or without the application of one of the parties or upon the request of the relevant minister and may also start arbitration of its own initiative or upon the request of the relevant minister or on the application of one of the parties if two months have passed since mediation began the dispute is still not settled.

Article 30 of the Public Corporation, Labor Relations Law, provides for the establishment of Local Mediation Commissions to take care of the mediation business locally. There are 9 Local Mediation Commissions. The Ministry of Labor appoints the mediation committeemen of Local Mediation Commissions with the agreement of the commission.

There is no special commission for the adjudication of unfair labor practice cases and dispute settlement in local public enterprise and so the Labor Relations Commission has the same function as the Labor Relations Commission. Unfair labor practice cases are handled by the commission in the first instance and an appeal against an order can only be to the courts for there is no administrative review procedure as there is in the private sector to the Central Labor Relations Commission.[19]

5. DISPUTE RESOLUTION THROUGH COURTS

The ultimate legal remedy for the settlement of an unresolved dispute is law court or adjudication. Adjudication involves intervention in the dispute by a third party appointed by the government for the purpose of settlement. In Japan, Labor Relations Commission as well as the law courts have jurisdiction over the legal problems concerning labor. There is no system of labor courts in Japan and so the ordinary courts, which are not specialized in labor problems, have to handle collective labor relations. Collective Labor Law in Japan has its foundation on the three fundamental worker's rights. It is divided into, the law regarding trade union organization, the law of collective bargaining and the law governing action in the course of disputes. The constitutional guarantee of these rights reveals another characteristic of Japanese collective Labor Law, i.e. that almost everything concerning organization; bargaining or labor dispute comes under the jurisdiction of the courts. As mentioned earlier the disputes of 'interest' between unions and employers are taken care of by the Labor Relations Commission—conciliation, mediation and arbitration, while disputes of 'vested rights' between employer and worker or union by the courts. The Labor Relations Commission plays a semi-judicial or adjudicatory role when it deals with unfair labor practice cases. It investigates the charges against the employer, finds facts based on the evidence and issues orders enforced by the punishment for violation.

In Japan the distinction between conflict of vested rights and conflict of interest has not been as clear as in the west. The Japanese industrial relations are not concerned with exact definition of the rights and obligations of the parties in a dispute. The provisions in collective bargaining agreements are obscure. On many occasions parties themselves find it very difficult to determine whether a conflict concerning the provision of a collective agreement is a conflict of vested right or a conflict of interest. Thus it is common for the parties to negotiate before they can agree on the meaning of certain clauses in the collective agreement. In such cases if agreement is not reached the dispute may be brought to the court. One might say that in Japanese industrial relations any problem or disagreement between labor and management can be dealt with either by formal collective bargaining or through the courts. These two approaches to dispute settlement are never clearly distinguished and can be pursued simultaneously.[20] I shall discuss the overlapping jurisdiction of the Labor Relations Commission and courts later in this chapter.

In the recent years there has been an increase in the number of cases at Japanese courts specially, to seek temporary injunctions. It is worth referring here, Matsuda's attempt in highlighting conflict resolution in the Japanese courts. One can notice three features of conflict resolution in the courts:

1. The emergence and predominance of provisional disposition orders,
2. The resolution of conflicts over the interpretation and application of collective agreements which are small in number, and
3. Resolution of conflicts arising out of an employment contract—are also small number.[21]

Table 6.13 highlights the number of civil cases completed by District Courts by manner of settlement. For example in 1988 out of 667 settled cases 617 belong to labor, 24 to employer and 26 others. Large (317) settlements reached by way of compromise, 172 dismissals and withdrawals, 171 (100 appeals accepted and 71 appeals rejected) settlements and only 7 determined and orders sought.

(a) Provisional Disposition Orders

A petition for a provisional order is granted when the danger to the petitioner is imminent that the plaintiff in litigation can not wait for the final decision and also when he is likely to win the case on merit. In Japan there is no special procedure or special labor courts like for example in India, however, the provisional disposition orders in civil courts has merged and become predominant for resolving both individual and collective labor disputes.

Japanese courts grant provisional orders as a temporary relief and encourage the parties for voluntary settlement, not as

TABLE 6.13
The Number of Civil Cases Completed at District Courts, by Manner of Settlement, 1984-88

Year	1984				1985				1986				1987				1988			
Plaintiff	T	L	E	O	T	L	E	O	T	L	E	O	T	L	E	O	T	L	E	O
(1)	(2)	(3)	(4)	(5)	(6)	(7)	(8)	(9)	(10)	(11)	(12)	(13)	(14)	(15)	(16)	(17)	(18)	(19)	(20)	(21)
Settlement (Total)	700	627	45	28	887	623	244	20	706	629	58	19	1240	675	550	15	667	617	24	26
Settlement	200	188	6	6	405	191	210	4	201	191	6	4	182	172	5	5	171	164	4	3
Appeal Accepted	129	125	2	2	322	111	209	2	145	137	5	3	117	110	4	3	100	95	3	2
Appeal Rejected	71	63	4	4	83	80	1	2	56	54	1	1	65	62	1	2	71	69	1	1
Determination and orders sought	6	6	0	0	14	9	5	0	4	4	0	0	4	4	0	0	7	6	0	1
Compromise	291	273	8	10	273	263	8	2	227	257	17	3	377	301	72	4	317	294	12	11
Dismissals and Withdrawals	203	160	31	12	195	160	21	14	224	117	35	12	677	198	473	6	172	153	8	11
Pending	1969	1100	832	37	1691	1025	626	40	1730	1102	577	40	1207	1103	54	50	1275	1171	62	42

T = Total L = Labour E = Employer O = Others

Sources : Hoso Jiho (Layers Association Journal), Vol. 41, No. 8, 1989.

a permanent resolution of conflict. Often employees seek to remove sit-down strikers from the company premises. Today the provisional orders have become vital for resolving labor dispute as they protect the loss of employment and wage of an employee. The court enjoys discretion in the way it chooses to handle cases. Why provisional order procedure has been used often? The reasons are simple. Because the provisional order procedure:

1. Encourages voluntary settlement (bargain in good faith),
2. Provides temporary relief,
3. Takes less time than required for suit on merit, and
4. Is simple and cheap.

On the contrary two major objections have been raised by critics:

1. Provisional order procedure by court discourage efforts toward voluntary settlement of dispute through collective bargaining as parties rely more on the courts.
2. Provision order procedure is not necessarily the most appropriate method for resolving all types of labor conflicts before court in the form of a dispute over vested rights.

The chances are great that the court will fail to quickly and appropriately reach and resolve the real issue in the case. In spite of these weakness provisional disposition orders have become dominant. Out of total civil suits on labor that are brought to district courts every year, about-half seeks a provisional disposition order (Table 6.14).

(b) Interpretational Application of Collective Agreements

It is interesting to note that the Japanese courts receive every small number of cases concerning interpretation and application of collective agreements. Matsuda found that out of more than 250 civil and administrative cases at all court levels reported in various law journals in 1976, only 12 involved a

TABLE 6.14
General Review of Civil and Administrative Cases Related to Labour Relations

Year	*1980*	*1982*	*1984*	*1986*	*1988*
Total					
New Cases	1554	3314	1903	2172	2045
Disposed	2003	2694	2002	2093	2021
Pending	2572	3274	2067	2858	2363
Civil Cases					
Normal Cases					
New Cases	777	2192	901	1043	1158
Disposed	793	1560	1927	1034	1093
Pending	1570	2245	2207	1981	1556
Provisional					
Disposed:					
New Cases	638	723	660	606	604
Disposed	759	703	728	722	640
Pending	424	429	366	432	325
Provisional					
Seizure					
New Cases	204	188	113	115	74
Disposed	204	183	117	113	72
Pending	4	11	4	3	4
Administrative Cases :					
Litigation :					
New cases	172	191	186	182	191
Disposed	223	206	214	203	285
Pending	556	523	46	423	453
Emergency Corder :					
New Cases	14	9	20	16	10
Disposed	17	9	13	13	9
Pending	9	6	16	12	21
Stoppage :					
New Cases	4	11	3	10	8
Dosposed	7	13	3	8	8
Pending	9	10	6	7	4

Source : Hosu Jiho (*Lawyers Association Journal*), Vol. 41, No. 8, 1989.

question arising out of collective agreement. In 5 of the 12, the issue was the interpretation and application of a clause providing for union-management "consultation on personnel matters", in a union-shop clause was the subject of dispute and in the rest the court was being asked to clarify wage provision, a re-employment agreement or a memorandum on promotion. The Table 6.14 shows the general review of civil and administrative cases related to labor relations. The factors responsible for small number of cases are:

1. The important feature of Japanese collective agreement, that they include a relatively large number of so-called "institutional" or "organizational" provisions, such as a consultation or a "meet-and-confer clause" as opposed to "normative" provisions that set out certain standards that each party must observe.
2. Japanese collective agreements also provide with the exception of the provisions on wages and hours, the procedural rules rather than substantive norms to be used in conflict resolution. This reflects the unwillingness of unions and managements to define in too much detail the standards to be applied to the working conditions of individual employees.
3. An employee finds it difficult to raise questions concerning the interpretation and application of a collective agreement unless an employer completely ignores consultation provisions.
4. Even when a conflict arises over the interpretation and application, the court will probably not be able to reach and deal with the underlying issue that prompted the dispute.

We can be therefore, convinced that in Japanese industrial relations, union-management consultation has a vital role in settling conflicts or question pertaining to interpretation and application of collective agreements. It is clear that parties rely more on consultation due to the following reasons:

1. The unwillingness of parties to set-up any clear

standards or rules that would automatically be applied in the day-to-day affairs of the employer-employee relations.

2. Grievance procedure are not popular, they are seldom used because employees are extremely reluctant to confront their foremen or supervisors individually even with union representatives presence.
3. From the employers' standpoint, too, preventing grievances by making use of the consultation system is desirable.
4. Consultation system serves the same goal as grievance procedure and provides an opportunity to maintain good personal relations between supervisors and workers.

The court remedies under Japanese provisional order procedure, have not been confined to the conventional ones available in a civil procedure, but have been expanded to include such orders as reinstatement of discharged employees, return of transferred employees to their previous positions, resumption of negotiations on a particular subject and revocation of almost every kind of employer decision including employee discipline.

(c) Employment Contract Conflicts

It is believed that Japanese people often neglect the binding character of a contract; universal standards for clear cut decisions are not popular in Japan. They rely more on personal relationship of mutual trust. Individual Labor Law has its constitutional basis in Article 27, section 2 of 1946 constitution of Japan, which provides that standards for wage, hours, rest and other working conditions shall be fixed by law. Apart from this constitutional requirement, individual relations between employers and employees are governed by the civil law rules on contract of employment-form and content, the legal capacity to conclude contracts.

As mentioned earlier traditionally labor litigations at courts are unpopular in Japanese industrial relations. More and more cases were reported by minority unions alleging discriminatory treatment and charging employers with breach of contract or violation of the rules of employment. This indicates that the courts have become familiar as a substitute for grievance machinery.

About 1,300 civil cases on labor have been brought at district courts every year since 1975-80. The vast majority of them or more than 95% are suits against employers, of which about 45% are filed by discharged employees. Among the cases that the district courts decide, employee discharge is the issue in more than 60% of the suits against employers.

Table 6.15 shows the number of civil cases according to the nature, brought by labor and employer and Table 6.16 deals with request pattern and provisional disposition. Table 6.15 shows that in 1988 out of 735 suits 685 (93.1%) suits are against employer by labor while only 50 (6.8%) suits are against labor by employer. Out of 685 majority 400 (58.3%) related to wages, 150 (21.8%) to reinstatement and 135 (19.7%) are others. Therefore, it is concluded that the rate of compromise or withdrawal is much lower in discharge cases than the dispute is

TABLE 6.15

The Number of Civil Cases According to Nature, Brought by Labour and Employer to District Court, 1984-88

Year	*1984*	*1985*	*1986*	*1987*	*1988*
New Cases	671	609	745	723	735
Plaintiff—Labour Defendant—Employer:					
Total	618	548	706	679	685
Reinstatement	213	165	178	194	150
Wages	374	334	426	405	400
Others	31	49	100	50	135
Plaintiff—Employer Defendant—Labour:					
Reinstatement and Compensation for damage	29	38	20	20	32
Others (Invalid of dismissal cases)	24	23	19	24	18

Source : Hose Jiho (*Lawyers Association Journal*), Vol. 41, No. 8, 1989.

TABLE 6.16

The Number of Civil Cases based on Request Pattern at District Court, Provisional Disposition, 1984-88

Year	*1984*	*1985*	*1986*	*1987*	*1988*
Total New Cases	598	517	735	671	518
Plaintiff—Labour Defendant—Employer:					
Total	555	414	692	637	490
Reinstatement	352	303	378	480	318
Wages	148	126	141	94	90
Others	55	65	173	63	87
Plaintiff—Employer Defendant—Labour:					
Prohibited for enterance etc.	31	15	29	22	15
Others (Pending)	12	8	14	12	31

Source : Hose Jiho (*Lawyers Association Journal*), Vol. 41, No. 8, 1989.

over any other issue.[22] Some other findings are also worth mentioning:

1. The percentage of discharge cases as a proportion of all cases filed against employer, has been declining recently.
2. The number of cases has been increasing where wages or other payment due, such as pay for overtime are the issues.
3. The steady increase in cases where an employer's order of transfer or discipline short of discipline discharge is challenged.
4. The number of damage suits against employers, brought by employee or unions on the ground of either breach of contract or breach still not high.
5. By and large employees are reluctant to go against their employers to courts except in case of discharge.

The Japanese courts respecting the idea of natural justice have favored employees in most cases. Employees are in fact better off under individual employment contracts or the rules of employment, even without a collective agreement, than they would be without contracts or rules. On many occasions the employee or the union brings their claims to court to strengthen the position and get a government acknowledgement of the employer's unfairness. The court is a stage for challenges. When a dispute is brought to Labor Relations Commission or court, these agencies are supposed to provide legal judgment. In case of courts they have to apply labor laws, while Labor Relations Commissions have to issue a policy decision which is determined by the spirit of the labor law. The principles of labor law are fundamentally Western natured. Often these principles are quite different from the usual standards of behaviors of the parties in Japanese industrial relations. In Japanese industrial relations, the role of labor law as a norm of action is minor one. The laws are never regarded as guide by whom behavior is regulated. Japanese unions fight for rights, which stimulate a consciousness of rights among workers. The settlement of almost all disputes by the Labor Relations Commission and courts are based on universal norms, i.e. rights and obligations of both parties.[23]

6. CONTROVERSY OVER THE JURISDICTION OF LABOR RELATIONS COMMISSIONS COURTS

We have already noted that the Labor Relations Commissions as well as legal courts have jurisdiction to handle the problems of labor in Japan. The orders of Labor Relations Commission and decisions of courts are very confusing. There is no doubt that these institutions have influenced the process of dispute settlement machinery. However, there is a controversy on the question of their jurisdiction. The relation between Labor Relations Commission and court in the field of industrial relations is complicated. Firstly, in the case of unfair labor practice cases, the functions of the Labor Relations Commission and courts overlap and secondly, the courts have the job of reviewing the commission's orders and this function seems to overlap with the existing review of the local commission's orders by the Central Labor Relations Commission. As said earlier Labor Relations Commission is semi-judicial and an administrative agency, which applies more flexible social norms. The courts need strictly to follow legal norms. Practically courts find it difficult to follow legal approach due to the nature of dispute. The disputes are settled often by going beyond legal norms.

The unfair labor practice cases can be brought before Labor Relations Commission or the court according to the wishes of the parties. The courts will judge the merits of the case from the stand point whether or not the worker's rights to organize has been violated. The Labor Relations Commissions are able to handle such cases more effectively, as they can issue any kind of order, not only legal remedies but also remedies such as ordering the employer to refrain from interfering in the administration of the union or ordering him to bargain with the union.

The procedure followed in Labor Relations Commission and courts are different. The original objective of the Labor Relations Commission is to provide more informal, more flexible, simpler, quicker and cheaper solution than court. The actual procedure followed by Labor Relations Commission is similar to that of the court. Since Labor Relations Commission's decisions are subject to judicial review, commissions are very cautious in their actions which would cause delay. It is criticized in case of judicial review, that courts do not understand the meaning of the administrative relief provided by commission. On many occasions the labor Relations Commission has challenged the court's stand. Recently, the Supreme Court had accepted the Commissions argument.[24]

Notes and References

1. Momoria, C.B. and Momoria, B., Dynamics of Industrial Relations in India, Himalaya Publishing House, Bombay, 1986, p. 272.
2. Grievance Arbitration: The submission of labor grievance to an impartial arbitrator for final determination. Sometimes they called arbitration of 'rights'. Grievances may involve a wide variety of issues. The arbitrator determines the meaning of the contract and clarifies and interprets its terms. Jurisdiction of the arbitrator is sometimes restricted to those disputes which involve the interpretation or application of the contract. Increasinglv, arbitrators are required to resolve issues involving the application of various public labor laws, such as unfair labor practices and charges of employment discrimination. Arbitration, in most contracts, is the last step in the grievance procedure.

3. Hanami, T.A., Labor Relations in Japan, Today, Kodansha International Ltd., Tokyo, 1978, p. 203.
4. Blanpain, R. (Ed), International Encyclopedia for Labor Law and Industrial Relations, Vol. 7 (Japan section is written by Hanami, T.A.) Kluwer Law and Taxation Publishers, The Netherlands, 1985, p. 46.
5. The law courts are only supposed to deal with disputes of vested rights but industrial disputes often simply can not be distinguished either as disputes of vested rights or as disputes of interest. The same dispute can be regarded both as one of rights and as one of interest. When a dispute arises about a wage claim by the union, and there is a relevant collective agreement, the union's demand could be settled by interpreting the appropriate provision. However, it is often the case that the interpretation of the provision is not really the issue; but that the union's real interest is the amount of wages to be paid in future. A few bargaining issues can be claimed as legal rights because of the peculiar legal construction of the rights to organize in Japan. Thus the courts are frequently required to settle cases by conciliation rather than by decision, not only because of the general preference of the Japanese for settling disputes by reconciliation, but also because of the very nature of industrial dispute.
6. Refer Taishiro Shirai (Ed)., Contemporary of Industrial Relations in Japan, University of Wisconsin Press Ltd., Wisconsin, 1983, (article by Matsudas: Conflict Resolution), p. 195 for a table dealing with distribution of labor disputes, by manner of settlement).
7. Rodosho, Roseikyokn, 1979, pp. 216 and 231 as quoted by Taishro Shriai, Contemporary Industrial Relations in Japan.
8. Refer Blanpain, R. (Ed.), International Encyclopedia for Labor Law and Industrial Relations, pp. 120-22.
9. Taishiro Shirai (Ed), *op. cit.*, p. 172.
10. *Ibid.*, p. 184.
11. Hanami, T.A., *op. cit.*, p. 208.
12. Kagawa, Kozo, Introduction to Japanese Labor Law, p. 60.
13. Momoria, C.B. and Momoria, B., *op. cit.*, 566.
14. Hanami, T.A., *op. cit.*, p. 206.
15. Pigou, A.C., Economic Welfare, p. 607 as quoted by Momoria's.
16. Kagawa Kozo., *op. cit.*, p. 60.
17. Momoria, C.B. and Momoria B., *op. cit.*, p. 595.
18. Kagawa, Kozo., *op. cit.*, p. 61.
19. Taishiro, Shirai (Ed.), *op. cit.*, p. 159.
20. Refer Hanami, T.A., Labor Relations in Japan, for a case which illustrates a typical obscure provision which led a dispute, p. 211.
21. Taishiro, Shirai (Ed.), *op. cit.*, p. 184.
22. *Ibid.*, p. 190.
23. Hanami, T.A., *op. cit.*, pp. 216-17.
24. Taishiro, Shirai (Ed.), *op. cit.*, p. 161.

7

Comparative Industrial Relations in Japan and India : A General View

1. INDUSTRIAL RELATIONS IN INDIA

My original intention for this book was only to describe Japanese Industrial Relations. However, in the process of writing I considered the necessity of this chapter in order to stimulate thinking. As I said earlier, it is not my intention to say which system is the best, but my assessment might help the readers to draw their own conclusions. Let us review in short the Indian industrial relations system, to equip and acquaint the non-Indian readers with minimal knowledge. The important basis of comparison is on the concept of employment, trade union and wage system and other aspects are also dealt.

Indian industrial relations have been influenced by social, economical and political factors. After World War II Indian industrial relations assumed a new dimension. An important character of industrial relations in the post-independence period was the change, in government's attitude towards labor and their problems. Many labor laws were enacted to protect the interest of industrial worker. At present the plant level industrial relations has become highly regulated and to some extent it is dominated by legal laws. The government made efforts to promote a bipartite collective bargaining and there are many instances of companies having a harmonious and strong bipartite relationship.

Due to increase in the modernization of Indian industries, today the recruits to industry need to have appropriate skills and qualifications, necessary for the job unlike their counterpart in the past. The large number of workforce constitutes the migrants from rural area. The new industrial worker's educational background and aspirations are much higher than those of his predecessors. They prefer to stay on an industry and improve their prospects. This indicates their commitment to work.

One of the major problems of the Indian trade union movement is the fragmentation of unions. Several unions associated with different political parties and groups have entered the national scene. This multi-unionism has posed a serious threat to the industrial harmony in India.

Labor legislation is another important area which has a great impact on the industrial relations system and has been instrumental in shaping the course of industrialization in India. In India establishment of social justice has been the guiding principle in the development of labor legislation. Broadly speaking there are three objectives of labor legislations: 1. Protect workers from exploitation 2. Strengthen industrial relations, and 3. Provide machinery for settling industrial disputes and welfare of workers.

Worker's participation is another issue of Indian industrial relations. This concept of worker's participation emerged within the frame work of the tripartite system of labor-management relations in India. The three major 'actors' of Indian labor-management relations are the government, the employer and the employee. The issue of worker's participation has great relevance in the Indian industrial relations scene, because it has emerged as a measure for promoting harmony between labor and management. The government with its concern for social justice plays a vital role in the shaping of labor-management relations and policies.

The government has played a major and dual role, one as an initiator of policy and other as an employer or owner of large public sector. On the industrial relations front, to protect weak employee the government enacted a variety of labor laws. These laws have not only covered rights and privileges but also guaranteed certain level of income and better conditions of working environment. The government is also trying to build bridge of partnership through the various schemes of participation between the management and the employee.

The First Five Year Plan stated that the worker's rights of association, organization and collective bargaining has to be accepted without reservation as a fundamental basis for mutually satisfactory relationship. Due to imperative political and economic factors the state could not encourage voluntary negotiations. Instead it favored to refer disputes to an arbitrator or an adjudicator, if parties fail to reach a mutually acceptable agreement. In 1952 collective bargaining was introduced in India. Collective bargaining agreements are concluded at plant level, industry and national level theoretically but it has not yet decentralized beyond the plant level.

According to the Industrial Amendment Bill, 1982, no employer, workmen or trade union can commit any unfair labor practices. The party committing such a practice shall be punishable with imprisonment. The Bill prescribes a long list of unfair labor practices for each party.

The industrial relations scene in India has not been very encouraging over the years due to industrial unrest. Since labor falls in the concurrent list, the state government also passes their own labor laws. The Industrial Disputes Act, 1947 is a backbone to promote industrial peace. It provides dispute settlement machinery. The following authorities are named for the purpose of investigation and settlement of disputes: Works Committee, Conciliation Officer, Board of Conciliation, Court of Inquiry, Voluntary Arbitration and Adjudication (Labor Court, Industrial Tribunal and National Tribunal).

2. CONCEPT OF EMPLOYMENT, TRADE UNION AND WAGE SYSTEM IN JAPAN AND INDIA

(a) Different Meaning of Employment

Indian labor 'partially committed worker', one who looks at industrial employment as something permanent but he maintains his contact with his village, while the Japanese worker 'specifically committed worker', who is permanently attached to a particular occupation. Unlike in India, we find in Japan discipline and devotion to work on the part of worker and a degree of paternalism on the part of management. The Japanese worker is educated, skilled, more loyal and cooperative than the Indian worker. These features have great value which cannot be easily measured in terms of money.

Under life time employment system in Japan, it is the responsibility of private enterprise to assure employment, in a sense granting life time membership in the company. It is my impression that life time employment practice is not forced either by labor law or by contract but widely accepted and applied by employees and managements for their mutual benefit. For the Japanese worker, the company itself is occupation and life. In Japan's highly structured labor market, with its seniority wage (nenko) system, the worker's basic interest particularly in their employment, income security and opportunities to advance, depends on the prosperity of his company. The Japanese worker often stays in the same enterprise until retirement. In contrast the degree of commitment of Indian worker is not as high as would be desirable even though he is provided the living wage, satisfactory working conditions and security of employment. There is high labor turnover at least in medium and small industries than in Japan. In my earlier study I found that 76.12% of Indian worker's first expectation from the management was higher wage and second bonus (48.39%).[1] This suggests the higher expectations in terms of quality of life and standard of living, which necessarily results in the pressure for more wages. Therefore, wage issues are a major concern in Indian industrial relations.

Whenever Indian companies face a recession, they often reduce their production by decreasing the input of factors of production, including labor causing unemployment. It is a matter of regret that for many Indian companies' worker is just a means of earning, so they kick out the worker during a slump and call them back when they need. However, in recent times it has changed. In India it is the government's responsibility (for example, Employment Guarantee Scheme of Maharashtra) to take care of workers who are no longer needed by providing unemployment benefits.[2] Such a system is harmful to the economy and contributes heavy financial burden to the government. On the other hand as I indicated earlier in Japan, managements consider it as their responsibility to assure employment and go to great length to keep their employees working even during recession avoiding dismissal, by resorting to various employment adjustment mechanisms such as: suspension of new recruitment, decrease in overtime working hours, a temporary rest with pay and reallocation and transfer of workers. By providing employment security the employer acts as a father who recognizes his child as a permanent member of his family and in turn worker offers unlimited commitment and loyalty to his employer.[3] If the management faces an inevitable problem of surplus labor, it will look for volunteers to retire rather than dismissals and on many occasions provide alternative opportunities for employment with different companies or public institutions.

The strength of Japanese culture of production is seen to be based on its powerful socio-cultural support system of people's deep love and concern for their nation, family ethos of enterprises and social harmony. Spiritual orientation of people and a strong climate of cooperation amongst production actors, i.e. industry, trade, labor and government is high. India needs such productivity culture and overcome barriers such as parochial divisiveness, defective socialization and spiritual malasie.[4]

Blue-collar workers in the large firms in Japan resemble white-collar workers in India, particularly in respect of wages, fringe benefits, labor mobility and prospects for promotion.

It is widely accepted that the Japanese workers perform much better than the workers in India and industrialized nations. For example, their attendance rate is very high and labor turnover is very low. It is therefore, evident that Japanese managements have utilized their workers successfully and in a most efficient manner.

(b) Different Meaning of Wage System

Employees' wage in any country is governed by various factors, some controlled by the employer and some by the external constraints. The wages that a company is willing to pay depend on its philosophy, its capacity to pay, its competitive position and its ability to attract and retain work force by factors other than that of wage alone.[5] On many occasions the companies face problems of recessions. It is interesting to see the way they confront with much an unpleasant situation. Generally the Indian companies go for traditional method i.e. reduction in the input of factors of production including labor, resulting unemployment and loss of wages. These companies in unanimity strongly criticize that their workers are unwilling to exert more to improve productivity.[6] By decreasing the number of workers they're able to continue to pay dividends to share-holders and bonuses to company executives.[7] In fact such companies take pride that they can continue to pay dividends even during recession and while workers are laid off. The philosophy of such company exhibits that they exist for the sake of stock-holders and consider the worker just as means of production. Indian industrial relation is vested in terms of profits, dividends and preoccupied with wages, bonuses and allowances. This is a big philosophical difference between Indian and Japanese companies.

In contract the Japanese company's philosophy of wage depends on its sincere attempt to retain a work force and pay wage rather than its capacity to pay. The companies follow egalitarian philosophy in which the worker, employer and shareholder benefit in the long-run. The companies are considered as a community of interest for employees and not the shareholders and to a greater extent the company's policies are influenced by the company executives rather than the shareholders. To them profits are secondary while the workers' interest is primary.

The Japanese wage system differs from that of India and exhibits a unique character.[8] One of the characteristics of the Japanese wage system is the distinction between the portion earned for one's work and the portion paid by virtue of just being an employee. The Security of Wage Payment Act, 1975 protects the payment of wages and other monetary interest of employee in the case of their employer's insolvency. When there are cases of insolvency, the civil law gives priority to wage claims against other claims. Wages in Japan are accepted as permanent and lasting for the employee's entire career. Japanese companies rarely lay off workers even during severe periods of recession, because they exist for the sake of their workers rather than stock-holders. They would reduce if necessary, halt dividends or bonuses and even cut management salaries in order to retain their workers. They try to overcome a recession through the adjustment of margin of profits and dividends. For Japanese companies workers are more than just means of their earnings, they are assets having the technology and information on which business runs.

I firmly agree with Odawara,[9] that Japanese companies have found that the 'no-layoff policy pays off'. Workers who enjoy job security even during the period of severe recession, are more loyal and cooperative with their company and loyal workers are apt to be more productive. This loyalty is a very natural response originating from a feeling of gratitude to the company. It is a mistake to interpret it as a feudalistic attitude. In the long-run the no-lay-off policy brings greater profits and larger dividends. At the same time the company can achieve its social responsibility to ensure continuity of employment of workers. Dividends and bonuses should be paid only when a company is making a profit. This Japanese concept of profit is in line with profit and loss principle and competition principle of capitalism. It is no exaggeration to say that Japanese companies are more welfare and social justice-oriented and much closed to the principle of true economic democracy than the Indian companies.

(c) Different meaning of Labor Union

As I have indicated earlier, the third most distinct

difference between Japanese and Indian industrial relations is organization and behaviors of unions. The unionism in one country is not comparable to that of another country because of varying approaches, roles and functions assumed by it. Unions in India and Japan are non-revolutionary. They can be considered as reformist unions based on industrial democracy, those which aim at the preservation of the capitalist society and the maintenance of usual employer-employee relationship and competitive production. They seek no comprehensive change. Indian unions are similar the 'Business Unions' while Japanese unions are 'Friendly or Uplift Unions'. On the one hand Japanese unions' political activities seem to be ideologically highly leftist in tone, yet on the other hand in their dealing with managements especially at the enterprise level, they appear to be quite submissive, cooperative and practical. The picture is completely different in India where unions are not so friendly.

The Indian unions are craft-based, industry-wise and general union, unlike the Japanese unions. India has unions of blue-collar and white-collar workers, while Japan does not make such differences. Many Indian unions are not affiliated to an industry level or national federations. They are thus like Japanese enterprise union, independent local unions centered on a particular plant or a multi-plant organization. Indian unions are characterized by a three-tier structure, the national, the state and the unit level, where the policies flow down-wards from the top. The state level units are generally more influential. In contrast most Japanese unions are organized at the enterprise level. Though 72% of the enterprise unions are affiliated with some type of federations, sovereignty is retained almost exclusively at the local enterprise union. Indian unions are horizontal in character and are job-based, industry-wise national organizations, while Japanese unions are vertical and enterprise-based.

The success of a union depends upon certain pre-requisites such as:

- enlightened attitude of labor force,
- a well defined constitution and objectives, and
- a honest leader.

which Japanese unions I think possess. For many scholars Japanese unions are weak, feudalistic, friendly and more cooperative with management, while horizontal, job-based and industry-wise national organizations are considered to be strong and superior with more bargaining power. Why then does Japanese enterprise unionism still exist? To me the main reasons are: firstly enterprise unions are suitable in protecting the interest of Japanese worker under prevailing life time employment practice; secondly, Japanese Industrial Relation has been amicable under enterprise union, in which workers are more cooperative with their enterprise.

The Japanese enterprise unions unlike Indian unions reinforce the worker's feeling that his fortunes are tied to those of his company, motivating him to work hard and increase efficiency, which has far reaching effects. The wage demands are always tied to the productivity and are determined on the basis of the company, unlike India, where unions normally pressurize and demand equal pay for all members doing the same job. Since the Indian worker does not feel that his fortunes are intertwined with his company, he is least interested in increasing his efficiency. In such cases workers in relatively unproductive companies even get the same wage as worker in a more productive company. This puts a tremendous burden on the less efficient companies, they even face insolvency. Thus I can safely say that Indian unions do not seem to follow the principle of competition. Generally the unions are big, strong and nationally organized, as a result of which the companies are often unable to cope up with their labor unions.

The Japanese unions which are vertical enterprise unions can not make unreasonable demands because, the Japanese system puts the unions in direct competition with one another, and while Indian unions are monopolistic organizations where the competition mechanism does not operate. India has a different and startling picture. In the private organized sector on an average, a per capita wage is approximately three/four times higher than the national per capita wages.[10] In labor surplus Indian economy, once a worker is in organized sector, his wages and other benefits soar irrespective of productivity. In India there are no proper guidelines and wage increases are often the result of union bargaining strength on many occasions than productivity, profitability, increased cost of living and governm‿nt regulation. Wages in Japan are determined through bargaining mainly at enterprise level, thus the differentials caused by differences in the size of enterprise and regional differences are common. It is true that Japanese wages have shown constant increase, not because of union pressure like in India but because of modernization, rationalization, high quality of labor force, high adaptability to new techniques, high level education, stable and harmonious labor-management relations, limited disputes, low absenteeism, etc. Further more Japanese workers unlike India workers are not much interested in knowing what the other company pays. He is concerned about himself and his company.

The most unique nature of a Japanese union is the spirit of cooperation. Since the fortune of workers and company is interdependent, unions and managements face challenge with competing companies jointly. Japanese companies and unions function on the basis of principle of competition, which is a key for success in free market regime and sustain capitalistic dynamism. Indian companies and unions do not follow these principles of cooperation and competition.

3. SIMILARITIES AND DIFFERENCES BETWEEN JAPAN AND INDIA

Japan and India started industrializing about the same time in the middle of the nineteenth century. Japan was an independent nation and homogeneous culturally, while India was under British rule with heterogeneous character.

(a) Labor Laws

Most of the major labor law legislations are enacted shortly after World War. II and amended later both in India and Japan. In Japan the legislations include the Trade Union Law, which are often called the three major labor laws. Other laws which were introduced later are the Labor Safety and Hygiene Law of 1972, the Employment Measures Law of 1966, the Vocational Training Law of 1969, the Employment Insurance Law of 1974, the Workmen's Compensation Law of 1947, the Worker's Asset

Building Promotion Law of 1971, the law concerning the Guarantee of Wage Payment of 1976 and the Women Worker's Welfare Law of 1972. Another group of laws include, the Seamen's Law of 1947 and Public Corporation and National Enterprise Labor Relations Law, Local Public Labor Relations Law, National Civil Service Law and Local Civil Service Law. Apart from these statutes enacted by the parliament, both the ministry of labor (ordinance for the Enforcement of Labor Standards Law, the ordinances about the Labor Standards of Women and Minors and many ordinances and rules regarding the Labor Safety and Hygiene Law) and Central Labor Relations Commission, issue orders and by-laws based on the statutes, which have a validity that is inferior to that of the statutes.

In India during the same period, after World War II a number of labor legislations were enacted and amended. For example, the Indian Trade Union Act, 1926 was amended in 1947, 1960, 1962, and 1964 and in 1982 a comprehensive Trade Union Act was passed. Though genesis of the Industrial Employment (Standing order) goes back to 1944 but it was passed and enforced in 1947—known as The Industrial Employment (Standing Orders) Act, 1946. The law relating to industrial relations in India is contained in the Industrial Disputes Act of 1947, which is amended several times. The Payment of Wages Act, 1963 which was passed in 1936 was also amended a number of times to seek the remedies of the evils. The most important legislation related to industrial relations is the Factory Act of 1948 which is an improvement over the Working Act, 1934. The Factory Act of 1948 not only consolidates but also amends the law regulating labor in factories. Apart from these major labor laws in India one finds many miscellaneous legislations such as: the Mines Act, 1952, the Plantation Act, 1951 and the Contract Labor (Regulations and Abolition Act), 1970, etc.

(b) Labor Administration Machinery

The government of Japan is very strong in the field of business but in contrast it refrains from intervention in the field of industrial relations. The Ministry of Labor is responsible for industrial relations. It has five bureaus: Labor policy, Labor

Standards, Women and Minors, Employment Security and Vocational Training. At local level Ministry has prefecture bureaus. The Labor Standard Bureaus are authorized to inspect working places and other facilities, to examine records and documents, to interrogate employers and employees and to exercise the right of a judicial policy officer with regard to the crime of violating protective labor law. The most important government institution pertaining to industrial relations in Japan is Labor Relations Commission. The Labor Relations (including Local Labor Relations Commissions) Commission has two functions: one is a semi-judicial function with regard to unfair labor practice cases and the other concerns labor dispute settlement through Conciliation, Mediation and Arbitration.

The entire legal system including labor laws in India is based on the ideology of social justice. Both central and state governments enact and administer labor laws. The jurisdiction between the state and centre is provided in the constitution. It is the centre which plays the main role in passing laws, acts as a coordinator and the state assists in their enforcement. The Ministry of Labor and Employment of the central government is the main agency for policy formation and administration in all labor matters. Together with the state governments, the local bodies and the statutory corporation/boards, it sees to the implementation these policies and decisions of the tripartite committees.

(c) Collective Agreement and Bargaining

Though collective agreement between union and employer have the effect of autonomous legal norms in Japan, it is often pointed out that they are simple and vague, which is true to some extent in India. The Trade Union Law in Japan provides that every individual contract or work rule which contravenes the standard of working conditions established by the collective agreement is null and void. However, the Trade Union Law admits that it has legal binding effect beyond this limitation under certain condition. If three quarters of the employees in a certain plant are covered by the collective agreement, the agreements automatically extended to cover all the remaining employees, at least as far as the working conditions are concerned. Work rule also acquires the nature of legal norms in relation to the individual contract. According to the Labor Standard Law, a labor contract stipulating conditions inferior to those fixed in the work rule is null and void. In Japan today the role of the individual contract is very limited.

In Japan all bonafide unions have the right to bargain; even minority union can practice within the boundaries of each individual enterprise. The employer cannot refuse to bargain with a minority union just because it is a minority union. The employer often imposes rules on the bargaining sessions. Japanese unions regard the bargaining session as a stage of confrontation with the management. The courts and labor relations commissions have to decide whether the managements deliberately avoid bargaining or for lack of rules. They have to decide also, whether it is violation of right to bargain or unfair labor practice. In many cases, rules are either laid down in written agreement or established by practice. The Japanese law does not specify issues for bargain. Almost all issues come under the scope of bargaining issues that affect working condition. The Shunto (spring wage negotiations) is the most important activity of Japanese collective bargaining. The important areas of collective bargaining are—bonuses, hours of work, employment security and participation. The political issues and other problems between collective bargaining and the worker's consultation is not very clear, so bargaining and consultation are carried by the same union, even though different people may represent the union in each case. Japanese labor law does not recognize unfair labor practice on the labor side, in other words, Japanese labor law is one sided which favors labor. Collective agreement will be effective when it is in the form of a document either signed by or under the hand and seal of both the parties. The terms of collective agreement is 3 years or the term agreed by the parties? The parties in Japan have reached a necessary degree of maturity and skill of collective bargaining which India has to improve.

Despite much controversy, the collective bargaining was introduced in India in 1952. The growth is very slow though some data show that collective bargaining practice is in use to determine the rates of wages, working condition, workers' participation in management and in the arrangement for the settlement of disputes through voluntary agreements. Collective bargaining agreements can be reached at plant, industry and national level. The collective bargaining at plant level has gained around. There are three important reasons as to why collective bargaining has not gone beyond the plant level:[11]

1. The varying sections of the plants/firms and the consequent dissimilarities in productivity and technologies which do not permit uniform employment conditions;
2. The absence of homogeneous labor market owing to lack of uniform skills and pattern of training which does not promote free mobility of labor or that uniform employment conditions could be evolved for the industry as a whole; and
3. The plant union leadership which at present enjoys enormous powers and faces prospects of political climb is reluctant to get integrated into an industry-wise union where its powers are likely to be restricted.

There are three types of collective bargaining contracts in India:[12]

1. Bipartite agreements which are totally voluntary for the purpose of implementation;
2. Bipartite settlements negotiated and settled primarily by the parties but registered before a conciliator in settlement; and
3. In the case of consent awards, when the parties have dispute pending before a tribunal yet they negotiated a contract which is recorded by the tribunal, the contracts so negotiated acquire legal status.

The Industrial Disputes Act, 1947 requires the parties to register the agreement with the conciliation officer, if they want it to be binding on themselves. The involvement of the government labor machinery as a third party imposes greater restraint on the parties. Many managements and unions first arrive at collective bargaining agreement and then ratify it, in the presence of the conciliation officer, in view of the binding effects of Industrial Disputes Act. Due to prevailing legalistic, political and authoritarian labor relations culture in India which contrasts with the spirit of mutual give-and-take, collective bargaining is not encouraged by Industrial Dispute Act.

(d) Acts of Disputes

In Japan 'labor disputes' means "disagreement over claims arising between the parties concerned with labor relations, regarding labor relations and resulting in either the occurrence of an act of dispute or in conditions where there is the danger of an act of dispute occurring". 'Act of disputes' means "strikes, go-slow, lock-out and other acts and counter-acts, hampering the normal courses of work in an enterprise and performed by the parties concerned with labor relations with the object of attaining their respective claims". The constitutional guarantee of the right to act collectively only applies to workers; the employer's right to lock-out suffers badly from being very restricted. The acts of disputes should be carried by a bonafide unions not necessarily registered or qualified. Though some feel that every act of dispute by union should be recognized as legal, but majority claim, a proper act of dispute be based on economic reasons and acts taken for political motives should not be given indemnity. Trade Union Law prohibits all acts of violence. Japanese acts of dispute are unique in a sense that they are very short, variety of types and are mainly to attract the employer's attention. Sometimes strike does take place even before bargain, without serious economic damage. The Constitution of Japan and labor union law does not admit the employer's right to lock-out, but the Supreme Court holds that the lawful lock-out of an employer is permitted to keep the balance between employer and employee. In public sector any act which hampers the normal course of operations in public corporation, a government enterprise or the public service of the government, is completely prohibited.

According to the Industrial Dispute Act, in India an 'industrial dispute' means "any dispute between employer and workmen or employers and employers or workmen and workmen, which is connected with employment or non-employment or the terms of employment or the condition of labor of any person". Generally a dispute should be a collective dispute. Collective support by the workmen is essential for making an individual dispute an industrial dispute. However, in disputes related to termination of service dismissal, discharge, retrenchment or other an individual can raise an industrial dispute. Even non-recognized and unregistered or minority unions may raise an industrial dispute, on any matter connected with the employment or non-employment, term of employment or the conditions of labor. The 'Act of dispute' includes strike and lock-out. Strike means "a cessation of work by a body of persons employed in any industry acting in combination or a concerted refusal to continue to work or to accept employment". Lock-out means "the temporary closing of a place of employment or the suspension of work or temporary refusal by an employer to continue to employ any number of people employed by him". Unlike in Japan, lock-out is often used by an employer as a weapon in his armory to compel the workmen to accept his proposals just as a strike is a weapon in the armory of the workmen to compel the employer to accept their demands. There are general and special (public utility) prohibitions. Once the dispute is referred to adjudication, strike or lock-out is prohibited.

(e) Unfair Labor Practices

The Labor Union Law in Japan prohibits unfair labor practices in order to protect the rights of workers to organize, bargain collectively and engage in industrial actions under the constitution. The administrative organs such as Labor Relations Commission in Japan are composed of labor, employer and public members and its procedures are closer to the court procedure. As a measure to protect union activities, judiciary relief by the court is also available. The employer usually commits for types of unfair labor practices which are prohibited by Labor Union Law, they are: discrimination or unfavorable treatment, refusal to bargain, domination or interference and yellow dog contract (employer should not make condition on employee of joining union). The labor unions and the individual worker can file a complaint with Labor Relations Commission. The employer will be the defendant before the commission. The commission will investigate the facts and hear witnesses and issue an order either rejecting or sustaining the complaint. This procedure is done mainly by a public member of the labor commission although the labor and management members participate. If union or individual employee and employer are dissatisfied with the order of Local Labor Relations Commission they can appeal to the Central Labor Relations Commission for rehearing and for judicial review from District Court, High Court and Supreme Court.

The measures of conflict resolution of India differ from the Japanese system. Broadly speaking India has statutory and non-statutory measure and government sponsored guidelines. The statutory measures provided in Industrial Disputes Act are: 1. Works Committees for prevention of industrial disputes; 2. Courts of Inquiry for investigation of industrial disputes; 3. Conciliation of Boards of Conciliation; and 4. Labor Courts, Industrial Tribunals and National Tribunals for settlement of industrial disputes through adjudication. Non-statutory measures encourage resolutions through negotiation between parties and thus by their nature speed up the process and cut short the long procedure. The provisions such as strong trade union, works committee, standing orders, labor welfare officer and government labor officer act as preventive measures. Apart from these, non-statutory measures include—Code of Discipline, Workers' participation in management and Collective bargaining which are voluntary in nature. They are encouraged by the government in conflict resolution. Unlike in Japan, the Government of India plays vital role in regulating industrial relations and maintaining industrial peace. For planned economic growth industrial peace is a pre-requisite. The Industrial Amendment Bill, 1982 prohibits unfair labor practices and covers employer and workmen or trade union. Some of the important unfair labor practices listed in the Industrial Disputes Act Amendment Bill, 1982 are: A. by employer: 1. threatening workmen with discharge or dismissal if they join a trade union or threatening a closure or lock-out if a trade union is organized; 2. wage increase to workmen at crucial time of trade union with a view to undermine the efforts of the trade union; 3. establish an employer's sponsored trade union; 4. encourage or discourage membership in any trade union by discriminating against any workmen; and 5. discourage or dismiss workmen by way of victimization due to the exercise of the employer's rights by falsely implicating workmen in a criminal case for misconduct of a minor or technical nature. B. By workmen or trade union—1. force workmen to become member of a trade union; for a recognized union to refuse to bargain collectively in good faith with the employer; and 2. to stage, encourage, coerce actions such as wilful go-slow, and to stage demonstrations at the residence of the employers or management staff members. The parties committing unfair labor practices shall be punishable with imprisonment for a term which may to six months or with a fine up to Rs. 1000 or with both.

(f) Dispute Settlement Machinery

The Labor Relations Adjustment Law in Japan provides three types of adjustment: Conciliation, Mediation and Arbitration, which are carried out by the Labor Relations Commission. Apart from these normal adjustment procedures there is an emergency adjustment system which the Prime Minister uses when a dispute threatens the national economy and life. The Labor Relations Commissions are set-up in each prefecture while the Central Labor Relations Commission is located in Tokyo. The Labor Relations Commissions have two main functions: 1. adjudication of unfair labor practice cases; and 2. dispute settlement by conciliation, mediation and arbitration. It also undertakes dispute settlement in public welfare work. Theoretically disputes of 'interest' between union and employer are taken care of by the dispute settlement procedure (conciliation, mediation and arbitration) while disputes of 'rights' between employers and individual workers or the unions are the responsibility of the courts. Unfortunately these distinctions often fade away. The relationship between law courts and Labor Relations Commission regarding dispute settlement is rather complicated and overlapping.

The principle legislation in India which regulated the collective relationship between the employer and employee is Industrial Disputes Act, 1947. As said earlier conflict resolution machinery in India includes statutory and non-statutory measure.

The Code of Discipline is primarily an ethical instrument designed to prevent disputes (both in public and private sectors). The Code prescribes many do's and don'ts based upon the central premise that to maintain discipline in industry, managements and union agree on various issues. The Code also includes criteria for recognition of unions, rights of recognized unions under the Code Discipline, inter-union Code of Conduct, Code of efficiency and welfare.

Joint Management Council is a voluntary bipartite instrument, in which labor plays a vital role as a partner in the common task of development. The functions of Joint Management Council includes: 1. to endeavor to improve working conditions; productivity; to encourage employees' suggestions; to assist in administration of law and agreements; to serve employees and to create in the employees a live sense of participation; 2. be consulted by managements on matters like general administration standing order, introduction of new methods of production and closure, reduction in or cessation of operations; 3. to exercise the rights to receive information, discuss and give suggestions on economic conditions of the firm; state of market, production and sales; general administration of firm; methods of work and manufacture; annual balance sheet and profits and loss statement; plans for expansion, etc. Apart from these functions, councils will also have responsibilities of administration of welfare measures; supervision of safety measures; operation of rewards to employees, etc. Matters such as wage, bonus, etc., which are subjects of collective bargaining are excluded from the scope of council. It also cannot deal with individual grievances.

The Government of India has taken steps for joint negotiation to maintain dialogue with its employees, which reflects erosion of the doctrine of master and servant relationship. The Joint Consultative machinery covers the entire body of government employees. All the Central trade union organizations set-up screening committees for screening cases before filing appeals in courts. This has helped to minimize litigations.

Industrial Disputes Act, Section 10-A provides for voluntary arbitration (like USA) on the basis of a settlement between the employer and the workmen before the dispute is referred to the adjudication. In voluntary arbitration, both the parties show the willingness to go to an arbitrator and submit to his decision, whereas in compulsory arbitration the parties are forced to arbitration by the power of the state. This method is applied only when parties fail to reach settlement mutually. The compulsory arbitration is called adjudication. The presiding officers of labor court can be appointed arbitrators. Only industrial disputes can be referred for arbitration. The arbitrator's powers are determined by the party's agreement; however his awards are binding on the parties.

The tripartite wage (non-statutory) boards are constituted by the government, whose members (representatives of employer and workmen) are appointed by the government. An independent member usually an economist or a politician is also appointed. Such boards have become principle machinery for wage fixation in selected industries since 1957. One of the main reasons for setting wage boards is that workers were dissatisfied with the method of compulsory adjudication for wage determination. The wage boards also sometime deal with the question of bonus and gratuity.

The appropriate government appoints all statutory authorities except Works Committees. The Works Committee is the most suitable mechanism for the prevention of industrial unrest by providing an opportunity for consultation at the level of undertaking for mutual settlement of differences. The Industrial Disputes Act provides for the setting up of a Works Committee, consisting of a number of representatives of management and no less a number of representatives of employees in every undertaking, employing 100 or more workmen. The Works Committees are to deal with matters which directly affect the conditions under which workers function. Wages, bonus, etc. are beyond the scope of Works Committee. The restriction has helped trade unions not to regard Works Committee as substitutes for trade union. In my earlier studies,[13] I found that majority of workers have great hope on Works Committee to deal with industrial disputes, wages, bonus, working conditions, etc. There is a general feeling among labor specialists that the Works Committees have not proved effective. The management, workers and trade unions should honour each others interests and should imbibe the spirit of participation and work as active and willing co-partners.

A court of enquiry is another authority set-up by the government under Industrial Disputes Act. It is a body of one or more independent persons appointed by the government to inquire into any matter appearing to be connected with or relevant to any industrial dispute. It is essentially a fact-finding body to enlighten the government and public opinion on the disputes. It is meant for voluntary settlement of dispute. A court of enquiry has to submit its report in writing to the government within 6 months from the commencement of its enquiry. Its proceedings are judicial in nature. However, its report is not binding on the parties, since the courts function here is to enquire and not decide. However, these reports have great influence on public opinion.

The Industrial Disputes Act provides two types of conciliation machinery: Conciliation officers and Boards of Conciliation. Conciliation has been the most frequently used machinery for settling disputes. The conciliation officer is permanent and very frequently used, while Conciliation Boards are appointed as and when the government decides. Conciliation can be defined as "the practice by which the services of a neutral third party are used in a dispute as a means of helping the disputing parties to reduce the extent of their differences and to arrive at an amicable settlement or agreed solution". The main purpose of conciliation machinery is to provide a mediator who by separate or joint meetings with the parties attempt to narrow the range of differences and assist them in reaching mutually acceptable and expedited settlement. He has no decision-making power.

Conciliation is compulsory for public utility services while it is not so in private. Conciliation officer has power to compel the presentation of documents and enforce the presence of persons. However, if either party request in writing that information presented be treated as confidential, the conciliation officer must honor and guard such information as professional secret. The conciliation officer has to mediate on a particular case within 14 days and then send a report to the government giving details of the steps taken to settle the dispute, listing the reasons for success or failure in reaching an agreement. If a settlement is reached between the parties, conciliation officer must send a report of the proceedings and a memorandum of the settlement signed by the parties and himself to the appropriate government. A settlement reached through conciliation has a high legal status. It binds not only the members of the union involved in the dispute but all other workmen. Conciliation officer lacks power and authority. His very lack of authority and power is actually a help to the skilful and effective conciliator, for his chief asset is power not authority, but his personal integrity, fairness, acceptability to the parties and persuasive ability.[14]

In addition to the appointment of conciliation officer the government can also appoint Conciliation Boards consisting of a chairman and two to four other members. The Conciliation Board is a rare appointment and most of the work is done by conciliation officer. The functions of Conciliation Board are similar to those of Conciliation Officer except. that when a settlement is not possible between the parties, the board can send its recommendation to the government for the determination of the dispute. The Conciliation Board must follow the procedure of courts and tribunals. It has additional powers such as: to enforce the attendance of any person and examine him on oath, to compel the production of documents and to conduct judicial proceedings in respect of prescribed matters including investigation or inquiry. The Conciliation Board must submit its report within two months unless there is an extension granted by government or parties have agreed in writing for an extension.

Since conciliation efforts call for an atmosphere of flexibility, understanding and compromise, lawyers are prohibited to represent parties as a legal practitioner, however, they can provide consultation or advice.

The Commissioner of labor, additional commissioner and deputy commissioner of labor, who are notified as conciliation officers deal with disputes arising in undertaking employing more than 20 workmen at the state level. Labor Officers act as conciliation officers for disputes arising in industries, for which the Central government is the appropriate authority which are undertaken by the state branch officers of central labor which commissioner's office. The Central Industrial machinery, with the chief labor commissioner as the Head of Department, carries out various provisions of the Industrial Dispute Act—for prevention, investigation and settlements of disputes in the industries under the central sphere. The Central Machinery located at Delhi has 13 regional offices.

The process of bringing an amicable settlement demands the high skill and sincerity of conciliation officer. It is therefore, necessary to provide refresher courses to update conciliation officer's knowledge of laws and industrial relations and to break the monotony of their job.

The legal remedy for the settlement of an unresolved dispute is its reference to adjudication by the government. When conciliation machinery efforts fail to bring a settlement, the dispute is referred to adjudication (Labor Court, Industrial Court and National Tribunal) for award or decision which is binding on both the parties. The three adjudication authorities are the same except the type of dispute upon which each adjudicates. An Industrial Tribunal however, can adjudicate on any matter that a labor court can but a labor court cannot adjudicate upon matters proper to a tribunal except in disputes where less than a hundred workmen are likely to be affected.

The Labor Court and Tribunal are not courts of law but of social justice, not merely looking at the legalities involved but always looking to what is fair and reasonable i.e., not only can they interpret existing rights but also they can create new rights by their own decision. A lawyer can represent the parties with the consent of other party and permission of the adjudicator. An award or decision of the adjudicating authority becomes enforceable 30 days from the date it is published. Normally an award remains in operation for one year, however, three years is the maximum period of operation.

All courts and tribunals consist of only one person (a High Court judge or judges fit to be so) appointed by the appropriate government. The centre always appoints the national Tribunal. These authorities are not hierarchical; it is the government's prerogative to refer a dispute to these. No contending parties can refer any dispute for adjudication directly; however, the parties can move a dispute to the High Court or Supreme Court, if they are dissatisfied.

In the past 20 years, the adjudication machinery has exercised considerable influence on several aspects of labor-management relations and has provided an acceptable alternative to direct action and to protect and promote the interests of workmen. On the other hand, many labor specialists feel that in spite of elaborate legal framework and government intervention, adjudication machinery has failed, partly because of red tapes, bureaucratic delays and complicates procedures. These delays make the parties impatient and encourage to resort for other measure to resolve their conflicts.[15] The procedure of adjudication needs to be simplified, make economical and introduce pre-hearing trials. The Indian Labor Courts, Industrial Tribunals and National Tribunal need labor specialists with practical knowledge of labor law and industrial relations. Like in Japan the government of India should restrict its interference in conciliation and arbitration and set-up an industrial relations commission on the Japanese pattern.

Despite the progress made so far, the standard established by the Indian labor statute continue to fall short of the international standards. India has not been able to ratify a number of conventions partly because they impose costs that the industry might not be able to bear but also because they would be unrealistically high in comparison to the spectacle of unavoidable neglect in the unorganized sector.[16] There is also much to do in the areas of contract labor, decasualization schemes, bonded labor system, child labor and abolition of sex discrimination.

4. CAN WE LEARN FROM JAPANESE EXPERIENCE?

After examining the industrial relations of Japan, it would be interesting to explore the possibilities of the Indian Industrial Relations system learning from the Japanese experience. Indian social scientists and even practicing managers often consider such basic questions as: Why have jobs become chores rather than sources of creativity? Why does a person who spend more than one-half of his life in an organization still feel no measure of equality, understanding or even friendship in his work place? Why in spite of their interdependence there is more distrust, conflict and confrontation rather than trust, cooperation or support between groups of employees and their collectivities[17]? The following section attempts to find some tips to these fundamental questions and value lessons on the basis of Japanese experience. It has been found that Japanese management practices may work well in Japan, they are not likely to be successful elsewhere. Therefore, careful and sincere efforts are needed.

No one can deny that the principle key factor for Japanese success is her unique industrial relations, which has attracted the attention of many western scholars. There are some fundamental differences between Japanese and Indian concept of employment, trade union and wage structure. Dore Vogel and OECD report, all agree that Japanese industrial relations have certainly valuable lessons. In fact Vogel, recommends for America to look to Japan and find out how it can improve the performance of her productivity and even social organizations. This is also true for India. Though there are many similarities between India and Japan, still India could get some useful tips from Japan's experience. Japanese industrial relations system need not be the only model for India even if it has opened for the adoption of foreign technology capital. India is also unique as it has different social, political and economical environment. Like Japan India should never allow becoming blind imitators of western or Japanese model, instead it should constantly try to find the best possible ways of adoption suitable for its situations. Japan has certain inherent strength in her existing value structure, necessary for rapid industrialization and economic development, which India can not easily achieve. It is difficult to believe that we could apply Japanese practice in ditto. Japanese society is based on Confucian ethics, in many ways superior to the west (also India) in the pursuit of industrialization, affluence and modernization. "A properly trained member of Confucian culture will be hard working, responsible, skillful and ambitious and creative in helping the group". There is very less emphasis on advancing individual (selfish) interest.[18] Indians certainly will benefit if a strong and strategic "Nippon Connection" is established. It can look for some tips in the field of industrial relations and cooperation in the field of capital technology and efficient management.[19]

1. Today in India at least in the organized and public sector, a kind of life time employment practice and enterprise unionism prevails without any force. It would be therefore, beneficial for the Indian worker to consider that his company itself is his occupation and life and union on its part encourage and make him understand that his future is tied to that of his company. Multiple rival unionisms are an important feature and one of the greatest weaknesses of the Indian union movement. Why not try enterprise-based union in India? They may affiliate to national federations to deal with political and institutional problems which are beyond the scope of enterprise union.
2. The Indian concept of employment and wage are close to the western concept where the level of employment and wages are determined on the basis of profitability. They are short-sighted and fail to understand the principle of cooperation and competition. Indian companies too should believe in "no-lay-off policy pays-off" and job-security which produces loyal and cooperative worker, who can ultimately bring greater profits. India needs to produce a kind of flexible supply of manpower for her growing industries. If companies practice permanent employment, promotion by seniority and on-the-job training system, they can go for smooth labor transfers within a company and between affiliated companies and avoid lay-offs. Indian companies perhaps also have to learn from Japanese companies, the career enlargement and job security concepts. Career enlargement involves the preparation of career paths and the availability and application of company resources, especially training to individual employees so that is profitable for both the company and the employee to actualize these career paths. This can be possible at least in large and medium scale companies in India.
3. Union-management relations are always strained in India. They lack cooperation, compromise and competition which are essential for industrial

democracy. These ingredients prevail in Japan. In India, to a large extent, managements consider union as a nuisance, while unions believe managements are exploiters. What is needed is consensus decision-making system and moderate labor movement. The organizational structure of Indian unions or any country, matters little in industrial relations. To me, the union's behaviors or attitude is vital. Indian unions must protect and promote the interest of workers but limit their excessive demands of higher wage and bonus. Unions should learn to know the financial position of their companies and competitive situation with regard to rival companies. After all their entire prospect depends upon their company's health. "Both have to sail in the same boat". Therefore, union and management jointly face the challenge and practice the principle of competition. After all the Indian domestic market too is competitive.[20] Apart from these it is worth learning how Japanese unions teach their employee his duties and impress on him to work with dedication and sincerity through regular meetings and training sessions. Japanese labor will never participate in a kind of sympathetic strikes, which have nothing to do with his work. In short, India should attempt to maximize the harmonization of individual and organizational goals on the basis of the Japanese experience.

4. The Indian government is extra cautious about unemployment problem, of course, it is an excellent insight, but it has many other priorities. I personally feel that it should encourage managements to take up various employment adjustment mechanisms based on the Japanese experience, whenever there is a threat of recession. Employees in Japan are subsidized by the government through a variety of devices during economic downturns, so that he can be maintained on the payroll.
5. The Indian worker who is partially committed to his job and who is less loyal and less cooperative than Japanese worker needs to improve his attitude.

6. There is an increasing trend towards greater use and appreciation of collective bargaining in India but there is very little genuine voluntary collective bargaining. Due to various reasons collective bargaining has not gone beyond the plant level. The most important pre-requisite for the success of collective bargaining is high degree of maturity of parties which Japan has achieved already. It is needless to emphasize the importance of strengthening collective bargaining in India. It would not be advisable to abandon compulsory arbitration that is prevalent in India at a time when the country is in the process of economic growth and the employer still has conservative attitude. India could learn the techniques and skill and develop her own system on the basis of Japanese experience.
7. Industrial unrests in India have very far-reaching effects on the workers, employers, consumers the community and nation. Japanese acts of dispute are unique in a sense that they are very short, not violent and mainly to attract employer attention. The responsibility of creating conducive industrial climate depends on the management, the union and the government. It would be possible to attempt tuning the existing Indian methods to that of Japan. India lacks cooperation, compromise and competition which are essential ingredients. The parties should chalk out progressive development programs such as: liberal fringe benefits, full and efficient utilization of all the available resources. Good employee communication, grievance procedure and settlement, workers education, etc. will go a long way in paving the way for industrial peace. While unions try to minimize strikes; employer should not declare lock-out, closure, etc. unnecessarily.
8. The Labor Union Law protects only worker's rights to organize bargain collectively and engage in industrial action in Japan. It would be out of place to consider such an arrangement in India, however, while protecting the interest of the employer and the trade union with reference to unfair labor practice; it is

advisable to keep strict vigilant check on the party's behavior towards unfair labor practice. The managements and unions must learn to respect each other's rights and perform their duties sincerely.

9. Japan does not have labor courts. The disputes of 'interest' are taken care of by the Labor Relations Commission, while disputes of 'rights' are the responsibility of the court. There is confusion and their stands are overlapping. The present Indian dispute settlement machinery is good. Still there is a necessity of retaining compulsory arbitration and stage for free collective bargaining can not be considered seriously at present. However, existing dispute settlement machinery can be improved by: reducing undue government interference, improving the efficiency of conciliation and arbitration and setting up an independent industrial relations commission, etc. on the Japanese lines.

The Government of India as a custodian of public interest is always concerned about industrial peace by formulating laws and brings the employee and the employer closer. From management perspective industrial peace is needed because it's efficiency, capability and its very survival depend upon it. The unions are not against the idea of industrial peace but the manipulations by managements and government, encourage unions to take up acts of disputes. While every one wants industrial peace, it is essential to make sincere attempts although there will be some degree of conflict. If government or/and managements try to bring industrial peace 'somehow' without taking union into confidence, unions will become violent. Here Japanese experience can help India. In Japan while labor is loyal to his company, company acts as a guardian, labor and management are integrated as a family, and state intervention is less but is able to bring industrial peace and economic prosperity. Indian has a benefit of having traditional social values and modern democratic ideas such as freedom and human rights like Japan. What is needed is sincere mutual trust, understanding and positive cooperation between the union and management.

5. REVIEW OF JAPANESE INDUSTRIAL RELATIONS

A critical remark is often heard these days even by many Japanese scholars that the Japanese industrial relations practice is backward, feudalistic, inefficient, irrational and undemocratic. My response to this criticism is that the Japanese industrial relations do have their own peculiarities, but basically they are not at all abnormal. However, one can identify few weaknesses. Enterprise unions are too dependent and dominated by managements and they are undoubtedly more cooperative than industrial unions. There is no need to replace enterprise unions by western style industrial unions but the present national centers of union should be strengthened. Unions today are required to participate more actively in management and industrial policy-making, pay attention to the well-being of society, instead of protecting well-being of workers only. Japanese industrial relations should become more tripartite and welfare-oriented.

While I appreciate life time employment practice, discrimination between regular and temporary workers, and male and female, needs immediate prevention. There is a strong feeling that Japanese workers are exploited and are forced to sacrifice their freedom and human dignity on the job. Though scholars like Koshiro proved through their studies that Japanese firms particularly large ones, not only keep worker's motivation and productivity very high but at the same time provide them with a high degree of satisfaction and a sense of security, however, there is a room for meaningful improvement in the quality of the life of workers in the rest of the economy.

Notes and References

1. The characteristics of 'Best Management' in order of worker's preference: Good salary 76.12%, Promotion on merit 44.52%, Grant of leave when required 46.45%, Food; Fringe benefit 46.45%; Less hours of work, equitable distribution of work according to capacity 100%.
   Refer: Zechariah John, *Administration of Labor Disputes*, Ashish Publishing House, New Delhi, 1984, pp. 53-55.
2. Maharashtra government (one of the Indian state) introduced the Employment Guarantee Scheme in 1972-73. The scheme was the first of its kind to give recognition to the 'right to work' to a person who comes forward to offer labor. Maharashtra government alone spent about 1.8

billion rupees in 1982-83. (as quoted by Rudder Datt and K.P.M. Sundharam, Indian Economy, S. Chand and Company, New Delhi, 1984, p. 561).

4. Taishiro Shirai (Ed.), *Contemporary Industrial Relations in Japan*, University of Wisconsin Press Ltd., Wisconsin, 1983, p. 8 (Shimada's Article: Survey of the English Language Literature.
5. In India several methods are employed in fixing the worker's wages. Different bodies such as the pay commission, wage boards, industrial tribunals and labor courts as well as High Courts and Supreme Court, perform this task. Wages are often fixed through collective bargaining and job evaluation.
6. For example productivity in Indian Cement Industry as measured by the quantity of cement produced per man-day or per man-hour or the installed capacity or production per employee, was very low in India compared to leading cement manufacturing countries such as USA, Belgium, Japan, U.K., West Germany.
7. Dividend Policy of a Firm, Manufacturing Potteries and other ceramic items

Year	*Dividend Paid out (Rs.)*	*Net Profits (Rs.)*	*Dividend Percentage (Rs.)*
1962-62	6,30,000	6,85,000	91.96
1967-68	4,97,119	2,05,345	242.09

Economic and Political Weekly, Vol. XIV, No. 2, January 13, 1979, p. 51 (as quoted by Ruddar Datt and K.P.M. Sundharam, Indian Economy, S. Chand and Company, New Delhi, 1984, p. 561).

8. In Japanese wage system personal evaluation system can not be ignored. When a worker works hard, he can get more wages under the judgment of supervisor on the basis of his ability and behaviors. This brings competitions among the workers. This competition is one factor responsible for high productivity and economic growth.
9. Kenichi Odawara, *The Competition Principle in Japanese Companies and Labor Unions: A Premise*, Research in Asian Economic Studies, edited by M. Dutta, Vol. 1, 1988, Part B, Greenwich, Connecticut, London, England.
10. The 1984 National per capita income—Rs. 2,494, while in the same year average annual earning of Manufacturing of Chemicals and Chemical products—Rs. 10,266. In fact in some Manufacturing companies it is still more.

    Economic Survey, Government of India, 1989-90, pp S-4 and S-5 and Pocket Book of Labor Statistics, 1989, p. 50.
11. Momoria, C.B. and Momoria, S., *Dynamics of Industrial Relations in India*, Himalaya Publishing House, Bombay, 1986, p. 561.
12. Monappa, Arun, *Industrial Relations*, Tata McGraw Hill Publishing Company Ltd., New Delhi, 1987, p. 118.
13. Though the purpose of Works Committee is to settle day-to-day differences, study reveals that 54% of workers feel that the Works Committee can settle major industrial disputes, Secondly, 20% of workers

feel Works Committee can promote good relations between employees and the employer. The third and fourth functions of Works Committee preferred by the workers are to discuss day-to-day problems and to deal with matters like wage, working hours and discipline.

14. E.H. McGrath, S.J., *Industrial Disputes: A guide to the Industrial Disputes Act, 1947*, Prentice-Hall of India, Pvt. Ltd., New Delhi, 1985, p. 25.
15. Monappa, Arun, Industrial Relations, Tata McGraw-Hill Publishing Company Ltd., New Delhi, 1987, p. 202.
16. Blanpain, R. (Ed.), *International Encyclopedia for Labor Law and Industrial Relations*, Kluwer Law and Taxation Publishers. The Netherlands, 1984 (Portion on India, written by C.K. Johri) item 723.
17. Chaturvedi, Abha, *Man. ging the Divide*, The Times Research Foundation, Poona, 1985, p. 117.
18. Punekar, V.B., "Work Values and Industrial Development: A comparison of Indian and Japanese Experience", *Indian Journal of Industrial Relations*, Vol. 24, No. 3, January 1989, p. 248.
19. Zechariah, John, "Japan can be Indian Partner", *Southern Economist, Bangalore, India*, Vol. 29, No. 112.
20. In public sector competition is avoided, while in private sector competition prevails under state regulated—controlled capitalism.

Index

Accident, 67
Acts of Disputes, 189, 277
Annual Vacation with Pay, 52
Arbitration, 237

Basis of Seniority Wage, 174

Chikio, Hayashi, 32
Child Labor, 27
Collective Agreement and Bargaining, 274
Collective Agreements:
  Interpretational Application, 254
Conciliation, 234
Conflict in Japan :
  Manifestation, 191

Dismissal/Lay off, 65
Disputes Resolution through Court, 251
Dispute Settlement Machinery, 212, 280

Education and Training, 55
Emergency Disputes Settlement Machinery, 248
Employees and Employer :
  Rights and Duties, 37
Employee's Duties, 37
Employee's Rights, 42
Employer's Duties, 38
Employer's Rights, 43
Employment Contract Conflicts, 257
Employment :
  Different Meaning, 266
Employment Structure, 85
Enterprise-based Union, 112
  Nature, 112
  Classification, 112
Enterprise Trade Union :
  Future, 137
Enterprise Union, 104, 140
  Functions, 124
  Characteristics, 123

Foreign Workers, 28

Go-Slow and Work to Rule, 196

Higher Education, 12
  Distance Learning, 131
Hired Labor :
  Trends, 16
Holidays, 51
Human Resources Management System, 70

India and Japan :
  Comparative Industrial Relations, 263

India :
  Industrial Relations, 263
Industrial Disputes :
  Types, 187

Japan and India :
  Similarities, 272
  Differences, 272
Japanese Companies :
  Employment, 94
Japanese Industries Relations, 212, 292
  Basic Characteristics, 79
Japanese Job-Seekers, 30
Japanese Labor Unions, 117
Japanese Work :
  Characteristics, 32
Japanese Worker and Management :
  Changing Trends, 32
Japanese Worker, 5
  Work-Role, 92
Japanese Worker and Japan, 1
Japan's Background, 1
Japan's Major Labor Federations, 118
Job Rotation :
  Reasons, 88

Kazuo, Koike, 22
Koshiro, Kasutoshi, 5

Labor Disputes, 180, 205
  Prevention, 206
Labor Force and Rate of Employment, 7
Labor Laws, 272
Labor Machinery, 273
Labor-Management Relations, 35
Labor Mobility, 68
Labor Relations Commissions, 222
Labor Relations Commissions Courts :
  Controversy over the Jurisdiction, 260
Labor Standard Act, 39
Labor Union :
  Meaning, 269
Life Time Employment, 79, 101, 103
  Nature and Practice, 81
  Life Time Employment :
  Employees Preferences, 108
Lock-outs, 200
LRC (Labor Relations Commission), 36

Means of Production :
  Control, 199
Measures for Obtaining Workers, 14
Mediation, 235
Mid-career and Part-time Workers :
  Hiring Channel, 17
Mid-career Workers :
  Reason for Hiring, 18
Minimum Daily Wage :
  Condition, 154
Minimum Wages Act, 40
Miyoshi, Masaya, 3
Mutual Settlement, 215

Newly-hired Employees, 15

Odawara, 269
Organization of :
  Japanese Company Union, 121
Over Time, 48

Part-time Workers, 23
  Reasons for Hiring, 24
  Problems, 25
Pasting Posters 199
PCNELR (Public Corporation and National Enterprise Labor Relations Law), 203
Picketing and Sitdown, 197
Promotion, 60
Provisional Disposition Orders, 252
Public Sector :
  Dispute Settlement, 249
  Disputes, 202
  Working Conditions, 69
Public Sector Employeees :
  Legal Rights, 204

Recruitment :
- Schedule, 13

Rest Period, 50
Retirement, 63

Seniority (Nenko) Wage System, 148
Seniority Wage System, 168
Senior Workers, 25
Shanks, David, 34
Shinbun, Nihan Keizai, 58
Small Enterprises :
- Disputes, 201

Strikes, 192

Taking Holidays, 198
Trade Union and Employer's Association, 135
Trade Unions and Government, 131
Trade Unions :
- Unification, 132

Training Programmes :
- Reasons for Dissatisfaction, 61

Unfair Labor Practices, 223
Union Labor Practices, 278

Wage and Labor Productivity, 156
Wage Determination, 173
Wages :
- Meaning, 148
- Payment, 148

Wage System :
- Meaning, 263
- Characteristics, 162

Wearing Ribbons, 199
Women Worker, 19
Workers' Commitment, 96
Working Conditions, 43
Working Hours, 46
- International Comparison, 48